LOUIS XIV

Also by John B. Wolf

THE DIPLOMATIC HISTORY OF THE BAGDAD RAILROAD
EARLY MODERN EUROPE
THE EMERGENCE OF THE GREAT POWERS, 1685–1715
FRANCE, 1814–1919
LOUIS XIV
TOWARD A EUROPEAN BALANCE OF POWER, 1640–1715

Louis XIV

A PROFILE

Edited by John B. Wolf

WORLD PROFILES

General Editor: Aïda DiPace Donald

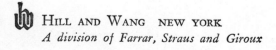

HILL AND WANG NEW YORK
A division of Farrar, Straus and Giroux

Contents

Note

OF THE THIRTEEN SELECTIONS in this volume, four have not previously appeared in English. Barbara Kennedy translated the selection from André; the remaining selections—Saint-Léger and Sagnac, La Force, and Lavisse—were translated by John Githens.

Introduction

WHEN TWENTIETH-CENTURY MEN speak of a king, the image that usually comes to mind is Charlemagne or Louis XIV; no other rulers so completely dominated their lands both in their own times and in the memory of posterity. For a century after his death Louis XIV was the model for strong rulers; both Frederick the Great and Napoleon recognized him as the prototype of the enlightened despot, and princes everywhere sought to imitate him by building châteaux more or less modeled on Versailles and establishing etiquette aping Louis's court. Historians no less than rulers have been fascinated by the reign of the Sun King. From the days of Saint-Simon and Voltaire to those of the congeries of republican, socialist, nationalist, monarchist, and academic historians, Louis XIV has been presented with varying de-

grees of scholarship in many different interpretations. Too often
in the books of these historians Louis XIV has become a protagonist
for this or that political party, or a whipping boy used to demonstrate the wickedness of this or that political position; it is often
difficult to find the king himself in the pages that have been written
about him.

Part of the problem is the fault of the king himself. Louis XIV
did not want to be remembered as an ordinary man who happened
to be king. He and Madame de Maintenon systematically destroyed
letters and memoranda that would reveal him as a man. The result
is that Louis XIV, the king, is nearly always seen with the diadem
and scepter, so much in the act of being king that he is almost an
institution rather than a man. This has allowed many historians
who write about his reign to interpret it to suit their own political
preferences rather than to present it in terms of the manners and
values of the period in which Louis actually lived. No one reading
the selections in this volume will miss the fact that several of them
—the Duke de La Force, Pierre Gaxotte, and Louis Bertrand, for
example—present the reign of Louis XIV as a most fortunate event,
while others, with Saint-Simon as their leader, give quite a contrary
view. The academic historians pretend to neutrality, but Lavisse's
republicanism and Goubert's sympathy with the fate of the common man tend to bias their judgments. G. P. Gooch uses Louis
XIV to show that hereditary monarchy fails because a great king
like Louis XIV is followed by a weakling like his great-grandson.
Saint-Léger and Sagnac, André, and myself try, with more or less
success, to present the reign as a part of the process that created the
characteristic forms of French society.

One of the intriguing questions about Louis XIV concerns his
motivation. Here was a man who spent much of his waking time
working at the problems of state. Most princes before and after
him found the pleasures of the court, the hunt, women, and all the
other distractions available to a man placed on the throne more
interesting than the mechanics of government and the problems of
politics. In his *Mémoires* for the education of his son, Louis tells
us that he enjoyed immensely the "trade" of king, that much
pleasure came from knowing the secrets of princes as well as of

courtiers, that he was happy to assume the task that God had given him: but he does not give us real insight into the character patterns that forced him or persuaded him to spend so many hours at his desk when other amusements could easily have distracted him. Also difficult to understand is Louis's exclusion of all women, even his beloved mother, from his councils. There is no evidence that any mistress ever had the slightest influence on his politics; even Madame de Maintenon, his second wife, discreetly avoided placing herself in a position between the king and his ministers, at least not until age and infirmities reduced Louis's ability to act. The writers of "scandalous histories" of the reign delight in the king's affairs with women, but none of them pretend that those women had any political impact on his government. At most, they secured pensions, favors, and gratifications for themselves, their families, and friends, but they were never responsible for the fall of a minister or the change of royal policy.

If we listen to the king he will tell us that he considered the most important aspects of the "trade" of the king to be: first, the choice of suitable servants to operate his government; then, the consideration of projects, plans, and policies; and, finally, the making of rational decisions for action. His reign largely confirms this set of priorities. Louis XIV was a man of plans; he was a king who made decisions, and he selected his ministers with care. The question that arises, however, involves the process of government, the actual mechanics by which decisions were reached. If we understand that Louis XIV tried to find ministers whose knowledge of the problems with which they had to deal was greater than his own, we can begin to see the inner workings of his regime. The king sought the advice of "experts" and forced them to debate their proposals in council. This did not always result in the establishment of a wise policy, but it did assure the king against the possibility that one of his ministers could dominate him and his government. Mazarin taught the young Louis XIV that he had in him "the stuff to make several great kings" if only he would "apply himself to the art of government" and refuse to allow any one, as first minister or minister favorite, to usurp the direction of the state.

Perhaps it was this fear of domination that led Louis to surround

himself with experts in the several fields of government while he
himself was the only "generalist" in the council. He did not pretend
to initiate policy, but he did insist upon the discussion of policy
before council and upon his right to make the final decision. Indeed, if there is one generalization that can be made about Louis
XIV as king, it is that he insisted upon picking his ministers,
supporting them, confronting their projects in council, and assuming final responsibility for the decisions. This was the "trade" of
king; it required careful attention to details, consideration of arguments, and willingness to assume responsibility for action.

French historians have come to recognize the three Bourbon
kings of the seventeenth century as *"rois éclairés,"* enlightened
kings, whose rule brought order and direction to French society.
Henry IV; Louis XIII and his minister Richelieu; Anne of Austria,
as regent for her son, and her minister Mazarin—all prepared the
foundations for the centralized monarchy that was in the process
of emerging under Louis XIV. These seventeenth-century rulers
faced enormous problems: the kingdom was a maze of provinces
and towns, of corporate interests, and of feudal anachronisms, all
eager to defend their "liberties." French liberties, like liberties elsewhere in Europe, meant the traditional rights, privileges, and im-
munities of towns, noblemen, magistrates, clergymen, and others
who resisted the processes building the centralized states and providing a sort of uniform order for the kingdom. Henry IV had
already started to recover some of the rights and powers of the
crown that he had been forced to surrender to secure recognition
of his claim to the throne. Richelieu and Louis XIII, as a result of
the Huguenot civil wars, wrested from the adherents of the "so-
called Reformed Religion" most of the military and political powers that had made the Huguenot party a republic within the kingdom. They also had moved against the powers of the great nobles
and the pretensions of the magistrates (*parlements*) that limited
the king's ability to act. Under the regency government and during
the first years of Louis XIV's rule as a major king, Mazarin skillfully plotted the course that broke the Fronde, brought the magistrates to recognize limitations on their authority, and created a
royal army so strong that rebellions of the type characteristic of the

preceding century were no longer possible. Thus, when Mazarin died and the young Louis XIV assumed control of the government as his own first minister, he had a throne endowed with the power to control the dissident elements in society, and the political base for the erection of a strong government.

Louis XIV and the men he assembled to help him govern the kingdom understood this fact. They were in the position to inaugurate a reform regime, a "new deal" that would continue to promote order to the chaotic structure of the kingdom. There were many areas crying for reform. The tax and tariff schedules were completely irrational. Tariffs were different from one port of entry to another, taxes fell unequally and unjustly from one province to another, and much of the king's income was lost or stolen in the process of collection. Public order was equally "disorderly"; the king's justice did not apply at all in many parts of the kingdom; in others murder, robbery, kidnaping, and other violent crimes were common and unpunished. The law itself was in chaos—a veritable mélange of traditional law, Roman law, and royal decrees differing from one part of the kingdom to another. The kingdom's economy was also in vague disorder. Dutch merchants controlled much of the commerce that passed through the Atlantic and Channel ports; the Marseille and Toulon commerce with the Levant always produced a deficit that drained gold eastward, and the Cadiz trade, which formerly had been profitable as a source of precious metals, was slowly dwindling under the reduced flow of gold and silver from America.

When Louis XIV appointed Colbert to his council, he had a minister whose sense of order and uniformity, ideals of public service, and ambitions for the prosperity and power of the kingdom practically guaranteed the introduction of reforms on a broad scale. Since Le Tellier, the war minister who had been responsible for building the army in the 1650s, was also in his council, the king could be assured that his military power would grow as rapidly as his fiscal prosperity would permit. The third member of the council, Lionne, was the foreign minister; he was no reformer, but as one of Mazarin's most competent "creatures," he was fully prepared to manage the king's affairs with the rest of Europe.

As with many reforming regimes, Louis and his advisers struck
out in all directions, sometimes successfully, sometimes not. Judges
sent from Paris held *"grand jours"* to try to capture malefactors in
the provinces; royal intendants of police, justice, and taxation mul-
tiplied and developed subintendants to attempt to force local officials
to do their duty or, in case of failure, to take over administration
or judicial problems in the name of the king's council. A court
sitting in Paris brought dishonest tax collectors to justice and forced
them to disgorge some of their pilferings. New tariff laws, new
controls over production of goods, and regulations to ensure standardization of products on the market—even a war against the
Dutch—aimed at the expansion of French commerce and industry.
At the same time, roads were bettered, a canal to join the Mediterranean and the Atlantic was undertaken, and royal officials and
engineers took interest in fortifications, harbors, and other port
facilities. The commission that undertook the codification of the
laws did not complete its work, but its studies and suggestions were
basic for the reformers who finally produced the Napoleonic Code
a century and a half later.

Indeed, many of Louis's reforms did not actually succeed very
effectively. There were always great distances in terms of the time
required for orders or goods to move about the kingdom, problems
of finding suitable and well-trained personnel to carry out commands, shortages of money for expensive programs. Anyone who
reads the administrative correspondence of this regime will soon
feel sorry for the ministers who were continually confronted with
almost insoluble difficulties. When the king's wars or the building
of Versailles added demands upon the time and attention of his
ministers and the flow of money into his treasury, the reform
projects suffered severely, for extraordinary fiscal measures do not
permit reasoned reforms.

While Colbert worried over the fiscal organization of the kingdom and attempted to introduce reform that would bring order
and abundance to the realm, the king himself was more concerned with the problems of foreign affairs and his military organization. Seventeenth-century princes, brought up under the shadow
of the Thirty Years' War, did not ask "Should a prince go to war?"
but "Against whom should I make war?" This attitude was shared

by the men who surrounded them in the court, men who saw in war the opportunity for wealth, fame, and advancement. Thus, Louis XIV tells us that he was uncomfortable with the "quiet" that reigned in Europe when he mounted the throne. Mazarin had done too well his work of bringing peace to the continent; there seemed to be no opportunities for exercising the military talents of the king and his nobility. The Treaty of Westphalia had ended the war in Germany; the Treaty of the Pyrenees, the war between England and France; and the Peace of Oliva, the war in the Baltic.

The young king, however, did have what seemed to be "legitimate aspirations," at least he and his ministers considered them to be. First was the problem of the "gates" to the kingdom; Richelieu and Mazarin before him had been concerned with fortifying existing frontiers and securing new, more defensible boundaries. This seemed to be a proper concern for the young king. His second "legitimate aspiration" came as the result of his marriage to Marie Thérèse, infanta of Spain. In spite of her renunciation of her father's throne, she and her descendants did have claims on the Spanish inheritance. It would be folly to assume that these two problems—the frontiers and the Spanish inheritance—alone accounted for Louis's foreign policy throughout the fifty-odd years of his government; yet they unquestionably were the constants in the flow of events that gave direction to his policies.

What made Louis XIV formidable was not his pretensions to territory that did not belong to him but the powerful army and navy that he developed to support his programs. His first excursion into the Spanish Netherlands to secure his wife's "rights" was followed a few years later by an assault on the United Netherlands to punish the "herring merchants." The formidable military power displayed in these adventures finally convinced the princes of Europe that they were confronted with the choice of submitting to French hegemony or building comparable military power for themselves. In the last two wars that Europe waged to check the ambitions of the king of France, French soldiers found themselves facing power comparable or even superior to their own. This, too, was one of the achievements of the reign of Louis XIV; his military strength evoked the emergence of strength in his neighbors, so as to establish a balance of power in Europe.

The reader of this book will soon come to realize that the resistance of Europe to the "pretensions" of the French king not only placed limits upon Louis's ambitions but also blighted the "new deal" reforms that had marked the early years of his reign. War forced his treasury to embark upon extraordinary fiscal policies, to adopt bizarre financial procedures to milk the kingdom so that the army could fight. War profiteers flourished, soldiers became rich, but the peasants, upon whom the heaviest burdens fell, suffered severely. Since these wars also engulfed the fiscal machinery of all Europe, the France that emerged from the conflicts in 1715 was perhaps no worse off than the rest of Europe. In fact, since the machinery of government that developed under Louis XIV functioned more effectively than that of most other European states, France probably came out of the disastrous wars as the best-governed state in Europe. But the promises of the reforms of 1661 were only imperfectly achieved by 1715.

Yet, we must not see Louis XIV only as a reformer or as a war lord; he also was a ruler with style, a conception of grandeur, and a willingness to support the vital cultural forces in his kingdom. Early in his career he built the great façade of the Louvre that bears his name, even though he hated the city and disliked living there. He understood that a powerful king impresses his own subjects as well as foreign princes by the construction of a palace that at once proclaims his wealth and his excellent taste. But it is not the Louvre that we usually associate with the name of Louis XIV: Versailles was his palace par excellence, and the millions of tourists who have flocked to see it since 1680 testify to its importance. Versailles was at once the home of a great king and the seat of his government—the seventeenth-century equivalent of the White House, the Pentagon, and the departments of state and interior. Europe had never seen its like. The façade is a third of a mile in length, the great park's fountains, reflecting ponds, statues, roads and alleys, clipped trees and flowers are all centered on the château. It was an enormously expensive undertaking, but France has recovered the cost many times over from the tourism that it has inspired. Versailles, too, became a model for the Western world: the plan of the city of Washington was inspired by Versailles; royal palaces from Portugal to Russia were copies of Versailles.

And the etiquette Louis XIV developed for his court to keep the great nobles busy and out of politics became the model for eighteenth-century princes everywhere.

We should note that Versailles undoubtedly reflected the wealth and power of a great king, but it was not a comfortable place to live in. Someone has pointed out that God may find his throne satisfactory, but grandeur can become oppressive for a man, even if he is also a king. This realization led Louis XIV to build several smaller, less pretentious châteaux, the most charming of which must have been Marly, where a complex of small buildings permitted the king and his intimate friends to spend a weekend at a seventeenth-century counterpart of an American motel.

Louis XIV was also a model patron of the arts and sciences. In the twentieth century scientists, writers, scholars, and painters are supported by universities, by foundations like the Guggenheim or the Rockefeller, or by royalties on books and sales of pictures or sculpture. Their seventeenth-century counterparts had to rely on wealthy nobles and princes. None of his contemporaries played out this role with the largess of Louis XIV. A host of literary men, scholars, scientists, and artists of France, as well as other countries, were regular pensioners, and a great many more were on the lists of men receiving "gratifications" from Louis XIV. Some were supported because they studied exotic languages (Turkish, Arabic, Persian, and the like); others, like Cassini the astronomer-mathematician, Racine the playwright, or Rigaud the painter, for reason of their fame. The theater as well as the opera received support from the king's government. This probably was the pattern that Louis XIV learned from Mazarin, whose taste and understanding of the arts and letters was somewhat greater than his own, or from Colbert, who believed that a great king demonstrated his importance through buildings and his support of the arts, sciences, and letters as much as through his armies and warships. In any case, except for those years when both famine and war contrived to reduce his revenue drastically, Louis XIV was a generous patron of men with distinction in many fields of activity.

It is, of course, impossible to sum up a career like that of Louis XIV in a few pages; even a book like this one can only scratch the surface of the materials available for understanding the Sun

King and his regime. If we judge him by twentieth-century standards or test his politics by liberal-democratic or communistic mystiques, Louis XIV and his ministers will often appear arbitrary,
arrogant, brutal, and many more such things; but neither Louis
XIV nor his ministers had any idea of these mystiques. They lived
in a world that was still theocentric, still dominated by God and
directed by His interests. They understood that God had created
society and it did not occur to them to question whether or not
there were accompanying injustices. Indeed, to raise the issue would
presume to judge God's intentions in the creation of the world.
But, like other "enlightened" men of his era, Louis XIV assumed
that there was harmony in the hierarchies of society; he warned his
son to protect his subjects in the third estate (bourgeoisie, artisans,
and peasants) as well as to respect the clergy and the nobility. He
also recommended to his successor a policy of peace with his neighbors, though even when disaster followed his armies, Louis XIV
believed that his "aspirations" were legitimate. He lived in a world
that had not yet heard the words "humanitarian," "cosmopolitan,"
"liberal," "democratic," "socialist," and a host of others associated
with the earth-centered civilization that was to follow.

It is not easy to find selections that will give the reader an over-
view of the reign of Louis XIV. I have presented two of my own
pieces; one should provide insight into the political and religious
education of the king, while the other is intended to illustrate the
assumptions of the era about the role of the king in society. The
chapters from Saint-Léger and Sagnac and G. P. Gooch discuss the
problems of governing the kingdom, while Louis André explains
some of Louis XIV's relations with Europe. The Duke de La Force,
Pierre Gaxotte, and Louis Bertrand introduce the court and cultural life of the reign. Lastly, Saint-Simon, Voltaire, Lavisse, and
Goubert give us summary interpretations that will indicate how
difficult it is to make a judgment about a reign that lasted seventy-
odd years. The reader will surely understand that he must probe
more deeply into the literature if he wishes a fuller understanding
of any of the questions that they raise.

University of Illinois,   JOHN B. WOLF
Chicago Circle

Louis XIV, 1638–1715

A MALE CHILD born to Louis XIII and Anne of Austria after more than twenty years of childless marriage was promptly hailed as *Louis de dieudonné*—the gift of God. Less than five years later his father's death gave the child the throne under the name Louis XIV. The government of the kingdom, and with it the conduct of the war, was in the hands of the queen mother and her minister, Cardinal Mazarin. The cardinal also undertook to supervise the education of the young king.

In 1648, just before the signing of the Treaty of Westphalia, which brought great gains to the kingdom of France, a rebellion known as the Fronde broke out in Paris. For the next four years the kingdom was in internal turmoil, and the young king learned the uncertainty that royalty must endure. It left a deep, unforgettable impression on him.

The Fronde was not broken until 1652, when Louis and Mazarin entered Paris as victors. But the end of the Fronde was not the end of the war with Spain; this lasted for another seven years. During this time Mazarin prepared Louis for his eventual role as king in fact as well as in name, by giving him an education such as few rulers ever received. Louis learned from the council table, from warfare in the field, and from long discussions with the cardinal and his "creatures."

In 1658, however, for a moment it appeared that all this effort might be in vain, for the king became so desperately ill that everyone expected him to die. Since his brother was not trained to succeed him, this crisis made it apparent that, for the safety of France, Louis must marry and have heirs.

It was not easy, however, to accomplish this marriage, for the king was at war with Spain, and it had been understood from his childhood that he should marry Marie Thérèse, the daughter of the Spanish king, Philip IV. A comedy that threatened Louis's marriage to the princess of Savoy brought Philip IV to accept both peace with France and Louis XIV as a son-in-law. The Treaty of the Pyrenees (1659) concluded the arrangement.

On March 9, 1661, Cardinal Mazarin died, and Louis announced to a surprised court that he would henceforth be his own first minister. It took the disgrace of Fouquet to convince the men around him that he really meant it to be that way.

The first half-dozen or so years after Mazarin's death were eventful for Louis XIV and for France. Reform followed reform; the aim of the king and his ministers was to bring *abondance* (prosperity) to the kingdom by administrative and economic reforms, so that it would be easier for the king's subjects to pay taxes. The new military organization that Louis and his war ministers were developing and the extensive and brilliant court that was to convince Europe of the importance of the king of France required extensive financial support.

In 1665 Philip IV died and opened to the French the possibility that the long-hoped-for annexation of the Spanish Netherlands could be at least partly achieved. The War of the Devolution (1667–68) allowed the king to annex a series of provinces and counties on the northern frontier. It also convinced the French government that the Dutch United Netherlands would forever stand in the way of annexation of the coveted provinces unless its power were broken. Thus, in the years 1668–72 Louis's government built a series of treaties to assure an easy conquest of the Dutch Netherlands. Unfortunately for France, the blitzkrieg of 1672 did not achieve its objective. In place of victory, by 1674 the French were confronted with a coalition of the Netherlands, Spain, and the Empire, and a war that lasted until 1678. The Treaty of Nymwegen may have seemed to be a victory for France, but the king knew that, in spite of the fact that his army was the most powerful in all Europe, he had not accomplished his ambitions of 1672.

These first decades of Louis's personal rule were also years in which his court was brilliant and the intellectual and artistic life of the kingdom so vital that it was compared to the age of Augustus. It was also a period in which the king's personal life was irregular. Marie Thérèse was a dull wife, and in a court inhabited by young women eager to make their way to power and wealth, the young king easily found consolation for his unfortunate marriage. Marie Thérèse died in 1683, when Louis was forty-five. He made a secret marriage with an intelligent, personable woman a few years older than himself—Madame de Maintenon. For the rest of his life he seemed to play out the role of a faithful husband.

After the Treaty of Nymwegen, his courtiers called him Louis the Great, and his government assumed an ugly face in Europe. These were the years of the "reunions," or arbitrary annexations of lands and cities on the frontiers, the years when French warships poured bombs on open cities that had offended the king, the years when Louis was at open war with both the papacy and the Huguenots in France. They also were the years when French armies took advantage of the Turkish invasion to force Spain and the Empire to sign a twenty-year truce that would allow France to retain all its "unlawful" annexations.

After 1685, when Louis XIV revoked the Edict of Nantes, the

international situation in Europe tilted the balance of power against France. The emperor's victories in Hungary were clear indication that a rejuvenated German Empire, armed with veteran soldiers, would soon be ready to contest the French king's annexations. When it became evident that the Ottoman Empire would have to make peace with Leopold, the French decided upon a blitzkrieg to force the Empire to recognize the new French frontiers as final. But events turned against Louis. In addition to the Empire's refusal to come to terms, a revolution in England brought William of Orange to power in the island kingdom, after which England as well as the Netherlands entered the new war against France. A long, difficult struggle followed that ended only with the exhaustion of both sides. However, it also marked a sharp reduction of French advances, for the Treaty of Ryswick (1697) set limits to the French expansion and established a new balance of power in Europe.

Unhappily for Louis, the peace that followed was short-lived. The death of Charles II of Spain and the subsequent war to determine the succession to his crowns filled the last years of Louis XIV's life. They were unhappy ones, for French armies suffered reverses that convinced the king that God had withdrawn His protection from the kingdom. These were the years when Louis wept bitter tears in Madame de Maintenon's chambers, although in open court he acted as though the disasters were not serious. A turn of fate in 1710-11 allowed France to recoup enough advantage to make the treaties of Utrecht (1713) somewhat acceptable to the kingdom.

His last years were further darkened by the death of his son, his grandson, and his wife, and even his eldest great-grandson. Thus, in the years before his death he saw the succession to his throne in doubt, since only the life of a delicate child, the future Louis XV, stood in the path of a serious conflict that could even again involve the kingdom in a European war.

JOHN B. WOLF

The Formation of a King

EARLY YEARS

THE BIOGRAPHER of a king and his portrait painter share a number of problems: neither can be sure of the final shape or tone of any of the royal features until the whole picture—the background, the costume, and the paraphernalia of office—have been completed. Nor is that the end of the difficulty. It is probably true that a man's personality and characteristics have achieved firm contours by the time he is twenty-five, but the historian trying to portray them finds that it is a formidable problem to sift the evidence that comes down to us from a seventeenth-century life

From *French Historical Studies,* I (1958), 40–72. Reprinted by permission.

and to separate the significant from the transitory. All personality studies seem to show that some experiences are enormously meaningful, others of little importance; and yet unless the man we study becomes articulate in his testimony, and his contemporaries record voluminously the things that happened to him, it is nearly impossible to assign weight to the important, and to dismiss the myriads of his ephemeral contacts with the world. This is particularly true in the case of Louis XIV since he has left us very little that can be called introspective evidence; even the remarkable *Mémoires,* intended for the instruction of his son, allow us only to infer his experience. Just as he cautioned his son never to say today what can be put off until tomorrow, Louis was reticent about his feelings and his motivations. This limits the historian; without the significant testimony from both the king and those who watched him grow up, it becomes difficult to study Louis the man or Louis the king *en* Dr. Freud, and therefore we must largely proceed with our inquiry *en* Dr. Watson.

Obviously, one must begin with a man's family. Louis XIV inherited the blood and the traditions of the houses of Austria, Spain, Burgundy, Florence, and France; both his father and his mother were descendants of the Hapsburg-Valois; Louis seems to have inherited the physical frame and features of his Burgundian ancestors. Unlike his own son, who was more completely a Hapsburg, Louis's genetic background was not the product of inbreeding. His social environment was as rich and varied as his genetic inheritance. In his ancestral traditions there were models for a king: Charles V, Philip II, Henry IV. These were great kings who had left their marks on Europe. His preceptors told him about the great rulers of France, but the early death of Louis XIII and the frictions between Louis's mother and the Orléans and Condé families made the Spanish Hapsburg influence of Anne of Austria more important in his immediate environment than the Valois-Bourbon traditions of his French forebears.

There can be little doubt about the fact that Anne and Mazarin were the two most important individuals in Louis's early life. We know very little about the contacts that he had with his father, and the stories that do come down to us are not of the type that could be used with any degree of assurance. Louis never talked about his father, never honored his father's memory; beyond this observation very little can be said with assurance about the part that Louis XIII played in his son's life. Anne's role is much less equivocal: Louis was born after more than two decades of a childless, loveless marriage, and his birth not only justified Anne as a woman and released great stores of emotional energy but also gave her a new status as queen. The haunting fear that she might be ignominiously sent back to Spain as well as the humiliation resulting from her failure to fulfill the role to which she had been born were both dissipated by the birth of the dauphin. Anne, who had so recently been a foreign princess suspected of treasonous correspondence with the enemy, became in a few short years not only the mother of the next king of France but also the regent charged with the task of maintaining the position and prestige of the realm. In her late thirties and long anxious for a child, Anne was able to give her son something quite rare for a royal prince—his mother's love and long hours of concentrated attention and care. Louis's personal stability in the face of adversity as well as the healthy structure of his ego may well be traced in important part to the influence of this vigorous, proud, attentive, and determined woman. Mazarin's influence upon the young Louis will emerge as a major part of this paper. As his stepfather and first servant, as preceptor and friend, as a respected and almost certainly beloved father figure, Mazarin must have been the most important masculine influence in Louis's life.

Two years after Louis's birth, his brother Philip came into the world. Brothers, as he wrote to his son, create a problem for the first born. "My care," he writes, "will be to raise them [the dauphin's nonexistent brothers] as well as you, but yours ought to be to raise yourself above them, and to make the whole world see that you merit . . . this rank that seems to have been given by the order of your birth alone." Elsewhere he warns that brothers of the king of France can become political problems. But Louis's own experiences with his brother Philip were conditioned by the fact that Anne was determined that her second son would not behave toward Louis XIV as Louis XIII's brother did toward him. Philip

was brought up to defer to his brother in all things; he was dressed
as a girl much of the time until he was well past adolescence, and
he continued occasionally to dress in women's clothing as an adult.
His latest biographer insists that Anne's rearing of this boy was
probably responsible for his homosexual tendencies. There may
have been some sibling rivalry between the boys, as the anecdote
of their wetting each other in bed might indicate, but neither
contest for their mother's affection nor feelings of inferiority vis-à-
vis his brother could possibly have bothered Louis. Poor Philip was
not so lucky; the mere fact that he, and not Louis, became the
ancestor of so many of Europe's nineteenth-century kings probably
would have been no recompense for the feelings of frustration and
inferiority that he must have had.

Louis had other relatives who taught him wisdom by their own
lives rather than by their precepts. His uncle Orléans had conspired
and revolted against Louis's father; the elder Condé had played
the same role against Louis's grandmother. Orléans's daughter,
la Grande Mademoiselle, was to fire cannons at Louis's own army,
and Condé's son, the Grand Condé, was to join the Spaniard in
war against France. Beaufort, a grandson of Henry IV from the
left hand, plotted to murder Mazarin and, along with the Grand
Condé's sister, joined the Fronde. Louis's aunt, Henriette of England, brought the tragic tale of rebellion climaxed by the execution
of her husband, Charles I. These relatives may not have had much
personal influence, but their lives were evidence that the throne was
no rocking chair, and that a king must look long to find men
whom he can trust.

The entourage of a minor king is a fluid, changing force. At one
time Anne's court seemed to Condé to resemble a ladies' circle
rather than the court of a great king; at another time Louis was
surrounded by boys and girls of his own age: the nieces and
nephew of Mazarin, the noble youths who were chosen to be his
companions. In the troubles of the Fronde and the years that followed, with the war against Spain, Louis found himself in a court
of intriguers, soldiers, bureaucrats, and, occasionally, statesmen who
turned his attention to the massive problems of the day. Each of

these in turn, as we shall see, contributed to the formation of the king.

GENERAL EDUCATION

What sort of an education did Louis receive? If we are to believe his testimony given in his old age, it was so scanty that he could almost pose as self-made man, a posture enjoyed by many men of action. Saint-Simon heartily agrees with Louis's estimate; Louis, in his eyes, was an ignoramus who did not even know how little he knew. Writing in the late nineteenth century, Druon reached the same conclusion. What did Louis know at twenty, he asks; the answer, "Nothing, or almost nothing!" Such harsh judgments must have some foundation; once found it is simple. Louis apparently knew little Latin beyond a schoolboy's translation of Caesar's *Commentaries* and a few exercises; thus, he was largely ignorant of the Latin and Greek classics common to the humanistically educated men of both the seventeenth and the nineteenth centuries. If a renaissance education is the criterion by which one judges a man's culture, Louis undoubtedly *was* an ignoramus. By other standards his education does not seem so hopelessly inadequate.

While his knowledge of Latin was weak, Louis did learn to use the French language with a degree of elegance. His achievement may be contrasted with that of the Grande Mademoiselle's faulty use of her mother tongue, and it is altogether surprising when one reads the ungrammatical half-Spanish, half-French written by his mother, or the Italian-French of Mazarin, and if one remembers that both Anne and Mazarin spoke French with atrocious accents. Druon believes that Louis learned his French from Anne's women, and it may well be the case; however, it seems unwise to discount completely the training of his teachers. In addition to his mother tongue, Louis learned enough Italian to speak it fluently and to appreciate Italian lyric poetry. He also learned, but imperfectly, to speak Spanish; of course, he had no trouble understanding it. English and German seem to have been *terra incognita* to him, but a man with three languages is hardly illiterate.

Louis's knowledge of geography was well beyond that of most

of the men of his day; both foreign ambassadors and his own correspondence testify to his considerable understanding of the geography of Europe. It is unlikely that the "school-book" geographies he used as a boy were more than the basis upon which this knowledge was erected. In the mid-seventeenth century "geographies" included a mélange of material about customs, politics, climate, and so forth. Louis had books available that discussed the cities and provinces of France, the kingdoms of Europe and the Orient, including the Ottoman Empire. His own travels as a youth never took him outside the kingdom, and it is difficult to assess the educational value of his journeys with the court, for it would be possible to travel all over France with the court and yet see very little of the country. Discussions with Mazarin, interviews with ambassadors, and the reports of French agents were undoubtedly of great importance in forming Louis's understanding of Europe.

In the instructions for the dauphin, Louis urges the importance of the study of history, but aside from an occasional recondite digression into the past that probably originated with the pen of Périgny or Pellisson, the *Mémoires* are largely written without benefit of historical learning. Nonetheless, we know that Louis was exposed to considerable historical lore. Péréfixe wrote for him *L'Histoire de Henri le grand* as a principal text for studying the "role of king" in France. Péréfixe's idea of history was admirably conceived for the education of a king; he studied Henry's decisions, the reasons for them, and the possible alternatives; this could be useful training for a man whose birth placed him in a position that demanded decisions. La Porte, Louis's *valet de chambre,* contributed his bit by reading to Louis from Mézeray's *L'Histoire de France,* which began to be published in 1643. We can believe with La Porte that Louis was incensed over the behavior of the early *fainéant kings* and determined not to be Louis *le fainéant.* Louis probably read Commines or at least discussed his work with La Mothe le Vayer, who joined Péréfixe as instructor, and during the Fronde he probably listened to reading from several chronicles describing the uprisings of the past. But how much could he get from his effort? As far as we can tell, most of his formal historical instruction was finished before he was fifteen; the professor of history who reads the test papers of even the twenty-year-olds should not be surprised that Louis's *Mémoires* were not buttressed by historical evidence.

There was another more or less informal source of Louis's education in history. When the court was traveling, it was customary to visit the church in any town where the queen stopped. This often meant a harangue by a clergyman or other important notable, and very often the theme of the address was taken from history. There were three kings whose lives and works were again and again paraded before the young king and his mother as models for action: Clovis, Saint Louis, and Henry IV. The reasons for the choice were simple enough. Clovis held firm to the Roman church and destroyed the Arians; the clergy hoped that Louis would end the toleration of the "pretended Reformed Religion." Saint Louis gave France a mild and just reign during which the church prospered; furthermore, Blanche of Castile, the regent during his minority, could be used to remind Anne of her obligations. Henry IV, whose alleged policy of peace and prosperity contrasted with the war and taxes of the era of Mazarin, made the third "model" for the young king. It is difficult to guess how much Louis understood of these discussions, but even if he did retain some, there remained great gaps in his historical knowledge, which, as Saint-Simon testily asserts, were never filled.

How much mathematics did he know? He had some instruction in the subject, but probably little more than simple arithmetic. His literary education was equally limited. He may have read *Don Quixote* and he did read Scarron's *Le Roman comique* (an early contact with that family); he also attended performances of the plays of Corneille and Molière, and the Italian theater that Mazarin brought to Paris to please Anne. His conception of *la gloire* was almost identical with that propounded in *Le Cid*. Marie Mancini introduced him to Italian lyric poetry, but this was hardly enough to make up for the lack of imaginative literature. No stories have come down to us to indicate that Louis as a child exercised his imagination in play; as a young man he occasionally took part in amateur dramatics at the court, but aside from that there is little evidence of his having a very lively fancy. It might be true that humanistic literature would have filled this gap, but it might also be argued that his natural disposition and temperament, and his lack of a sense of humor, as much as his education, dictated his turn of interests and his feelings about the world.

We have no direct evidence about any education in the fine arts, and yet as king he was a patron of painters, sculptors, and architects. It is probable that he was familiar with Mazarin's fine collection of Italian art, and he undoubtedly was influenced by the Italian decorators, some of whose work for Mazarin can still be seen in the Musée Carnavalet in Paris. Indeed, an art historian might be able to develop an interesting study by comparing the artistic tastes of Louis XIV and the cardinal. How familiar Louis was with Mazarin's magnificent library is also a matter for conjecture.

The instruction of the king also included fencing, dancing, riding, hunting, and some music. The Fronde interrupted the process of instruction, but Louis learned to dance, ride, and hunt with elegance. His marvelous physique and natural grace may have been more important than the formal education. Every picture that we have of Louis as a young man bespeaks his handsome figure, his athletic prowess, his natural charm; his teachers cannot be credited for these graces.

Religious Education

On February 10, 1638, Louis XIII issued *lettres patentes* announcing his intention to take the Virgin Mary as the protector of his kingdom. On the twenty-sixth of March he ordered the archbishop of Paris to proclaim his intention from all the churches "so that each could prepare himself to offer himself with me . . . and to join his prayers with mine so that it will please her to extend her powerful protection to her kingdom." Louis, *le dieudonné,* was born seven months later. In the celebrations that followed the fortunate event, religious services played an important part: indeed, it can be said that Louis *le dieudonné* came into the world with a chorus of *Te Deums,* hundreds of forty-hour devotions, and thousands of votive Masses rising from the churches of France. As Louis XIV, Louis *le Grand*, he continued to order religious services to thank God and the Mother of Jesus for benefits bestowed upon the kingdom. The medal that Louis XIII had struck portraying the king of France on his knees before a statue of the Virgin Mary offering to her his kingdom in gratitude for her favor was illustrative of the religious values of the French royal family in the mid-seventeenth century; Louis absorbed these values with the air he breathed and made them part of himself.

Anne, even more than Louis XIII, regarded the birth of *le dieudonné* as a miracle. Her religious background was strict and tinged with mysticism. Her father, Philip III, read his office daily with the spirit of a monk; he heard voices (in Castilian Spanish) from heaven, he pressed the pope to proclaim the dogma of the Immaculate Conception; reared in the court of the aged Philip II, he was more suited for the Church than for the throne. Anne's mother was at least as attentive to the services of the church as Philip III; she heard two Masses daily, took Communion every Sunday, and spent many hours on her *priedieu*. Under such influence Anne grew up reading books of devotion and religious mysticism, accepting the symbolism found everywhere in the Escorial as substantial idea, finding solace and meaning for her life in church services, and seeing religious mystery in the strange religious allegories of Lope de Vega. Before her marriage to Louis XIII her life had been wrapped in a texture of religious observances, cults, and mysteries that conditioned her thought and action until her death. This was not as apparent in her first years at the court of France, when youthful vigor and animal spirits encouraged playful, often frivolous, behavior, but one has only to read the de Motteville memoirs to see how much she changed after she was forty. Anne's Catholicism was Spanish: candles, hours at the *priedieu*, books of devotion and mystery.

Her most important declaration of faith was crystallized in the baroque church at Val-de-Grace. In the days of her near disgrace that cloister had been a place of refuge where she could talk about God in Spanish with sympathetic nuns; when the birth of a son gave her status, Val-de-Grace became the object of her

special attention. Her body was buried at St. Denis, but her heart
was sent to Val-de-Grace, along with many of her most treasured
possessions. The symbolism in the church identifies the mother
of the king of France with that other mother whose son was the
King of Heaven; in the chapel of Saint Anne at Val-de-Grace
the sculptor Michel Anguier glorified with mystic symbolism
the married state and divine love in marriage. St. Anne and St.
Joachim, the parents of the Virgin, suitably became the central
figures of the drama of marriage. Roman Catholics in the twentieth century will recognize the emotional force behind this sort of
cult of saints.

While not as pious as Anne, Mazarin, too, was a deeply religious man. For a long time the present writer tended to discount
as mere formalities the appeals for prayers, the expressions of
respect for God and his saints, and the religious tone in so many
of Mazarin's letters. Could it be that this man who seemed to fear
so little in the world was so respectful of God? However, it is
clear that Professor G. N. (now Sir George) Clark was unquestionably correct when he once remarked that we must take a seventeenth-century man seriously when he talks about God. Mazarin,
like Anne, must have encouraged Louis in the fulfillment of his
religious duties.

There were many priests and monks in and out of the court
during the childhood of Louis, but the man whose name occurs
most often as an intimate of the family was St. Vincent de Paul.
He prepared Louis XIII for death; he remained as friend and
counselor of the queen during the regency. His influence on the
Council of Conscience was often enough nullified by Mazarin,
but until his naïve attempt to end the conflict during the Fronde,
St. Vincent was well known at court. He was no theologian, not
even a "thinker," but his religion of good works, pious intentions,
and spiritual exercises suited the royal family; and it did not
seriously interfere with other activities that may have been less
pleasing to God.

The young king's formal spiritual education was entrusted to
Father Charles Paulin, S.J., who as confessor and friend directed
the conscience of the young man. Father Paulin's interest was

the saving of Louis's soul by giving him a Christian upbringing. How much he recognized Anne's part in the work can be seen from a letter written to the general of the Jesuit order at the time of Louis's first Communion: "There is no lamb more sweet, more tractable than our king. . . . He has in him the piety that the most Christian queen has inculcated in him from early childhood by her tender counsels and advice." Anne more than "counseled" her son; when Louis attempted to use some language that he had learned in the stables, Anne imprisoned him in his room in solitary confinement for two days. This punishment may or may not have been responsible for the fact that Louis's speech was never profane, but there can be little doubt about the influence of Anne's "counsels" on his later life. It was she who reduced him to tears over his weakness for La Vallière, and probably her introjected "super-ego" that forced him so often to try to give up de Montespan, and finally, when his queen had died, to take Madame de Maintenon as his wife. It is well to remember that Louis may have enjoyed the pleasures of the flesh in his early manhood, though not without attacks of conscience.

It is difficult to assess the impact of a single event on a man's life, and yet it is hard to believe that the ceremony of consecration performed when Louis was a boy of fifteen could fail to leave a strong impression on his mind. The *Sacre* was Mazarin's answer to the rebellious noblemen who could not be controlled by a regent and a minor king; the event itself, however, must have been an emotional experience for the young man. Louis prepared himself spiritually for the consecration the night before, much as a bishop prepares for his elevation. At 4:30 A.M. the high clergy robed themselves and began the ceremonies; by six o'clock the court and a great press of people filled the great cathedral of Reims, and then the bishops of Beauvais and Châlons, followed by the crowd, marched to the door of the archepiscopal palace, where the Duke of Joyeuse, acting as grand chamberlain, demanded: "What do you wish?" Beauvais: "The king. We ask for Louis XIV, son of that great king Louis XIII, whom God has given us for king." Upon the third repetition of this formula, the doors were thrown open, and the crowd marched to the bed where Louis, clad in

rich clothing, awaited them. With holy water, incense, and prayers
they led him to the cathedral for the age-old ceremony of anointing
with the oil that "came from heaven" for the consecration of
Clovis. The consecration emphasized the sacerdotal character of
the kings of France. "Your Majesty," he was told, "must recognize
by the maxims of piety as much as by the light of pure truth, that
if the kings of France are of a divine order . . . this striking
privilege flows from the sacred unction, the holy ampole of oil
that gives sacred character. . . ." Louis may have noted that
Condé and others were absent, in rebellion against his rule, but
he also knew that God had established kings as His rulers on
earth and that the church consecrated their rule.

Dubois tells us of the young Louis's strict attention to religious
duties; Fénelon assures us that the old Louis's religion was super-
stitious, devout, in the Spanish style. These two witnesses, over a
half century apart, can be corroborated by many others. Louis
probably understood no more than his mother did about the
theological differences that separated the Catholic and the Reformed churches; his conception of God as an object of worship
seems to have led him to perform acts of piety, to cause prayers
to be said, to thank God for His blessings. When things went
well with the royal projects, Louis knew that God had blessed his
labors and ordered *Te Deums* and Masses and other religious
services in thanksgiving. When his armies were defeated, when
drought brought crop failure, when his kingdom looked like a
land occupied by a hostile power, Louis feared that God had withdrawn His protection from his kingdom; then his prayers were to
supplicate God's forgiveness for his pride and to ask for a return
of favor.

It should finally be noted that Louis's respect for the church
and its ministers did not blind him to the fact that the church
and the churchmen played many roles in society. One can almost
hear Mazarin's voice in one passage of the *Mémoires*:

> I have never failed to call your attention whenever the occasion
> presented itself to the respect we owe to religion and the deference
> we owe to its ministers in the things that make up their principal
> mission, that is, the celebration of the mysteries of cult and the

spread of evangelical doctrine. But because the men of the church
are likely to take advantage of their profession . . . I am obliged
to point out to you certain points that may be important.

The "important points" concerned the property of the church and
the service of churchmen to the state. In other words, as Louis's
career indicates, he was brought up to respect cult, to give his
heart to God, but he also had a practical attitude toward the
clergy and its wealth.

PROFESSIONAL EDUCATION

Louis's general education may have been neglected, but his professional training was not. The times in which he lived, as well
as the devoted efforts of his mother and Mazarin, combined to
give Louis XIV an education in the art of government seldom
allotted to princes. It was professional education that would have
appealed to John Dewey: he learned by doing, by direct experience
with the problems of state. Louis could never be a doctrinaire
politician; his education gave him a practical, pragmatic approach
to the problems of government.

Anne once remarked that kings did not need to *study* history
since they *lived in* it. Louis certainly lived in history from the time
he could take note of things, even though it is improbable that he
understood what was happening at first. Minority governments
had long since been the "opportunity" for the "great ones" who
wished to reverse the centralizing tendencies of the royal authority,
and in the 1640s the "great ones" were joined by the regular officials of the kingdom (members of the sovereign courts and the
municipal and provincial officials) who resented and feared the
rising power of the king's council and its agents. The Fronde
really started almost as soon as Louis XIII closed his eyes. Beaufort
and the "important ones" plotted to murder Cardinal Mazarin;
parlement refused to register the edicts of the council; Condé demanded special favors for his son as soon as that young man won
victory for the king's arms; the boy king *had* to hold a *lit de justice*
and listen to the tense speeches; provincial as well as parlementary
officers complained about the activities of the king's *maîtres des*

requêtes on mission (intendants). His aunt Henriette of England, a refugee in France, did not need to tell of the troubles in her husband's kingdom for the young Louis to realize that the paths of kings are not easy. He had only to see his mother's anger and humiliation at the speeches of Omar Talon in Parlement, and hear her mutter, "My son will punish them when he grows up." The boy of ten who remarked on the occasion of a French victory in the Netherlands, "The gentlemen in Parlement will not be pleased," had absorbed much from his environment about the political process in the kingdom, and there was more to come.

The Fronde was well under way before the riots and barricades in Paris called attention to the problems in France. However, the drama of the rioting crowds demanding the release of the arrested parlementarians; the tense speeches and hasty conferences; the fears that the Palais Royal might be invaded and sacked; the intrusion of men demanding to see if the young king were really asleep in his bed and not spirited away; the nocturnal flight from the city with his mother and the cardinal obviously afraid of the possible consequences of their act; the siege of Paris and perhaps some knowledge of the awful things that men were writing and saying about his mother and Mazarin; the semihypocritical appeals for the king to return to "his city of Paris," which was at war with him—these and many more dramatic events of the first year of the Fronde were unforgettable experiences for the boy king, and there were more to come. Writing for his son some twenty years later, Louis says of this period:

> It is necessary to point out the conditions of things: terrible agitations throughout the kingdom both before and after my majority; a foreign war in which these domestic troubles cost France a thousand advantages; a prince of the blood and a very great name at the head of the armies of our foe; cabals in the state; the Parlements still in possession, and in taste for, usurped authority; in my court, very little fidelity without personal interest. . . .

This is a graphic description of the misery of the Fronde.

Charles Péguy once wrote a moving essay about *misère* in which he asserted that anyone who has ever experienced such total

privation can never forget it and can never act without its influence. Such a person will pile up money and any other security
beyond all need simply because of the memory of the pain. The
Fronde was *misère* for the young king of France, an experience
that he never forgot. Its memory colored many of his acts in later
years: the maintenance of a strict etiquette to control members of
the court, the treatment of a harmless brother asking for favors
or for a military command, the regulation of *parlement* and the
royal bureaucracy, and a host of others. This is not surprising. It
was humiliating to be shut out of his own cities. It mattered little
that the rebel soldiers also cried *"vive le roi"*; they still held
towns against the king's loyal forces. It must have been near to
terrifying to see his mother being forced to send Mazarin, the only
man she really trusted, into exile; it must have been disturbing
not to know whether a soldier like Turenne would be on the side
of the king or of the king's enemies. Nor did the humiliation end
with the victory over rebellious noblemen, parlementarians, and
the Spanish armies; years later when Louis was proudly showing
his recently forgiven cousin, La Grande Mademoiselle, a new
regiment equipped with kettledrums, he asked her if she had ever
heard the like before (he, Louis, had not). The answer: "Oh yes,
years ago during the war [Fronde] with the foreign troops." Even
the joy of a new military toy was blighted by memory of the
Fronde.

While the Fronde was a period of political *misère,* it was also
an object lesson in the art of government, a time when a young
man with his eyes open could learn much about the game of
politics. It was as instructive to watch a master politician like
Mazarin manipulate affairs, even from exile, as it was to observe
the twisting and turning of his uncle Orléans, of the wily Retz,
of the calculating Châteauneuf, and of others. Soldiers no less than
politicians had much to teach about politics as well as about war.
Louis learned well. His later dramatic arrests of the Cardinal de
Retz and Fouquet plagiarized the pattern set by Anne and Mazarin in the arrest of Condé; his famous response to all requests—
"je verrai"—probably originated in a youthful slip of the tongue
during this period.

Mazarin's role in the political education of Louis XIV was, as mentioned above, most important. He was Louis's godfather (at the request of Louis XIII); he was superintendent of Louis's education (suggested by the then dead king, the queen, Orléans, and Condé); he was probably Louis's stepfather; finally, he had a deep affection for the young man. Memoir writers and many historians have told stories about Mazarin's neglect of the young boy, of hostility between the two, of Louis's impatience to be rid of his minister. The facts seem to have been exactly the opposite. There was a deep friendship, a feeling probably near to love, between the two men. One has only to read Mazarin's letters to Anne to see the warmth, the fatherly feelings of the elder man. Like Anne, who always treated Louis as *her king* and gave him the homage due a king, Mazarin always showed great respect for the person of his "master"; even when he sent Louis letters filled with scolding words, recalling him to his duty as a father might write to an erring son, the formal tone of the letter was that of a courtier just as Anne's behavior toward Louis was that of courtesan. But neither Anne nor Mazarin were really "formal" toward Louis; their courtly ways were intended to teach him the respect due a king. Both of them thought of Louis as king and man, and were anxious that the boy should succeed in *both* roles. Mazarin wrote, "He [Louis] has in him the stuff of several kings and of an *'honnête'* man." On another occasion he wrote to Villeroy, "You know how many times I have said to you that we can expect that he [Louis] will be a prince as accomplished as any that one has seen in several centuries."

Le Confidant [Louis] was obviously Mazarin's pride and hope. He wrote to Anne: "The king is well—he has taken great pleasure in the letters that you have sent me . . . he knows the firm and tender love that you have for him . . . he never fails to embrace me in the evenings, and we talk in terms from the heart." Louis was privy to the secrets of the household; he knew that Anne did not wish to displease Mazarin "by deed or even by thought." When Louis and Mazarin were with Turenne at the front, the cardinal's letters to Anne sound like those of a doting father, proud of the achievements of his son. And when Louis was deathly ill in 1658, Mazarin wrote to Lockhart, "I want above all to hope that God does not wish to punish this kingdom by taking from us the one who brings it joy, being the father of the people. . . ." And to Turenne, when the fever finally broke, he wrote: "I rejoice again with you over the grace that God has given us in conserving for us the king." These letters during Louis's illness are filled with paternal love and anxiety; because of his confidence in the queen's love, it was not until later that Mazarin realized how much personal danger he might have been in had Louis's brother become king.

Louis's own feelings are more difficult to assess. Even as a small boy he was reserved and sober, yet the oft-quoted words to the cardinal at the time of the illness give some indication of his feelings: "You are a man of resolution and the best friend I have; therefore, I beg you to alert me if I shall be near to death; for the queen would not dare to do it for fear that it would augment the illness." Up until Mazarin's death Louis deferred to him and left all to his judgment, and Louis wept hot tears both after his last interview with the cardinal and when the news of his death was announced. Anne's grief was not the only reason for ordering full court mourning, heretofore reserved for members of the royal family. Furthermore, Louis's *Mémoires* and his government after Mazarin's death are a standing monument to his respect and his love for the cardinal. Lacour-Gayet was not wrong when he concluded that Louis loved and respected Mazarin so much that it almost seemed that the cardinal ruled decades after his death.

Mazarin's method of instruction gave the young king direct contact with affairs. In the first place, he urged him to read the state papers as they came in, accustoming him to the most elementary work of a ruler, namely the learning of the facts upon which decisions must be made. In addition, Mazarin gradually introduced Louis into council meetings, but only after the young king had read the papers to be discussed, and in slow stages so that the problems would be simple enough for him to understand. At first it seems that Louis attended only meetings at which decisions could easily be made; later he was to learn that it is not always possible to make a decision. In his *Mémoires* Louis explains that he would secretly make up his mind how the matter should be decided, and prided himself in the fact that very often the decision of older heads was the same as his own. When foreign ambassadors visited the court or when a French envoy was sent abroad, Mazarin had Louis assist him with the interview, thus instructing him in the art of high politics and the counters of diplomacy. The unquestioned skill and knowledge that Louis was to show as king are tributes to the success of this method of instruction.

Louis spent many hours closeted with Mazarin during the last half-dozen years of the cardinal's life. When the court was domiciled at one of the palaces, the young king would spend time in the morning and again in the afternoon in the cardinal's chambers; when the court was traveling, the two were together almost as much. What went on during these interviews? There is no direct documentary evidence, but much can be inferred from a study of Louis's *Mémoires*. These pages were dictated, written, and suggested by Louis for the education of his heir; some of the passages recount events and decisions that Louis had taken as king and therefore are the result of his own experience; other passages are general reflections about politics, society, the handling of men, and the like; others, insight into the art of government, rules for managing affairs. Many of these are much more sophisticated than one has the right to expect from a young man in his twenties, even a young man as bright as Louis. It cannot be proved, and yet there is undoubtedly a strong presumption that these passages are Louis's recollections of the advice and counsel of the cardinal and, perhaps, of his mother.

In a short essay it is impossible to analyze the content of the *Mémoires*; it is enough to note that parts of them are surely some of the best pointed and practical counsels that were ever written for the education of a prince. Here and there Louis falls into a high moral tone exhorting his son to "give his heart to God" or expatiating on "virtue," but for the most part he confines himself to practical advice. They deal with questions in the everyday life of a king as well as more difficult problems of state policy. "How shall a king live with his neighbors?" "How shall he choose his ministers?" "How does a king reward those who serve him?" "The importance of keeping one's given word." "Do not presume too much; it is better to wait until success is sure before announcing victory in politics." "Do not hope too much from fortune; indeed, be suspicious of hopes." "Wisdom and councils." "Faithful and faithless servants." "A king must be father of his people." "Factions: it is better to prevent their forming in the state." "Means and methods of dealing with the clergy." "All classes have utility to the state; protect the bourgeoisie and peasants from the soldiers." These and many more were topics for the dauphin: they must also have been Mazarin's lessons for the young king.

Mazarin's advice covered big as well as little things. He did not need to urge Louis to be his own first minister, but we know that he did so. Louis scrupulously followed Mazarin's policy of thanking those who served the king's government; this sort of letter bulks large in the correspondence of both men. Both managed people by indirection whenever possible rather than by force; both were polite to those about them. Perhaps even more important, Mazarin's discussions of foreign policy, the only policy that really interested him, must have left a strong impression on his protégé, for Louis's foreign policy for the next quarter century and more can best be understood by studying Mazarin's ideas about Europe and the role of the French Bourbon dynasty in Europe. Lastly, Louis's methods of work were unquestionably in part influenced by Mazarin. The cardinal insisted that no one can govern without studying the documents; he urged Louis to be attentive to work and praised him when his style of writing and his grasp of political problems improved. It may even be that Louis's *feuillets* from which he wrote or dictated the *Mémoires* were in imitation of Mazarin's *Carnets*.

Where Mazarin left off, Anne took over the task of preparing her son for the *"métier du roy."* Louis's love for his mother led him to see her often and intimately. Like those of so many attentive mothers, Anne's counsels were not always heeded by her son, and yet much of Louis's vision of himself and his part in the world cannot be explained or understood unless we infer that Anne, the Spanish princess educated in the Escorial in the days when the

memory of Philip II was still a vital force in that court, was a significant factor in his education. Anne's vision of royalty and the
role of king in society, as well as her conception of the honor and
respect due to kings, were not in the Bourbon tradition. Henry
IV's court had been managed with the easygoing manners of a
guerrilla captain; he got his way by backslapping, by cajolery, by
feigned intimacy, or, at last, by force. Louis XIII had run the
state and secured obedience by cold, surly, and at times brutal
insistence upon his policy; while Richelieu understood the meaning of diplomacy and indirection, both he and Louis XIII were
willing to rule by force. Anne and Mazarin, perhaps because they
had less moral authority, were less cruel, less willing to depend
upon the headsman's ax. She knew that men can be controlled by
etiquette, by imposed manners, by a system of values saturated
with ideas of rank and social position. She also had a vision of
a great king, Philip II, whose life might have been a failure, but
whose notions about the métier of a king surely *ought* to be the
secret of success. Louis does not follow all of his great-grandfather's
patterns, but the long hours over paper work, the attention to detail, the vision of the grandeur of royalty, and, of course, the obvious connection between Versailles and the Escorial all indicate
possible relationship between the two men. The student should
never underestimate Anne because of her love of cocoa, her self-
indulgence, her passion for entertainment, or even her indolence;
the mother of Louis XIV was the woman who stood up (with
the aid of Mazarin) against the storms of the Fronde, coldly
scorning and hating her enemies who did not share her vision of
her son, and finally triumphing (again with the aid of Mazarin)
over princes, and noble cabals, and sovereign courts that wished to
limit the royal authority. In Louis her scorn and hatred is translated into action that controlled the minds and bodies of men, and
forced them to play parts that were set by the king.

There were two important roles that Louis XIV assumed: those
of soldier and of administrator. Louis's own heirs failed to see
that when Louis the soldier was combined with Louis the administrator, Louis the great, Louis the enlightened despot, emerged.
Frederick II of Prussia did not miss this lesson. In the education

of Louis the soldier administrator many men, unmentioned here, contributed a share—bureaucrats and soldiers who trained the king in the arts of war and administration.

The French king was expected to be a soldier; indeed, that was his historic role in an age when war was the natural agency for curing anarchy and shaping political life. Louis's father, his grandfather, and the great kings of the Capet-Valois line had been soldiers; it was a role that French kings had to play. Le Tellier and Turenne were Louis's most important preceptors in military affairs; the one taught the art of command, the other the science of military administration. Turenne was a hardheaded teacher of the art of war: his cadets included the dukes of Luxembourg, Lorraine, Villars, and Marlborough ("handsome Jack Churchill"), and many other soldiers who fought for and against France in the era of Louis XIV. Louis's period of apprenticeship under the great soldier was not long enough to make him into a great captain, but Mazarin and Louis spent much time with the army between 1654 and 1659, and most of it was in the company of Turenne. Mazarin's letters tell us of the enthusiasm and ardor with which Louis followed the sieges and other operations. Turenne's counsels were reinforced by those of Le Tellier, the first bureaucratic war minister who, with his son Louvois, was the architect of the French standing army. Le Tellier, whose code name was *"le Fidèle"* in the Anne-Mazarin correspondence, was one of the few people whom the family could really trust. It is not unlikely that Louis not only learned enough from these two men to write the shrewd passages about military affairs that one finds in the *Mémoires* but also got from them his liking for wars of position, of sieges and maneuvers, as well as his fear of infantry battles in the field in which a war could be won (or lost) in an afternoon.

Colbert's influence upon Louis was undoubtedly important, but by the time Colbert became the king's trusted man, Louis's character and ideas were already fixed, so that Colbert's role was more that of a counselor and advisor than of a teacher; many historians who see Louis's wars as acts of the royal will regret that the minister of economics did not get to the king earlier. When Mazarin died, obliging him, as he wrote to his son, "no longer to defer that which I had hoped for and feared so long," Louis recognized himself as ready to assume the task of government. It only remained for him to use his education effectively.

POLITICAL PHILOSOPHY

Seventeenth-century men were more conscious of the problems involved in justifying political power than any European generation before their time; a galaxy of political philosophers—Hobbes, Harrington, Bossuet, Pufendorf, Spinoza, Grotius, James I, Locke, and Leibnitz, to mention only a few—proved how fruitful were their efforts. With his contemporaries so self-conscious about the problems of political philosophy, it was inevitable that Louis XIV should somehow be instructed in its secrets. But, as in his study of history, his philosophical education was neither formal nor structured. The fact that he was king was unquestionably an important factor in the formation of his ideas; both sycophants and sincere men combined to exalt the office in his mind. The structure of political society itself was also significant; centuries of political evolution under a monarchy in which the king was a consecrated officer had created a series of political assumptions that the young Louis absorbed in much the same way in which he breathed air. A politically self-conscious generation made it necessary to form these ideas into words.

Louis warned his son that "those people badly abuse themselves who imagine that the pretensions to this quality [the preeminent position of royalty] are only a matter of ceremonies. . . ." Yet the numerous ceremonies in which he either took part or which were held in his honor must also have been of considerable importance in the formation of his ideas about the role of king. Meetings in *parlement* when the government held a *lit de justice,* receptions of delegations, and, of course, the impressive consecration at Reims —all entailed implications about the role of king. The elaborate ceremonies after 1661 when the king's real or imaginary triumphs were celebrated with tableaux of papier-mâché, fireworks, trumpets, pantomimes, and extensive oratory were not as common during his minority and early years as king, but the number of receptions and speeches honoring the king is nonetheless impressive.

In the period of the regency not all the speeches were friendly to the government; if there is one thing that all of these ceremonies had in common, however, it was a full recognition of the idea that the king had been established by God as father of the people. Even Omar Talon, when his forthright words in *parlement* offended Anne, admitted freely that God had given France her king, and that the king should be obeyed. The large number of books and pamphlets published without royal permission during the Fronde manifest this same tendency; even though the authors hated the regent and her minister, they were almost universally royalist and ready to admit that the throne was established by God. In other words, both sides of the conflict in the mid-seventeenth century accepted the basic assumption that the king's power came from God, and both regarded the king as a sacerdotal officer.

There has been, however, considerable misunderstanding about the nature of that grant from God. Did "king by divine right" mean that the king could do what he wished? By no means. The Roman church has long expounded the doctrine of divine right based upon the sentence in St. Paul's Letter to the Romans (XIII:1): *Non est potestas nisi a Dei.* Men with as varied backgrounds as Mazarin, Bishop Bossuet, Claude Joly, and Antoine Arnaud all would agree on the church's teaching on this point. All power and authority, indeed everything in the world, came from God; and since hierarchical society was necessary for man's well-being, God therefore had created kings to rule over men. But in Catholic thought man had the free will to do right or wrong, and kings were no exception to this rule: it would make God the author of the evils committed by bad men if God were responsible for kings' actions. The problem was solved by making God the source of power, power that he bestowed upon kings with the right to act as His lieutenants on earth. But, just as Locke divided power (ability to govern) and authority (right to govern), giving one to kings and retaining the other for the people, so the doctrine of divine right left the authority (the right to govern) in the hands of God, giving only the *potestas* (the power to rule) into the hands of magistrates.

Jacques Maritain insists that the same relationship exists today between God and governments, even parliamentary ones. God, however, expected kings to do their duty, to carry out His work on earth, and if they failed to do so, He not only would punish them in the next world, but also would withdraw His protection from them in this one. Péréfixe had the young Louis translate into Latin the phrase, "I know that the principal duty of a Christian prince is to serve God and that piety is the basis for all royal virtues." Louis wrote for his son a long passage insisting upon the necessity for a king to submit to God's law and urging him to believe that kings have greater obligations toward God than other men. "Important obligations demand of us heavy duties," he wrote; "and since, in giving us the scepter, He has given us that which appears as the most striking thing on earth, we ought, in giving Him of our heart, to give Him that which is most agreeable in His eyes." Mazarin put it even more bluntly at the time of the Mancini crisis:

> God has established kings to care for the well-being, the security, the repose of their subjects, and not to sacrifice those goods and that repose to their own passions, and if that unfortunate situation does occur . . . the Divine Providence abandons them. The histories are full of revolutions and prostrations (*accablements*) and that they [willful kings] have brought down upon themselves and their subjects.

It would be hard to find a statement that better expressed the assumptions of the doctrine of divine right as it was understood in the mid-seventeenth century.

Louis's deductions from the idea that God established kings and endowed them with power to govern were in part his own and in part common to his society. Kings, he was sure, were a race apart, signally different from other men because of God's action. They are the "fathers of their peoples." God not only placed them on the throne but also gave them the wisdom necessary to do His work. Kings, created in the image of God, Louis believed, had a natural understanding of politics. He was certain that he could deal with affairs of state more surely and more deftly than his ministers, who were always anxious to be sure that their action would be acceptable.

Since power was the gift of God to the king, any division or sharing of that power, in Louis's opinion, tended to corrupt or degrade it. How many of the *mazarinade* pamphlets expressed this same point of view in urging the king to govern without a "companion" (Mazarin), to be the sole "father of his people." It was also the lesson of the valet, La Porte, who read histories of *fainéant* kings, of Mazarin, who urged Louis to become his own first minister. Louis writes about the plight of English kings: "This subjugation, which forces the sovereign to take the law from his people, is the last calamity that can fall upon a man of our rank." He went on to say that a prince who has to give power to a first minister is in a miserable condition even though he has the right to choose that minister, but infinitely worse is the lot of a monarch who has to depend upon a popular assembly because it is not "merely power that a people assembled attributes to itself: the more you give it, the more it pretends to; the more you favor it, the more it despises you; and when this power is once in its possession, it is held so strongly that one cannot take it away without extreme violence."

So brief a statement does not do justice to Louis's discussions about power and the use of power, and yet a fuller statement would only modify and expand his basic assumptions, namely, that God has established kings and endowed them with the ability to carry out His work on earth and, secondly, that this gift of power is personal and therefore the king should exercise it himself. However, a reading of Louis's *Mémoires* makes it clear that the expression of absolutism is tempered by the fact that Louis also understood that he ruled a kingdom in which history and tradition had created a matrix of rights, customs, and privileges limiting the action of power; royal absolutism did not imply the right to arbitrary political action even in the mind of so absolute a king as Louis XIV.

The Person of the King

Anyone who has watched children grow up to become men knows that there are important individual differences in physical and emotional inheritance; American environmentalist assumptions sometimes tend to ignore these genetic differences, and historians usually pay no attention to them. Nonetheless, inheritance is important. In Louis's case, he was richly endowed by nature; as a youth and as a man he was handsome, athletic, and vigorous; his emotional temperament was calm, at times almost lethargic, and even as a small boy he carried himself with a natural dignity, related perhaps to good muscular coordination. In spite of his tendency to hypochondria which caused him to take quantities of pills and potions, he was usually in excellent health. Just what the relationship of inheritance and environment was to the various characteristics of his personality we cannot, of course, say. Even more baffling are other aspects of his personality. The present status of personality psychology still leaves us at a loss to know which questions are the most important ones to ask, and even if we did know the proper questions, it is often impossible to find trustworthy witnesses to supply the answers.

Personality theorists are, however, largely in accord with an observation that wise men had long suspected, namely, that an individual develops the contours of his personality in part as the result of meaningful repetition of behavior that proves to be successful in effecting inner satisfaction. In other words, characteristic behavior patterns tend to become firmly fixed to the measure that the individual receives satisfactions in the form of social rewards, inner feelings of well-being, success in dealing with anxieties, and the like. It would be very difficult to produce evidence that would prove the connection between Louis's behavior patterns and his inner feelings, and yet the *Mémoires* are replete with passages from which we can infer that Louis *learned* to fill the role of king by successfully becoming king under the tutelage of Mazarin and his mother; that he "resolved" the threatening anxieties of the Fronde by being associated with the master politician whose skill pulled the teeth of the rebellion; that he absorbed the ceremonial pattern of the king by successfully acting out the role on a score of platforms. Such achievements alone probably would not have given him the conscience that *drove* him to try to fulfill his part as king, and yet they may well have been the added fillip that brought satisfaction to Louis the man when he acted out the part of Louis the king. We probably must look deeper to discover why Louis the king demanded of himself the effort necessary to live up to his *gloire*.

William James believed that a man's "self" is the sum of the different roles that he plays in the world; more recent psychologists, affected by Freudian concepts, have produced considerable evidence that strongly suggests that the interpersonal relations of a child with his parents or *qua* parents are of great importance in the fulfillment of roles, as well as of "ego" development. Of particular significance seems to be the love-respect attitudes of the parents toward the child and the consequent desire of the child, in order to be assured of his parents' continued love, to act within the patterns, values, and behavioral limits represented by the parents. In "important" (to the parents) and stressed behaviors, the child who is loved, respected, and guided with some consistency is said to "introject" the values of the parents. Louis was born to the role of king, but so were many other children born to the purple, and yet only a few of them have acted out their roles on the stage of the world, and fulfilled it as seriously and pervasively as Louis XIV did. Today when we think of a king, the stereotype is either Louis XIV or Charlemagne: why did he assume so well his role?

One thing that we can be sure of is the mutual affection between Louis and his mother, and it seems almost equally sure that a similar relation existed between him and Mazarin. Who knows the hundreds of daily and persistent contacts among these three people that may have been decisive factors in Louis's opinion of himself, his role, and his obligations toward God, man, and himself—in short, his *gloire*. We do know that Anne never ceased to impress upon him her desire that he should grow up to be a great king, as well as a good man: she had a sense for majesty, a feeling for the rights and obligations of rulers, and an ideal of *la gloire* that meant in effect the fulfillment of both the role and the inner potentials entrusted to a man. How she transmitted these to Louis cannot be told, but her attitudes and values and his later actions correlate so well that we do have the right to infer a strong relationship. We have also shown similar instances with regard to Mazarin.

Furthermore, Mazarin's intervention at the time that Louis wished to marry Marie Mancini has left us a series of letters that leave no doubt about his attitudes and influence. The deeply infatuated Louis was ready to throw over all the advantages of a royal Spanish marriage to marry Mazarin's niece. Louis's argument that the house of Bourbon was deeply indebted to Mazarin and that the marriage he wished to make would, in a way, repay that debt, speaks for Louis's ingenuity as well as for his feelings toward Mazarin (and Marie!). Mazarin's letters are those of a father using all the arguments he can muster to prevent a willful son from committing an act of folly. He speaks of Anne's feelings, of his own labors for the well-being of the kingdom, of Louis's duties as king, of his obligations to society. At one point he recalls that Louis had often asked what he must do to become a great king. Attention to duty, hard work, recognition of obligations— this was the formula for *la gloire*. The fact that Mazarin was willing to go further in his argument, balancing his own career and life against the will of the young king, may indicate his feelings more poignantly than the impersonal arguments; it may also indicate the extent of his moral authority over the boy, for Louis *was the king,* and Mazarin never questioned that fact. Indeed, it was to Louis the king that Mazarin appealed to check the passion of Louis the man.

These letters at the time of the Mancini crisis seem to be the most dramatic documentary evidence of the sort of influence that made Louis XIV seek so untiringly to fulfill his historic destiny, his conception of his *gloire*. All the formal education in the world cannot persuade a man to play his part, to fulfill his potestate, to achieve his *gloire*. But if a man has taken into the core of his self-concept, of his ego, if he has identified with himself the deepest values of his beloved and respected parents—in this case, his destiny as great king and an *"honnête homme"*—this may well drive him forward to accordant action. The fact that Louis gave up Marie Mancini may well be the great tragedy in his life, but the fact that he *did give her up* upon the insistence of his mother and Mazarin that in this way lay duty to kingdom and to *gloire* seems to argue that, among other influences that we do not know about, the relationship that existed among these three persons—Louis, Anne, and Mazarin—provides a most important key for the understanding of this man whose career was so fateful for the history of Europe.

A. DE SAINT-LÉGER AND PHILIPPE SAGNAC

The Administrative and Military Monarchy of Versailles

LOUIS XIV AND HIS COURT

THE VICTORY at Nymwegen wreathed Louis XIV in an halo of glory. The might of the true sovereign of Europe blazed forth in dreamlike setting far from noisy and unruly Paris, to which he had repaired in 1682. The small château of Louis XIII had become the vast palace of Versailles with its imposing façade on the park. The never-ending work of improvement and

Translated from A. de Saint-Léger and Philippe Sagnac, *Louis XIV* (Paris: Presses Universitaires de France, 1949), pp. 185–200. Used by permission of the publisher. *Louis XIV* is volume X of the collection *Peuples et Civilisations,* published under the direction of Louis Halphen and Philippe Sagnac, Translation copyright © 1972 by Hill and Wang, a division of Farrar, Straus and Giroux, Inc.

embellishment proceeded without halt in the halls and chambers filled with Italian masterpieces acquired by François I and the later kings of France; in the majestic Galerie des Glaces, which would be decorated by Le Brun and his pupils; and in the groves and terraces, where reliefs and statues of bronze and marble by Coyzevox, Girardon, Tuby, and the Keller brothers continued to multiply in an orderly, measured fashion, casting their reflections upon the tranquil waters of the pools or emerging artfully from the foliage.

From the high windows of his palace, Louis XIV could look out on the great terrace with its stone-rimmed basins surmounted with bronze gods and goddesses, images of the rivers and streams of his realm, and with little cupids bearing rosy garlands. To the right and to the left, toward the Orangerie, he might admire the beds of multicolored spring flowers that he had seen planted so lavishly and masterfully.

Beyond the central terrace his gaze might drop to the Latona fountain, and beyond that to the "green carpet" bordered with great marble urns; he would then observe the Apollo fountain, which a green strip, restful to the eye, separated from the long canal, that bright silver mirror in which the young trees of the adjoining alleys were reflected in their march toward the distant wooded hills rippling in the horizon. Behind the sculpted shrubbery and yews, which stood like figures about to descend toward Latona, masses of newly planted trees—a paradise for birds—surged up like waves on the sea. This was nature subject to order, for "Every path is an alley in Le Nôtre's* kingdom"; but all the same it was vibrant and unconstrained, with full possibility of expansion under that vast sky, which long summer evenings filled with phantasmagorias of white and pink clouds splashed with the slanting rays of the setting sun. The king, eager for diversion after a weary day with his ministers, spent precious, fleeting hours outdoors in the company of his lords and ladies, either in the marble court—that veritable stage setting in which he would present, to

---

* André Le Nôtre (1613–1700) was the most famous gardener-landscape architect of the seventeenth century. His designs were the basis for the park at Versailles. [ed.]

the astonishment and delight of the great of Europe and their ambassadors, a comedy by Molière or an opera by Lully and Quinault—or in Girardon's graceful colonnade, the most exquisite outdoor concert hall imaginable, or above all in "Little Venice," where, gliding along the illuminated canal in a richly appointed gondola to the strains of an orchestra stationed upon the bank, he gave himself over to the pleasures of the imagination, escaping for a moment from himself and his calling of king, which would soon be less delightful than he had declared it to be earlier.

Louis XIV seemed an Olympian god. Soon the famous War and Peace urns of the terrace and Le Brun's ceilings in the Galerie des Glaces would depict him as the lawgiver of the Empire and of Europe. In consequence of the principle that "the King alone governs," all the successes of his ministers and his generals were attributed to him, as their source and inspiration. In this sumptuous setting, perhaps the most majestic that man has ever created, Louis XIV dwelt amid a concert of praise that exceeded the limits of the human imagination. Some would eventually compare him with God, and even in this comparison God would be merely "the copy." Inflamed by victory and encouraged by his ministers and nobles, his passion for glory knew no bounds.

Love's fires had not been extinguished. The reign of La Vallière had witnessed the rise of the haughty Madame de Montespan, taken from her husband in a double adultery that bore fine fruit. This triumph was not without its darker moments: scenes of jealousy erupted; the king, who disliked being "embarrassed," drew back from the liaison; it seemed as if the rupture Bossuet had sought to bring about, thinking it a simple matter, was about to occur. Once again, however, the lovers were reunited. Nonetheless, a new woman began to rise in the king's favor, a lady in waiting to Madame de Montespan—Françoise d'Aubigné, daughter of the famous Huguenot Agrippe d'Aubigné and widow of the poet Scarron. Hers was a slow and skillfully conducted conquest. At first it was insecure—Montespan, on her way out, did not yield gracefully—and it was momentarily interrupted by the king's capricious passion for Mademoiselle de Fontanges, whom he made both marchioness and mother, to the great distress of all the court preachers and royal confessors (1680).

Louis XIV, at forty-two, continued to be obsessed by the passions of his youth. But soon the reign of Madame de Montespan was to end. The king had become accustomed to conversing with Madame Scarron during his visits to the favorite and was gradually won over: the lady in waiting finally took the place of the mistress and became his confidante, almost his counselor. Levelheaded and good-natured, mature through the harsh experiences and misfortunes that had schooled her for her role in the intrigues of the court, this widow was adjudged a good adviser. She opened "a new territory" of tender and intimate friendship to the king. To retain the affection of this king she had so long admired, she contrived to bring him to God, a political as well as a pious work in which she was supported by Bossuet and Father La Chaise, whose clever intuition had led him to hail the new day even before it had dawned.

The widow of Scarron became the favorite. She had already received the domain of Maintenon, which had been raised to a marquisate. After years of virtual abandonment, Marie Thérèse died in July, 1683. Louis XIV mourned his "good queen," but Madame de Maintenon was wise enough to mourn deeper and longer. Now there was no obstacle to marriage. Although it is possible that the king himself thought of it, there can be no doubt that this lady prodded him toward a regularization of her situation. She accompanied him in his travels, and without much delay the consort became his spouse in a secret ceremony, performed no doubt before Father La Chaise and Harlay, the archbishop of Paris. Rumors about the wedding immediately swept the court and the city; Louis XIV was forty-six years old; Madame de Maintenon, forty-nine.

From that very day—or even a bit earlier—Versailles was transformed. Only a short time before, the court and even the city had been shaken by sensational reports of the "affair of the poisons" —scenes of magic and black masses in which important persons were said to be implicated. Now, by the king's order, silence and caution reigned. "The kingdom is like a seminary," noted Primi

Visconti. "Few people enjoy themselves and all must be wary, especially at court." Piety was the rule: the Duke of Aumont, the Maréchal de Bellefonds, and many others made show of their devotion as they returned to God, or at least pretended to do so. The entertainments and the fetes became less frequent; soon the great diversion would be the plays performed at Saint-Cyr, the institution that Madame de Maintenon had founded for the daughters of impoverished noblemen and for which she was to win the king's active interest and support. Like religious devotions, attendance at these plays was another way to seek advancement, and the mere fact of being admitted to them was already a mark of favor. Only Molière was left to castigate the sanctimonious, although La Bruyère, too, might brand them with a searing remark. "A sanctimonious man," he wrote, "is a man who would be an atheist if the king were one." This maxim demonstrates the weight of the king's influence.

The Administrative Monarchy

The men who had rendered the greatest service to the king—Colbert, Louvois, and Le Tellier—had also sought to introduce the same harmonious arrangements that prevailed at court into the administrative apparatus of the realm. These ministers were not, of course, in full agreement with one another, but all worked for the monarchy with a dedication and assiduity that had been rarely seen in the history of France. All his life Colbert had been a prodigious worker. Louvois, too, was capable of startling expenditures of energy. "I have never seen a man work harder," said the Marquis de Saint-Maurice, the ambassador from Savoy, in 1667. His thirty years of service have bequeathed us five hundred volumes of correspondence in his own hand, which no historian has yet read in its entirety and which is as fully deserving of complete published edition as Napoleon's correspondence.

Secretary of state for war from 1668, minister in 1672, superintendent of the post in 1683, and finally superintendent of public works, Louvois was the major architect of the policies of the reign. By 1673 his power had become so great that he issued direct orders to Turenne and Condé This was the cause of loud complaint from these illustrious captains, and Le Tellier undertook to quell them. During the Flemish campaign of 1674 he ordered the sacrifice of Turenne's army, only to see it win the victory. He kept the Maréchal d'Humières and the Maréchal de Créqui securely under his authority. Only Luxemburg broke loose after the Battle of Nymwegen and undertook to quarrel with him.

In addition to his power in the army, Louvois also directed diplomatic affairs. When Pomponne succeeded Lionne, he conspired against him with the help of Courtin, who had succeeded to Pomponne's post in the embassy to Stockholm. In council he raised questions about various omissions on the part of the secretary of state, sought to catch him out, to make profit of his Jansenist affiliations, his absences, his trips to his estate at Pomponne, his lack of diligence and assiduity. The king came to believe what Louvois told him. Colbert stood by, waiting to profit by Pomponne's fall, and had the post assigned to his brother, Colbert de Croissy, while Louvois was away at his château in Meudon.

When Colbert died in 1683, Louvois took his revenge: Seignelay, Colbert's son and secretary of state for the navy, was excluded from the council; public works, which had been directed by his father, was transferred to Louvois; and the Le Perrier family obtained the appointment of their friend, the mediocre Le Pelletier, to the post of inspector general of finance. In the "high council" they were thus assured of three out of four votes. After that they were firmly in power. Now both the elder Louvois—who despite Colbert had been chancellor since 1679—and his son ran everything. Louis XIV was in Louvois's hands, and his policies became more and more violent, aggressive, and brutal. At the beginning of her new career, Madame de Maintenon tried in vain to give her support to the Colberts. After 1683 all restraints were gone; Louvois's personality dominated everything; the king saw only what Louvois saw and followed him blindly.

Thanks to these shrewd administrators, the new regime, which was still very imperfect in 1667, grew stronger. In the years after 1668, during the period of the Dutch War and especially after the victory at Nymwegen, the administrative monarchy may be considered definitively established. This system has been frequently called "absolute monarchy," because the authority of the king seems perfect and complete, even though the feudal bases of social institutions had not been altered, and the special privileges of persons, regions, and towns had not been abolished. What is more, a uniform code of law and uniform tariff regulations—both important characteristics of a fully developed state—had not yet been instituted.

A central government with councils, a chancellor, a comptroller general, and four secretaries of state had been established. The councils had assumed their definitive shape, especially the council of state. By the regulations of 1673 it was comprised of twenty-four state counselors and forty-eight *maîtres des requêtes*. The latter, all younger men, constituted an informal corps of administrative trainees, from which the king was to recruit the intendants of the *généralités*. The council of trade, however, which might have been extremely useful in this period of economic reconstruction, was dismissed by Colbert, who distrusted tradesmen because he frequently found them opposed to his views. This council was reinstituted only after his death, during a period of economic crisis. All important political and administrative measures were drafted in council; more and more, decrees of the council took their place beside royal edicts, ordinances, and proclamations.

The administration of the realm was now entrusted to the intendants, who were no longer the mere investigators or temporary deputies that they had been in 1664 but regular officials permanently residing in their *généralités*. There was nothing abrupt about the introduction of this new institution: Brittany did not receive its first permanent intendant until 1689. With the exception of this remote, very feudal province, in which a good half of the population was unable to speak French and which remained firmly attached to its ancient ducal privileges, by 1680 the king had his agents everywhere. "Letters of commission" gave them very broad powers; the wording of these credentials was so loose that they frequently represented the full authority of the king. Their ever-increasing authority, particularly in financial matters, was often exercised at the expense of the authority of the chief treasurers and of the army of financial officers who had purchased their posts and had hitherto presided over the assessment and collection of taxes: a statute of 1670 reserved this essential function to the intendants and their powers continued to expand, particularly in the territories along the frontier. This was partly a consequence of the wars, but also of increasing financial and economic difficulties. As the burden of work became heavier, they had recourse to "subdelegates." Colbert authorized the intendants to appoint a limited number of these in the various *"élections"* or "dioceses" of their *généralités*. These were people of the region—notaries, lawyers, mayors—who were well acquainted with local conditions. Although Colbert would have preferred to pile the greater burden of work on the shoulders of the intendant, who was in fact the sole agent responsible to the king, these subdelegates continued to multiply.

The intendants, far from Versailles, grew accustomed to resolving many urgent questions on their own, without waiting for instructions from the ministers; they strove to retain this freedom of action. More than one began to act as a "vice-roy," as the comptroller general of finance was later to call them: this was especially true of those who had long resided in one district. Lamoignon de Basville, for example, chose to remain at his post in Languedoc for thirty-five years. Moreover, the king intended that his "commissary," his only real representative, should exercise the full power of the state. He therefore sought to reduce the functions of the governors and even the various forms of respect that had been their due. These important noblemen who now held a merely titular office either ceased to appear or received orders to cease to appear in their governments. Henceforth, all were to submit to the authority of the intendant. Nobles, bishops, priests, municipalities, and corporations were to address themselves to him even in the least important matters. The "officers," whose offices soon became an empty formality, were not content but were nonetheless obedient. A numerous and influential class stood apart from the regime; the dissatisfaction that it dared not express became less discreet toward the end of the reign.

This new administration was more regular and on the whole

more equitable than that of the chief treasurers and "officers" of finance, which had been subservient to local as well as caste and clique interests. Under firm pressure from the comptroller general of finance—that is, from Colbert, who wanted to put everything in order—the new administration made and kept rules and raised standards of discipline. In its work of standardization, it encountered formidable resistance from people of privilege whom it in no way thought of injuring, although it did attempt to restrain the gravest abuses in the social order or render them less intolerable.

The feudal system remained very harsh, especially in the mountains of the Massif Central, in far-off Brittany, and in the regions close to Germany (Alsace, Trois-Évêchés, Franche-Comté). Louis XIV and his ministers tried to check the outbreak of crimes committed by the nobles of Auvergne against the peasantry, but the encroachments of the seigneurs continued to threaten peasant communities by stripping them of age-old rights to the use of manorial forests and commons. The seigneurs invoked a right of *"triage"* (setting aside), which permitted them to recover one-third of all goods and properties they had ceded in the past. The ordinance of 1669 restricted the application of *triage* to those cases in which the seigneur had made gratuitous concession of the contested property or rights to the rural commonalty. The intendants undertook to apply the new rule, but not without considerable hardship, for the seigneurs, who were masters of their villages and dispensers of their own justice, were often recalcitrant. Furthermore the king, as *"seigneur fieffeux,"* or overlord of the realm, following a tradition based on several of Richelieu's edicts and the subtle theories of the jurists, did not fail to claim his right to place the seigneurs, exactly like his common subjects, under his "universal direction," to consider, in some ill-defined way, all the landed property of the realm, even the ancient alodia, subject to the operation of the seigniorial system, and to levy taxes on the owners of islands and alluvions of navigable rivers, in defiance of the protests raised by the *parlements* of the south of France, which were deeply imbued with Roman principles. It was another way for Colbert to add to the crown lands.

Abuses within the fiscal system were by no means insignificant.

Prodded by Colbert, the intendants combatted the more unfair assessments of tallage and corrected the most glaring injustices. In their administrations they regularly undertook the defense of the lowly and of the common interests of the country, which did not prevent them pleading the cause of their *généralités* when they felt that they were overburdened with taxes or when acts of God had diminished their resources. In this way monarchical absolutism discovered within itself a system of balances that was less a consequence of inherent principle than of day-to-day practice.

The intendant emerged as the instrument of an absolutism that was preoccupied with the general interest. This concern for the general interest implied the curtailment of special privilege, but it also implied the abolition of the last vestiges of liberty. It reduced persons and guilds to obedience; it took charge of municipal administration and put an end to all freedom of choice in the election of the town magistrates. The free choice of mayor, which had long been more apparent than real since the man elected was in every case the king's candidate, disappeared in most towns around 1683. The mayors, now purchasers of their office, were converted into permanent magistrates.

The subdelegates carried on the work of administration in the rural communities. The choice of the parish syndic was entirely in the hands of the seigneur, whose authority and influence were not contested, not even by the subdelegates. How could this bourgeois, a notary or procurator in the little town in which he lived, possibly issue commands, even in the name of the king, to a Duke of Rohan, the ostentatious lord of the manor of Josselin and seigneur of dozens of towns large and small, including Pontivy, where he had his own courts, judges, fiscal procurator, and an entire army of agents? Subdelegates and intendants shrank from the task of "absolute" regularization of which Colbert was dreaming and which they themselves recognized dimly as a goal for the future, although it was blocked for the present by insurmountable obstacles of social privilege. Little by little, they laid the groundwork for the modern state, but they were powerless to achieve it by themselves.

Such were the king's provincial "commissaries" and their helpers. From the very first years of the reign their powers grew; they had supplanted the "officers" in all essential tasks and had become the most active agents in the process of administrative centralization. In their work they were guided by new laws and instructions issued by the secretaries of state, by the chancellor, and, above all, by the comptroller general of finance—Colbert—who, by an extraordinary accumulation of powers, had become virtual minister of the interior and master of the national economy.

THE LEGISLATIVE ACCOMPLISHMENTS OF LOUIS XIV

After 1667 the laws that the king's agents were to enforce became more and more numerous, precise, and peremptory. Inasmuch as the legislative power belonged solely to the king, it was the king in his councils who wrote the edicts, ordinances, and proclamations; it was he who charged the *parlements* and "high councils" of the realm to enter these acts in the registers so as to give them fixed date, publicity, and executory force.

With his major ordinances, the king had the power to effect some gradual harmonization of monarchical legislation with conflicting systems of ancient law: Roman law, feudal law, and canon law. The struggle with the last was already a very old one. It continued, less sharply than Colbert might have wished, but nonetheless steadily. The ministers, magistrates, and intendants were, of course, on the side of the monarchy and frequently hostile to the clergy. For the most part, however, the status of persons remained under the jurisdiction of the church. Marriage was considered a sacrament as well as a contract, and the registration of births, marriages, and deaths remained legally in the hands of the parish priests.

The assault upon the political power of feudality was over, and the monarchy did not dream of launching a new offensive against the feudal system of land ownership, for it did not wish to ruin the nobility, which was one of its staunchest supporters. Roman law was much admired and taught in the universities. It still governed half of France: common law in the south was based upon it, and in those instances where common law was silent, Roman law remained the point of reference. Everywhere it seemed to be held in greater esteem than common law, which in its diverse forms such as the custom of Paris and the custom of Orléans was entirely absent from the curricula of juridical instruction in the universities of the north, at least until 1679, when a chair of French law was finally instituted at the University of Paris. The age-old struggle against Roman law came into the open, and certain jurists denounced it as a foreign system. And so it fell to the age of Louis XIV to dream at last of founding French law.

A uniform code of civil law was out of the question. France still had over four hundred minor civil codes, each reflecting the traditions of some small locality in questions of the status of persons or property. Property, inheritance, and marriage all escaped the efforts of the legislator, although it might have been possible to impose greater uniformity in the regulation of marital status. In any case it *was* possible to reform and unify civil procedure. This was Colbert's first thought, and it was strongly supported by his uncle, Counselor of State Pussort, an honest, firm, and clear-sighted man who disliked contradictions. In 1665 a commission composed of counselors of state, masters of appeals, and lawyers—in anticipation of their opposition, the magistrates had been deliberately excluded —drafted an ordinance that would simplify cumbersome procedures throughout the realm. Despite the urgings of his entourage, the king decided to deal more tactfully with the magistrature and ordered the final drafts of the articles to be reviewed by a conference of parlementarians under the presidency of Lamoignon. Out of this painstaking reexamination came the *Ordonnance civile* (1667).

A criminal code was no less necessary. An understanding was easily reached on the question of the unification of procedure, but beneath the surface, opinion remained divided. Some were intent on maintaining old inquisitorial forms. Oblivious of the haunting problem of judicial error, they gave no thought to what we call today the guarantees of the rights of the accused; they were of no mind to eliminate the more extreme penalties, which they felt to be an important affirmation of the state's right to punish. Pussort was their leader, and he was the spokesman of Colbert. The others wished to grant the accused a defender in order to reduce the part of error. In good conscience, as magistrates and Christians, they repudiated excessively harsh penalties, taking pains to reconcile these humanitarian sentiments with their respect for the forms of justice. Their leader was the president, Lamoignon; he spoke as a philosopher in advance of his times. Authority carried the day: the *Ordonnance criminelle,* promulgated in 1669, unified procedure without introducing further reforms.

Colbert also wanted to introduce uniform regulation of trade by land and sea. He called upon traders like Savari and ship owners as well as counselors of state to draft the *Ordonnance du commerce* (1673) and the *Ordonnance de la marine* (1680). His spokesman, Pussort, again presided over both commissions. The result was a clear, methodical codification of existing trading practices with no important innovations. Judging by the minutes of one of the preparatory sessions—the only such records that have survived—a small revolution in jurisprudence had been planned—authorization of lending at interest. This innovation would have permitted merchants to raise capital and expand their enterprises.

Although recognized by law in Spain and Italy, both Catholic countries, and in France, too, by the *parlements* of Toulouse, Bordeaux, and Metz, lending at interest was formally prohibited by church law. Three members of the commission—the merchant Savari, the banker Bellinzani, and the lawyer Gomont—were reluctant to attack this doctrinal conflict directly and, against the advice of Pussort, decided to consult with the theologians and casuists of the Sorbonne, who were all too happy to step into the debate. They cited a vast number of texts for and against, only to arrive at a negative conclusion or a suspension of judgment. The members of the commission, fearing to offend people of timid conscience, or perhaps to come into conflict with the Sorbonne or the papal nuncio, prudently decided to avoid the question altogether: jurisprudence would continue to tolerate lending at interest, and practice would come to the aid of the law, which, as in the past, would remain mute.

Important sectors of the social economy were the exploitation of forests and waterways and the exploitation of Negro slave labor in the colonies. The *Ordonnance des eaux et forêts* (1669) reorganized the administration of the forests. It reduced the number of super-intendancies, punished unauthorized lumbering (which for the most part had been the work of the "officers"), and by 1683 succeeded in making the royal forests yield six times more earnings than they had in 1662 (1,028,000 livres). Colbert could now obtain the "good hardwoods" he needed for his fleet. The system of forest administration, codified in the ordinance, was one of his greatest achievements.

The *Code noir,* regulating the status of Negro slaves, was published in 1685, after Colbert's death. Slaves were not persons, they were chattel. In his own interest the master was advised to keep them well fed; his right of life or death was restricted. Although the code demonstrated a modicum of humanity toward the slaves, the only religious considerations that entered into it were its intent to establish the dominance of the Catholic religion, its refusal to Protestants of the public practice of their cult, and its expulsion of the Jews as "declared enemies of the Christian faith." Despite these stains of intolerance, the new code marked a slight step forward in the treatment of the slaves and permitted the intendants of the colonies to protect them from the cruelty of their masters.

ENFORCEMENT OF THE LAW

Never before had the monarchy enacted so many important laws. But enacting good laws was not enough; the chief thing was to enforce them effectively. Who was to make them known and respected? That was the problem. The king, of course, had his dedicated agents, the intendants, who had been recruited from the council of state. But what of the magistrates, the officers who administered justice? Their attitude toward these "commissaries" charged with supervising their work was hostile. They had not participated in the drafting of these new laws and had recorded them with utmost reluctance. They were still a rich and powerful group, quite capable of obstructing reform. They shut their eyes to the malfeasances and even the crimes of the great nobles; they ignored the new civil procedure and for the most part thought only of bribes and *douceurs.* Although there were a large number of honest and enlightened men among them, a still greater number were ignorant and inept, if not frankly dishonest. The problem was very serious, and radical solutions—among other things, the suppression of venality or the purchase of office—proved infeasible.

At the very least, it *was* possible to introduce a certain measure of discipline into the magistrature. This is what Le Tellier and his successors attempted to do, with the help of the intendants. Although the task was comparable to that undertaken by Louvois and Colbert in the army and the navy, the results were considerably less brilliant. There were far too many infractions to be corrected. In Toulouse, in Pau, and even in Paris certain magistrates refused to apply the *Ordonnance civile*. In 1667 the king exiled three refractory members of the *parlement* of Paris. The chancellor issued the following warning to the chief presiding magistrate of Toulouse: "It is essential that the king hear no further reports of contravention of his ordinance." There were even graver abuses. The courts employed a double standard in meting out criminal justice. Nobles under sentence of torture were left in peace on their estates, where they continued to commit further offences and crimes; in other cases, officers of the law gave them time to escape. The chancellor would reprimand the procurator general of the region, although it is unclear whether sentence would be subsequently carried out. Presumably, if the chancellor did not personally intervene in the case, he would not be obeyed. Money had to be advanced to defray the costs of arrest; otherwise, there would be no hope of action.

Whenever we encounter in the various edicts and ordinances the same monotonous repetition of prescriptions, we may assume that the king's orders remained a dead letter. It took a long time to teach the French to inform themselves of the law and to submit to it. What is more, as the authoritarian Pussort so pointedly observed, this widespread attitude of insubordination could only exist in consequence of complete lack of discipline on the part of the magistrates and the great seigneurs; unnecessary complexity within the judicial system; unresolved conflicts of jurisdiction; blatant injustices within the seigniorial courts, where the seigneurs were at the same time judges and litigants; and, finally, mounting contempt for the magistrature as an institution.

How then were the laws to be enforced, when, despite the significant improvements that the chancellors had made in judicial discipline, the king still could not fully rely on his officers? As we have already seen, the principal method of enforcement was the action of the intendants. An even better method was found for the big cities, first of all for Paris, that immense city so feared by the crown that Louis XIV had deserted it for Versailles: in addition to the civil lieutenant of the provost at Châtelet, a court of first instance much overburdened with business, the post of lieutenant general of police was created in 1667. The first appointment went to Nicholas de La Reynie, a diligent, honest, and extremely capable man. Although the king had not clearly set forth the scope of his powers with respect to the existing powers of the Hôtel de Ville or the *parlement,* the entire administration of justice within Paris soon came to rest on his shoulders. It was not the custom of those days to worry about the limits of competing spheres of public authority.

Faced with the weakness of his rivals, the energetic La Reynie did not hesitate to assume full responsibility for all police functions of the city: supervising trade and corporations, public health and utilities, and hospitals; suppressing mendicity; censoring the press; and guarding public morals. He did a great deal to establish order. He ordered the streets to be lighted by night and made the city a safer place for the honest bourgeois. The city was no cleaner, however; it would be a long time before even the most elementary rules of hygiene could be enforced. On the whole, the king was satisfied: for the first time Paris was securely in his grasp. The police lieutenant became one of the essential institutions of administrative centralization. The success of this innovation soon inspired the creation of similar posts in all the principal cities of the realm.

The justice of the police lieutenant, although swift, was still not enough for the king. Faced with rampant irregularity in the ordinary administration of justice, Louis found it necessary to expand his own justice. In any case, such justice was quite appropriate to his own conception of the monarchy. The king's justice was more expeditious than that of the magistrates and, despite its arbitrary character, no harsher. It was willingly sought and accepted by families who wished to avoid the scandal of an ordinary trial. The king, after a detailed examination of each case, would issue *"lettres de cachet,"* containing secret orders of arrest and imprisonment in the Bastille or in some convent or hospital. The "insane" soon filled the Hôpital Général in Paris. One of its oldest residents was a helpless cripple deemed capable of "perverting recent converts to the Church." The Bastille was reserved for those who had shown want of respect for the king. One was a young woman who had confessed to a priest her wish to make an attempt upon the life of Louis XIV. Then, too, there were many writers whose licence in speech had aroused the king's displeasure. People were already accusing the king of tyranny, and the Bastille was fast becoming their symbol.

LOUIS ANDRÉ

Louis XIV and
Foreign Affairs

I T HAS BEEN SAID that "when Louis XIV took the reins of
government into his own hands he was in the prime of life,
possessing a combination of qualities rare in kings—the advantages
of youth allied with experience." The major role he played from
that time on, in affairs of state in general and in the direction of
foreign affairs in particular, cannot be disputed. The young king
had permitted Mazarin to be all-powerful as minister until the
time of his death. But during the cardinal's long illness, he had

Translated from Louis André, *Louis XIV et l'Europe* (Paris: Editions
Albin Michel, 1950), pp. 14–45. Used by permission of the publisher. *Louis
XIV et l'Europe* is part of the Bibliothèque de Synthèse Historique, founded
by Henri Berr and published by Editions Albin Michel, Paris. Translation
© 1972 by Hill and Wang, a division of Farrar, Straus and Giroux, Inc.

given much thought to how he would organize the ministry. As early as January 25, 1661, the rumor circulated that "there would be no more ministry of state, and that the King himself would govern." On March 23 Anne of Austria told Madame de Motteville that Le Tellier, Fouquet, and Lionne "were not going to govern but to serve the King." On the 5th of March, according to the Abbé de Choisy, Louis XIV apprised Le Tellier, who some people were sure would be the cardinal's successor, of his intention to govern by himself.

Hence, it is not surprising that, according to the Dutchman Van Benningen on the 9th, when Mazarin died, he sent for "the Prince of Condé, the Duke of Longueville, the Chancellor, the marshalls of France, and other chief officers and ministers of the realm." His Majesty declared that "he was resolved to undertake the cares of government himself with the aid of a council such as he himself would see fit to establish." Thereupon he dismissed his counsellors "very courteously," according to Brienne the Younger, who was present, telling them that "when he needed their advice he would send for them." He enjoined the chancellor to affix no seal and the secretary of state to dispatch nothing without his orders.

Thus, by suppressing the post of first minister and establishing a very limited council, Louis XIV began a personal regime of his own creation. The court was startled by this coup, for it was a truly revolutionary act. . . .

At the same time the court was skeptical, never imagining that the king could sustain such a posture for long. That Louis XIV kept his word is well known. In 1670, when he was dictating his *Mémoires* for the year 1661, he was able to give this reply to those who had been doubtful of his perseverance: "Time has shown what should have been believed in the first place, and it is now the tenth year that I am treading, pretty constantly it seems to me, the same path, without ever a halt in my diligence." And what he said at that time was still true when he presided over the council of finance eight days before his death.

LOUIS XIV AS KING: HIS IDEAS

Who then was this king whose contemporaries had been so prone to deceive themselves about him?

Le dieudonné, the God-given, as he was called at his birth on September 5, 1638, was not yet twenty-three when Mazarin died. He was popular because, aside from being extremely young, he was considered very handsome and exquisitely polite. According to Saint-Simon, he never "said anything that could hurt people's feelings." Aside from his charm, which was both natural and deliberate, he won the affections of his subjects by his easy, sparkling outlook on life.

He loved pleasure, any form of pleasure. First of all, like all the Bourbons, he loved hunting. It was one of the reasons for his attachment to Fontainebleu, where he lived, at the beginning of his reign, almost the whole year around, except for the winter months. He also loved dancing. He not only danced at the great court balls but especially loved taking part in the magnificent ballets organized by Benserade, official superintendent of these spectacles since 1651, with whom he collaborated and on whom he settled a pension. To be applauded in the role of Apollo or Jupiter was one of his favorite amusements, "the perpetual apotheosis of his grandeur and his weakness."

He was also of an amorous disposition and refused to heed his mother's reproaches. . . . He finally got married on June 8, 1660, at Saint-Jean-de Luz, to Marie Thérèse, daughter of the king of Spain, Philip IV. But a few months later, while respecting his duties to the queen, he developed a new passion for one of the ladies in waiting of Henriette d'Orléans—Louise de La Vallière. . . . This is not to say that the king ever forgot the resolves taken by him at the time of Mazarin's death to direct affairs himself. Even during the summer of his romance with La Vallière the ministers and secretaries of state did nothing without his orders. In his *Mémoires* for the year 1668 he declared, "The time we give to love must never jeopardize our work, because our first aim must always be the preservation of our glory and our authority."

In actual fact his passion for *la gloire* was much stronger than his passion for romance, and much more real. He often referred to it: "The love of glory assuredly takes precedence over all other [passions] in my soul." He said in his *Mémoires* that "Kings, who are born to possess all and command everyone, should never be ashamed to submit to public opinion. . . . Reputation alone often accomplishes more than the most powerful armies." The words he uses to describe this cult of glory are the same as those with which he justifies passion:

> The hot blood of my youth and the violent desire I had to heighten my reputation instilled in me a strong passion for action; but at the same time I realized that the love of glory requires the same delicacy, if I may say so, the same sort of timidity as the most tender of passions: for my eagerness to distinguish myself was just as great as my fear of failure. . . . I found myself holding back and pressing on in almost equal measure, impelled by one and the same desire for glory.

Even more significant is the following phrase: "*La gloire,* when all is said and done, is not a mistress that one can ever neglect; nor can one ever be worthy of her slightest favors if one does not constantly long for fresh ones."

Louis XIV did not specify the consequences that the desire for glory had created and developed in him. In regarding himself as the master of all, the representative of God on earth, he could not escape the extraordinary arrogance he received from his mother, Anne of Austria, and the notion that no sovereign could be his equal. This pride can explain some of the more disagreeable aspects of the Sun King's many actions. On the other hand, he failed to understand the precise nature of his "proud" glory. "I no doubt have the same feelings in my heart," he writes d'Estrades, April 6, 1663, "as every prince has for glory. But they are not distorted by a voracious desire for conquest and the extension of my dominions, since God has given me such a generous share of His blessings that I am content if I can render those who are envious of me forever powerless to do me harm." This statement does not correspond to the facts. After 1663 we see that Louis XIV was not satisfied with the domains already in his possession, and he tried to increase them at the expense of the Hapsburgs. His pride and his passion for glory forced him to strive for success through armed conflict and, above all, to make conquests. Here again the king was of one mind with his subjects who were also obsessed by glory, especially after the Peace of the Pyrenees. It was the general opinion that "the title of conqueror is considered the noblest and highest of all."

Another passion that developed early in Louis XIV and persisted until the end of his life was the love of the craft of kingship. His remarks on the matter are well known. "The *métier du roi*," he told his son, "is great, noble, and delightful when one feels oneself capable of worthily performing all the tasks it involves. But it is not free of sorrow, weariness, and anxiety." That he did not consider this métier, for which he acquired so rapidly a taste, particularly difficult, we see by his further statement:

> You must not imagine that the affairs of state are like some of those obscure and thorny parts of science, which may have wearied you and where the mind strains to rise above its reach. The function of kings consists principally in relying on common sense, which always works naturally and effortlessly. . . . All that is most essential to this kind of work is pleasant at the same time: in fact, my son, it means keeping the whole world under your gaze, receiving news each moment from every province, every country, learning every court secret, the moods and weak points of every prince, every foreign minister.

This precise definition enables us to understand exactly everything that happened during his long personal rule. Louis XIV wished and had, to his full satisfaction, "the whole world under his gaze." He was able to take real pleasure in this because of his role as master. Everyone, Protestants and Catholics alike, told him that God's lieutenant on earth could do what he pleased. Of all the concurring opinions one of the more characteristic is that of Montausdex: "Your Majesty had no need of teachers or advisors. God inspired you with the science of kingship just as He inspired the first men with those arts and techniques necessary to mankind."

Undoubtedly, Louis XIV followed a policy that was always his own. Nevertheless, we are not obliged to believe that it was entirely of divine inspiration, and we may even ask ourselves whether, when he assumed power after Mazarin's death, he was capable of exerting it with full knowledge of its implications. The cardinal, in fact, who had had himself appointed superintendent of the king's education, was accused, in the seventeenth century and afterward, of having completely, or almost so, neglected this task. There is no need to insist that the cardinal gave strict supervision to the activities of the tutor or teacher. But he found himself before a sovereign to whom "even as a child the mere mention of the *rois fainéants* or the mayors of the palace caused visible pain when pronounced in my presence." Full of regrets that he had not made better use of his time when he was young, "I forced myself, in order to please him," wrote Louis XIV in his *Mémoires,* "to work regularly twice a day. It is difficult to put in words the benefits I reaped as soon as I had taken this resolution. I felt my spirits and courage rise as though I were another person; I discovered in myself things I had not know to be there, and I joyously reproached myself for having remained so long unaware of their existence."

He found in Mazarin an excellent teacher for this political education. From the year of his coming of age in 1651, but long after the Fronde, we see Louis XIV visiting the cardinal, listening for hours on end to the reports of the secretary of state, spending his afternoons attending council meetings, becoming acquainted with the innermost secrets of the affairs of state. According to Brienne the Younger, "The cardinal hid nothing from him." Colbert confirms this assertion stating that "as long as the cardinal was alive, nothing of consequence took place without the king's being fully informed." Later the question was more accurately stated by the well-known English statesman Bolingbroke: "Louis XIV received an inadequate education from every point of view except one—the initiation by Mazarin to the mysteries of his politics."

Meantime, the cardinal was observing his pupil. "You'll see," he would say, "he has the stuff of four kings in him; he may get off to a late start but he'll go much farther than anyone else would." To one of his teachers, Péréfexe, who was showing some anxiety about him, he gives the advice: "Don't worry. He's going to know more than enough. Whenever he attends the council he asks me hundreds of questions about the matter in hand." During June and July of 1659, after approving the decision of Louis XIV to rule by himself, the cardinal added a few words, later to be paraphrased by the king himself: "If you succeed in enjoying the business of governing, I can assure you—and this is not idle flattery—that you'll go farther in a month than another in six months. The good Lord has generously endowed you with all that is necessary to become one of the greatest princes of the world, and you will have only yourself to blame if you don't become one."

One might be tempted to believe that Mazarin was simply indulging in flattery. But we have the testimony of various foreign ambassadors that the king followed his advice and permanently dedicated himself to ruling. While the Venetian Morosini went so far as to say that the prince vetoed resolutions approved by the members of the council "because they are not truly in his interest," his compatriot Mani, in 1659–60, remarked to the contrary that Louis XIV inquired about state affairs but "considers himself too young and inexperienced to be capable of making decisions." In 1662 a Dutchman, Boreel, observed that the prince "inquires with great curiosity about old maxims from the days of Henry IV, especially those concerning the United Provinces, and he speaks about them so knowledgeably that one can hardly restrain one's astonishment." In 1662, the Brandenburger Blumenthal stated that Louis XIV presided over councils every day and worked from morning till 2 A.M. of the next day. Another Venetian, in 1665, claimed that the king "takes a passionate interest in all he undertakes . . . to the point of exhaustion, when he succumbs to the most terrible headaches."

All this is very interesting evidence, especially as it is confirmed by Colbert, according to whom the king worked six to eight hours a day. Nevertheless, the most precise and detailed information we have comes from a confidential letter written by the minister Hugues de Lionne, on August 14, 1661: "Those who thought that our master would soon tire of affairs of state have been proved very wrong. The more time goes by, the greater his application and pleasure in dealing with them wholeheartedly." Lionne read the king all the most confidential dispatches he received. Louis later summoned him to communicate "his reactions and the way he wishes me to answer, which answers I prepare in his presence and His Majesty corrects me whenever I have misinterpreted his intentions." Louis XIV completed the picture himself by showing us that he wished the foreign powers to know all about his daily occupations. "The aforementioned Gravel," we read in a royal instruction dated April 6, 1661 (one month after Mazarin's death), "will be furthermore able to describe how he has witnessed His Majesty assiduously at work more than four hours a day without ever an interruption, hearing the reports of his officers or ministers on all affairs and giving them their orders, not to mention the rest of his day, almost entirely given over to similar pursuits having to do with the governing of the realm."

"The revolution that occurred at Mazarin's death," it has been justly remarked, "was merely the culmination of an internal process that had been at work for several years." What then was going to be the nature of the French monarchy?

"What I like about France," Sophia of Hanover wrote in 1679, "is that the king has absolute power and that he wields it with the greatest of ease." Her aunt, the Palatinate princess Elizabeth Charlotte, second Duchess of Orléans, confirmed this in 1712: "It is not like England here; no one, with the exception of the ministers, is allowed to speak of affairs of state." Thus, she reflected the ideas of her brother-in-law, her idol, Louis XIV, who criticized at some length, in his *Mémoires,* the relationship between Charles II and Parliament. "This subjection . . . [is] the worst calamity that can befall a man of our rank; for it is a perversion of the order of things to assign decisions to subjects and submission to the sovereign." According to him, "It is the prerogative of the head to decide and act." The king reserved for himself both initiative and decision. For a long time he was uncertain, making up his mind in secret and "confiding in no one," reflecting alone over matters as they took place, happy when he discovered that his conclusions coincided with those he considered "skillful and experienced." But the Peace of 1659, the marriage of 1660, and Mazarin's death in

1661 obliged him, he assures us, "no longer to postpone what for so long I both wished and feared." He then for the first time suppressed the role of first minister so that the king could shine in solitary splendor.

The king, for Louis, was second only to God, whose will is that "whoever is born a subject must blindly obey." Moreover, the revolt of subjects against a king, even an evil one, is a crime. Implicit obedience is an idea that Louis XIV managed to convey even to his top officials. In 1671 he chided Colbert: he must serve him "as I desire and believe that I do everything for the best." More crudely, he wrote to Duquesne in 1682: "Since the orders I give are always carefully thought out, I wish them to be carried out without protest and without the presumptuousness of trying to interpret them." How could it be possible not to obey the orders of the kings of France, the oldest, most powerful kings in the world, since "our crown was the first in all Christendom" and therefore rightfully takes precedence over all others?

From 1661 Louis XIV could be sure that his ideas were right and that he could be "a real king in every way." His subjects did not consider any kind of opposition, satisfied as they were that he had kept peace and abolished poverty, and that he was strong enough to maintain order. Seeing him so hard at work on affairs of government—something that had never happened before—they responded with displays of joy and hope. The cult of the king had started. No praise was spared for the sovereign. In December 1666, Portier de Morais presented him with the *Portrait of Louis XIV,* a portrait not only of his body but of his soul, his mind, and all the perfections that were the life force of this "consummate chef-d'oeuvre of nature." Even more exaggerated declarations were to come. But it does not seem too unnatural that Louis XIV himself gave the following portrait of a sovereign: "All eyes are fixed on him alone; it is to him that men address their aspirations, hopes, and respects." Everything comes from him; "everything else is servile, impotent, and sterile." Louis XIV pondered his relationship to the foreigner in one of his characteristically unambiguous phrases: "Just as he is the admiration of his subjects, he will soon become the wonder of the neighboring nations, and, providing that he is able to use this advantage, there is nothing either within or without his empire that, given time, he cannot master."

ORGANIZATION AND CHANGE: REFORM

The monarchy of Louis XIV was not completely organized by 1661; it continued to change all through the half century of his personal rule.

At first, foreign affairs were not treated separately. All important matters, whatever their nature, received equal attention from the king, and an informal organization was set up. The king gave less consideration to the competence of those who assisted and counseled him in his work than to the confidence they inspired in him, and he made a point of sharing this confidence between them "without singling out any particular person." At first he shared it among three of Mazarin's assistants: Le Tellier, Lionne, and Fouquet. He explained in his *Mémoires* his conception of their role: "In the most important and secret affairs of state, although these affairs demanded more time and application than all the others put together, it was important and desirable to involve as few people as possible. Not wishing to rely on a single minister, the three I believed could be most useful were Le Tellier, Fouquet, and Lionne."

Thus, Louis XIV does not distinguish among "important and secret" affairs. The same observation is made by Colbert in the "journal kept each week to assist in recording the history of the king": "In whatever concerned the most important affairs, the king resolved to use the same people as the cardinal had used." As we know, Louis XIV quickly lost confidence in Fouquet, whom he had watched, then replaced in September, 1661, with Colbert. Thus, the first group of men whom the king consulted for the most secret affairs was formed, "the Triad"—the first cabinet as we would say today—since Le Tellier, Lionne, and Colbert were all ministers of state.

Besides them, however, were those who executed the royal orders, drafted and dispatched correspondence. These were the four secretaries of state: Loménie de Brienne, assisted by his son and heir to his office; Le Tellier and his future heir, Louvois; Du Plessis Guénégaud; and La Vrillière. The beginnings of specialization started to affect the two secretaries of state for foreign affairs for war. There was only one secretary of state in charge of diplomatic correspondence—the Count of Brienne—whereas Louis XIV discussed external affairs with Hugues de Lionne. The situation seemed somewhat strange and illogical. It was not going to stay that way.

Little by little, foreign affairs became separate from others in the council meetings. Brienne the Younger, who for several months kept the minutes of the council, gives us the clearest account imaginable. The king, he says, "ordered two council meetings a week for internal affairs of state. . . . His majesty ordered me never to speak of foreign affairs except in the presence of himself and the three Messieurs. There was to be no special day fixed for them, but I was to come along any morning he was meeting with the Messieurs to speak of these matters as they arose." The ambiguity of this report can perhaps be attributed to the fact that until that time the kind of work the ministers had to do had not yet been clearly and precisely defined. It is not surprising that information furnished by Colbert for the same period does not entirely agree with that of the secretary.

In short, it is likely that in the beginning the meetings between the king and his ministers of state were quite frequent without there being days and hours fixed in advance for what were considered foreign affairs. Nevertheless, the tendency to regularity, which accorded with the temperament and character of the king, revealed itself rapidly enough; at least three meetings a week began to be dedicated to foreign policy.

In the eyes of the court, these meetings assumed the aspect of a regular council without ever being designated by any official name. They were what today one would call a cabinet meeting. Spanheim, Brandenburg's representative in Paris, in his report on the French court in 1690, calls the council "the secret council of the ministers' council." But the language of the times employed different names for the little gathering: "royal council," according to Dangeau; "state council"; "high Council," according to the *États*

de la France. For most people it was just "the council." When
Brienne the Younger stopped attending the meetings, Le Tellier
acted as secretary until Fouquet's fall (September, 1661). But because Louis XIV demanded absolute secrecy about all decisions,
it is impossible to know whether the meetings were devoted to
specific issues, whether they dealt, as Colbert claims, with foreign
affairs and "other, more secret and important affairs," or whether
they were limited only to foreign policy.

However, as Spanheim notes, Louis XIV was "extremely jealous
of his authority, sensitive beyond measure to everything that concerned him or could hurt him." So as not to be contradicted or
diminished, he made certain changes during the early months,
which we can read about in the *Mémoires,* intended to ensure that
all matters be referred back to the king. On May 9 French repre-
sentatives abroad were informed that in future they must send
"their diplomatic reports" to the king and that the letter must be
accompanied by another one to the secretary of state containing
those details that "out of respect for the king they did not feel
they should include in the letter to him." On August 13 Louis XIV
resolved that he would answer his ministers abroad when "there
was a matter of importance requiring great secrecy," and he began
to do this with Gravel, his representative to the Diet of Regens-
burg. A few days earlier, he was so displeased by any show of
initiative that he ordered Le Tellier to advise the secretaries of
state "not to issue any more decrees (*arrêts de commandement*)"
without a royal order.

These changes created a paradoxical situation. The execution of
royal orders in external affairs, the sending and receiving of dispatches, was actually the job of the secretary of state "of foreigners,"
the Count of Brienne, or of his son, heir to his office. Louis XIV
did not react very favorably to these two men in his *Mémoires.*
The father was "old, presumptuous, and usually saw things neither
my way nor according to the dictates of reason." "Nor could the
father's job" be entrusted to the son, who, though well-intentioned,
was too young to handle matters with the necessary secrecy. It
would have been logical, it might seem, for the king to force the
Briennes to sell their office. Perhaps he did not wish to use co-

ercion toward such devoted servants, preferring the use of a singular device. The son was ordered to always work together with one of the ministers of state, Hugues de Lionne, who had had an extremely brilliant diplomatic career, to repeat what he told him when writing to ambassadors, and to sign his name.

But at the same time the French ambassadors were to continue addressing their official dispatches to the Count of Brienne, while accompanying them with enclosures of their most secret reports to Lionne, that is, to the king. In fact, whatever there was of importance in the diplomatic correspondence went to the minister of state without the nominal secretary of state knowing anything about it. Brienne continued to receive and answer unimportant dispatches even though he had no orders from the king to transmit. At first, Brienne lent himself to this humiliating game. Then, tired of playing the dupe, he resigned himself to selling Lionne an office which, in actuality, he was no longer performing. Beginning in April, 1668, Lionne was both minister and secretary of state, like Le Tellier. He alone received dispatches from abroad, had them deciphered, gave an account of them to the council, and entered in the record the replies which the king wished given. Thus, the organization of the "foreign department" seemed more or less complete. "The entire government of the state," concluded Père Rapin, "was confined to the person of the king and the three ministers who formed his inner council. Each of them kept within the limits of his ministry and its functions with no thought of furthering himself."

Nevertheless, foreign policy retained a rather surprising flexibility and resourcefulness. For example, the council did not always intervene. There was nothing to stop the minister-secretary of state from reporting on some matter *directly* to the sovereign or from taking orders *directly* from him. On the other hand, it was allowable for the king to consult persons other than the three ministers, and during the early years he often did so. He could still call a special session of the council. On March 10, 1661, he excluded his mother, who was never again summoned; his brother, Philip of Orléans, who was much too lightheaded to be trusted with confidential matters; the Prince of Condé, still suspect despite his complete submission; the marshals, even Turenne, although he had held the title of marshal-general of the armies and had been minister of state in the time of Mazarin. The brutal exclusion of these people caused astonishment. "The great ones of the court," remarks the canon Hermant, "and amongst them Monsieur de Turenne, were not too satisfied and asked how it could happen that three bourgeois should have the principal part in the government of the state."

Perhaps Louis XIV repented his hasty decision, which seemed almost to overreach its aim. Or perhaps he wished to get advice from as many people as possible and be able to turn for it to whomever he wished. The fact remains that on March 16, seven days after Mazarin's death, Condé, who corresponded with the queen of Poland, Louise Marie, wrote her: "The king continues to employ Monsieur Fouquet, Monsieur Tellier, and Monsieur de Lionne. These gentlemen are the only ones whom he employs for ordinary business, and when he holds a special council, which happens fairly often, he pays me the honor of summoning me as well as Monsieur de Turenne, Monsieur le maréchal de Gramont, Monsieur le maréchal de Villeroi and Monsieur le maréchal du Plessis-Praslain." This observation is really truer for the early days. Council meetings of this sort were soon to become much more infrequent, and later Louis XIV called them only to strengthen serious decisions with additional opinions.

The only exception among these counsellors is Turenne. The Dutchman Benningsen described his participating on March 16, 1663, with Le Tellier, Lionne, and Colbert: "These are the people," he tells us, "who at present have the most credit with the king and in whom he confides the most." Louis XIV gave him an especially important place in the conduct of foreign affairs. Article 3 of the Peace of the Pyrenees had forbidden Louis XIV to come in any way to the aid of Portugal, which was in revolt. Turenne helped him overcome the obstacle that he himself had created to his own policy. Theoretically, there were no observable dealings between governments. But Louis XIV persuaded Charles II of England to close his eyes to the levying of troops, which was proceeding in great secrecy within his realm. Turenne was in charge of assembling them together and conveying them to Portugal.

On the contrary, as long as the marshal had not converted to Catholicism, he was authorized to keep up a personal correspondence with the Protestant princes of Europe. Evidently, it was his task to dispose them favorably to the king's designs. The king, while discussing all sorts of affairs with Turenne, asked him to draw up memoranda, still extant, on current problems. One even finds instructions to certain ambassadors, prepared by the marshal, joined to those of the secretary of state. Turenne also intervened in the drafting of certain treaties. At the top of the draft of an agreement with the Elector of Cologne and the Duke of Neuburg (1666), Lionne entered this remark: "The preamble should be worded as Monsieur de Turenne did it."

During the campaign of Flanders in 1668 the Marquis of Saint-Maurice, ambassador of Savoy, visited the marshal "because he wishes to be considered for a ministerial post; he does in fact, play a large role in affairs." The correspondence between Turenne and Lionne justifies the statement of the Piedmontese, and "this great role" of the marshal proves that, although Louis XIV ordinarily used only three ministers, he did not limit himself to them. The following fact confirms this yet again. When Louis XIV decided to put Condé in charge of an army that was to proceed to the conquest of the Franche-Comté, Turenne was informed of the fact well before the prince. "The king," Lionne writes him (September 29, 1667) "told *Monseigneur le prince* yesterday of a decision that I know you have been aware of for a long time. He was delighted at the unexpected news." It was therefore useful and just to make a special place for Turenne since in fact he really occupied one.

THE WORKINGS OF DIPLOMACY

"Louis XIV," it has been said, "ruled Europe as much by his diplomacy as by military force: he negotiated even more than he fought." He indicated, in his *Mémoires,* certain principles according to which he was to conduct himself. First of all, he thought, one should reflect without haste and take advice from a variety of people. "This is not, as fools would imagine, a sign of weakness or dependency, but rather of prudence and strength." The chief function of kings is "to give scope to common sense, which always arises naturally and effortlessly, leads to success in all affairs of the world, and thus produces an agreeable satisfaction." The king's thoughts are expressed so frankly, they are so curious, that it is worth quoting the full passage despite its length:

> In a word, my son, a king must keep an eye on the whole world; he must constantly be gathering news from every province, every nation, learning every court secret, the temperament and foibles of each prince and foreign minister. He must take note of an infinite number of things that people think we do not know about. He must look around for what is most carefully hidden from him, uncover the most secret concerns of his remotest courtiers, discover those who have come to harm. I really cannot think of a pleasure one would not sacrifice for this one, if only our curiosity could really be satisfied.

The king, after being so thoroughly informed, must then "make decisions" and, "however enlightened and able his ministers, must put his own hand to work in the matter without seeming to do so."

For Louis XIV, the best method to use was Richelieu's: "to negotiate endlessly, everywhere, openly and in secret," and without haste. "Better," the king reiterated, "to complete one's work late than spoil it by hurrying." Richelieu also had written, "Kings must be careful about the treaties they make, but once made, they must observe them religiously."

Some historians have seen fit to accuse Louis XIV of duplicity and treachery, of constantly violating his word. Although he acknowledged that one must have "given careful thought" to keep "one's word inviolable," he also maintained that "treaties are not always to be observed literally"; they contain "no clause so clear that it will not be subject to some interpretation, and as soon as one has made up one's mind to break it, one will easily find a pretext." Elsewhere the king repeats that "treaties are always subject to interpretation." He goes so far as to compare "the words of a treaty to those polite phrases that are absolutely essential to living together" in the world "but are far less complimentary than the words would imply."

Spanheim thus seems to have correctly gauged the "inclinations" of the king, which tended toward integrity, justice, and fairness unless they had been deflected or hindered "by considerations of interest or glory—in short the grandeur of his reign." Thus, Louis XIV took over from Richelieu the principle that "proper action requires people who follow the middle road between the two extremes" and who act according to circumstances, sometimes "parading their power with fanfare" to impress their enemies, sometimes "assuming a modest look and espousing moderate sentiments in order not to arouse jealousy." Were one to believe his foreign critics, he would have acted only in the first way; we shall demonstrate that the king of France also used the second way, though less often than he might have done.

He was constantly concerned about matters of state, and he was telling the truth when he said, "I was always seen dealing with foreign ministers, receiving dispatches myself, composing some of the replies, and giving my secretaries the gist of the others all at one and the same time." His contemporaries all give similar accounts: Pellisson, in his *Histoire de Louis XIV*; Colbert, with some tendency to flattery. While recognizing that the king is not a great genius, Spanheim found in him "great devotion to affairs, close attention to the councils, discretion in deliberations, and great firmness in carrying out his decisions." Primi Visconti and Spanheim both attributed to him "good native judgment." Someone far closer to him—Lionne—informs Queen Christina of Sweden (September 19, 1662) about his master, who, he assures her, is "firm, inflexible, energetic, unceasingly devoted to affairs," and, above all, "sensitive in the extreme to anything touching his honor . . . considering neither state, life, public tranquility, or pledged word as important as his honor when he believes it injured."

This constant activity, this concern about government, this desire to keep France in the foremost rank resulted in Louis XIV becoming, for subjects as eager for glory as their sovereign, the leader they had been waiting for.

THE MINISTERS OF STATE

Right after declaring that he did not want a first minister, Louis XIV proceeded to find men who would carry out, under him, "those things with which he had resolved to charge them." He explained to his son why he did not search for people of higher rank:

> To show you all my thoughts on the matter, I believed that it was not in my interest to look for men of greater rank; for, since I needed above all to establish my own reputation, it was important that the public should understand, by observing the rank of those whom I appointed, that I had no intention of sharing my authority with them, and that they themselves, knowing what their position was, would not have higher hopes than I wanted to give them.

This determination to act as he liked made a strong impression on his contemporaries; for them it appeared that the king wanted to show that he was in no way "under the sway of his ministers." There is a story that Le Tellier, in order to describe this royal absolutism, said that, of twenty items that any of the ministers might present to the sovereign, nineteen would be accepted without objection, but the twentieth would never pass. Anecdote or exact account? We do not know.

Louis XIV also set great store on the solidarity of his first set of advisors. His contemporaries appropriately had a single name for them—"the Triad." There was no formal division of labor between the ministers—Le Tellier, Lionne, and Colbert. They each dealt with all matters, whether domestic or foreign. They were also held to the greatest secrecy; hence, we cannot, in their joint work, distinguish the role any one of them had played. According to several witnesses, Lionne was in disagreement with Turenne. Conversely, there was not always complete trust between Lionne and Le Tellier on the one side and Colbert on the other, Colbert having a more ruthless temperament. Such differences, however, were not perceptible to the outside. Whenever rumors of them got around, the ministers would make a public show of their good relations. The Piedmontese Saint-Maurice notes the following episode: "On Sunday morning the ministers left and, to the astonishment of all Paris, including those best informed, they left together, in the same carriage, and at that from Monsieur de Colbert's." The author adds: "Political observers believe they are being treated to this show because there had been rumors of this last minister's having fallen from favor." The Triad, to be sure, had no power of decision; but whenever the ministers agreed to give the same counsel to the king, as in the peace negotiations of 1668, it became difficult for him not to follow their advice. On the other hand, during the first fifteen years, it often happened that Louis XIV was absent and was accompanied by only one minister; in 1667 it was Le Tellier. The latter's influence would then temporarily increase, but even in this situation the ministers who had remained in Paris did not have their functions curtailed.

Nonetheless, the king and the secretary of state for foreign affairs had a predominant role in the conduct of foreign policy. Along with the secretary of state should be mentioned those who helped him in his daily task, his clerks and particularly the head clerk. These clerks, who were always selected more or less in the same manner, depended solely on their employer. Their stipends were not fixed but derived from various privileges conferred on them by the king. Few as they were, it was their task to prepare all matters of diplomacy. They might be summoned to accompany the king on his travels, or they themselves might be sent on temporary missions abroad. They were indipensable assistants in preparing the work of the secretary of state. These valuable aides deserve the praises that Sainte-Beuve in the *Nouveaux lundis* has bestowed on them: workers "industrious, well-informed, discreet, knowledgeable about the highly complex finances of the states of Europe." Louis XIV expressed his judgment of several of the ministers of state, and it is of interest to note these opinions, as a rule tersely phrased.

Of Lionne, who for ten years was the man to whom he listened most, he said that none of his subjects "had been so frequently used as he for foreign negotiations." Elsewhere, in 1671, Louis XIV wrote: "A minister has died. He was a man of talent if not without faults. He made it difficult to find an adequate replacement for his post, which is of great importance." We do not find the same royal discretion in a little-known but elaborate portrait drawn by Jean-Yves de Sainte-Prest, head custodian of the Archives, in 1711. Commissioned by Torcy to compose a history of the reign of Louis XIV after the Peace of the Pyrenees, he had to stop at the year 1663 "because the frankness of which he was so proud in his writing was not appreciated." He discussed the unusual talents of Lionne without hiding his weaknesses. On the one hand, he mentions the great industriousness, the "subtle and shrewd" mind, the courtesy and lack of vanity: he was a "true father and protector of the king's ministers abroad." On the other hand, he mentions the "constant adulation showered on his master and an unfortunate tendency to indulge him in his passions. . . . The minister, who would have been better equipped than most people to cure a young prince of these passions, nourished them, on the contrary, with the same care that a virtuous man would have spent combatting them."

Le Tellier, like Lionne, was often judged by his contemporaries, both French and foreign. The king summed up the different opinions as follows:

> Cardinal Mazarin often told me that he found him to be capable and loyal in delicate situations; I also observed these qualities myself several times, and I saw that the responsibility he had exercised for twenty years gave him a vast knowledge of affairs. He had always been employed on matters of extreme secrecy. His conduct was prudent and circumspect, revealing a modesty that I much appreciated.

Of Colbert Louis XIV says only that he has placed him in Fouquet's office to be in charge of financial administration. He was "a man in whom I had the fullest possible confidence because I knew that he had great diligence, intelligence, and integrity." Nothing is said about the role played by Colbert, who was the one to reveal Fouquet's dishonest conduct to the king; but about Fouquet he says that his "thieveries" were known to him. Nor is there any mention of Colbert's brutal and violent character, noted by all contemporaries. "Dry and cold," Primi Visconti was to say, "he immediately freezes those who come to him with any request." This quality prompted Madame de Sévigné to call him "the North Wind."

Louvois is never mentioned in the *Mémoires*. He became minister of state only in 1672, but even earlier he was at Louis XIV's side and accompanied him to war. According to the Venetian ambassadors, the king regarded him as his pupil. Le Tellier's son, pushed by his father, was present at the council from 1661 on, along with Brienne the Younger. From 1672 to his death he was to play a top role. For a picture of this minister we must look to sources other than Louis XIV. Primi Visconti, Spanheim, and Madame de Maintenon speak of his tough, uncivil, violent nature, while acknowledging his tireless diligence and great energy. For the king's favorable opinion of him, one must refer to his letters.

On the other hand, Louis XIV devotes a whole passage to the gentle Simon Arnauld de Pomponne, whom he chose in 1671 to succeed Lionne because he was acquainted with "the assignments I had given him and executed them well." But the job, notes the king, turned out to be "too big and demanding for him." Over the years he formed an adverse opinion of the minister because of his weakness, obstinacy, and laziness. "At last I had to order him to resign, because anything that passes through his hands loses the grandeur and strength required for carrying out the orders of the King of France, a prince not unblessed by fortune." It is beyond the scope of this discussion to establish whether this fall from favor, which caused a great stir and provoked widely different reactions at court, was justified. It is enough to observe that Pomponne was to be recalled in 1696, when circumstances had changed from those of the king's early reign and the presence of a conciliatory, tactful minister was required.

Just as with Louvois, Louis XIV left no record of his attitude toward Colbert de Croissy for the years 1679 to 1696, though this was a very active period in diplomacy. According to Le Pelletier, Croissy was a sensible man, but he was not a hard worker and "he was rather limited." Furthermore, he did not have influence. Le

Pelletier was too close to the Le Tellier family to have much sympathy for Colbert's brother. According to Spanheim, who had occasional dealings with him, Croissy was honest, just, and good-natured. "He is rather banal and not as clever as he might be; nevertheless, he is perceptive and able to form opinions." He is a true Colbert, "easily carried away, which is apt to prevent him from maintaining all the calm and moderation appropriate to a job such as his."

His son does not at all resemble him in this respect. Louis XIV congratulates Torcy on the fact that his character is more like that of his father-in-law, Pomponne, than of his father, Croissy. Moreover, in the critical period of the Spanish Succession, Louis XIV developed full confidence in this young minister who had proved himself both able and devoted.

In short, for almost his entire reign, the king had a remarkable set of collaborators; it was with them that he accomplished the deeds that made him the first sovereign of Europe. But in 1691 Louvois, last survivor of Louis's first team, died, and the situation changed considerably.

On July 23, the Marquise d'Huxelles noted that the king was spending his time with the clerks of the deceased minister and added: "The other day I heard him tell Monsieur de Pomponne that he was better acquainted with the affairs of state than any one of his current ministers." Pomponne was immediately called to the council and five years later, after Croissy's death, resumed the direction of foreign policy. This reappointment, the only one during his reign, indicates the increasingly personal character of government. As he grew older, Louis XIV chose only colorless figures: Beauvilliers, Pontchartrain, Chamillart, Desmaretz. For a quarter of a century he worked terribly hard—eight to nine hours a day—keeping all initiative in matters of administration and diplomacy for himself. As La Bruyère said in his speech on entering the French Academy, "He is his own first minister." This became an even more onerous task when, after 1700, he had to deal with Spain as well. Le Pelletier did not think this a very good arrangement. "The king," he says, "wants to do more by himself than a prudent ruler should. . . . I knew deep down that the king was flattering himself and was seeking the flattery of others. He sub-ordinated everything to his own convenience to show everyone that he was doing everything by himself." Voltaire, for his part, notes that Louis XIV in his sixties "was no longer such a good judge of men," and "his faith in his own wisdom betrayed him."

THE "GOLDEN AGE" OF DIPLOMACY

Two attempts were made during this period to proceed with the organization of the ministry of foreign affairs. Torcy was planning to institute what he called an academy of statecraft, where young men who were later to enter the diplomatic service were to study. This proved to be a short-lived institution. More successful was his idea of transferring all papers prior to the year 1713 of possible interest to the secretary of state for foreign affairs from Versailles to the Louvre. This was the origin of the Archives, which were endowed with a special guardian whose task it became to arrange the documents and to compose memoirs of a historical nature.

This arrangement had become inevitable because ever since 1661 French diplomacy had entered into a new phase of intense activity. Rousseau de Chamoy, secretary to Pomponne, even felt inspired to write a book entitled *L'Idée du parfait ambassadeur* (1697), where he suggests that diplomats must be motivated by love and natural devotion to their monarch. The basic quality of a diplomat must be integrity, not the deception and hypocrisy that "make a scoundrel out of a man to whom character and the reputation of a gentleman are as necessary as in any other profession." But this first treatise was not enough. One of the diplomats, Callières, wrote a very interesting work entitled *On the Method of Negotiating with Rulers* (*De La Manière de negocier avec les souverains*, 1716), and Antoine Pecquet, first clerk under Torcy and secretary-general of the council of foreign affairs under the regency, sanctioned these technicalities in his *Art de négocier* (*The Art of Negotiation*).

One would like to give an account here of the ambassadors—both the permanent ones and those on a single mission—including the manner of their appointment and their compensation. Actually, there was no firm rule at first. It seems that the king thought that the expenses of a diplomat's service should be borne by the person who had had the honor to be chosen for the post and who was obliged to represent his master abroad with pomp and circumstance. During the second part of the reign one notes that salaries were paid, varying in amount, according to the city of residence, from 24,000 to 72,000 livres. There are similar variations in travel and furniture allowances. To cite only one example, Grémonville received 6,000 livres for furniture and two payments of 12,000 and 6,000 respectively for "extraordinary" expenses. This, however, proved insufficient, and Lionne suggested to Louis XIV in 1669 that this excellent representative should receive a present of 12,000 écus to enable him to pay off "a portion of his debts."

By 1715 there were fifteen ambassadors, fifteen envoys, and two residents. Among these were some outstanding diplomats who rendered important services to the monarchy. There were Grémonville, who accomplished "wonders" in Vienna; Courtin, backed by his relatives, the Le Telliers, who did remarkably well in England and Sweden; Bonrepos, who almost became Seigelay's successor; Cardinal Bonsi, who was mentioned as a possible successor to Lionne; the Bishop of Marseille, Forbin-Janson, who distinguished himself in Poland. Among the noblemen were d'Estrades, who served in Holland, Fouquières in Stockholm, his son Rébenac in Brandenburg and Spain. Needless to say, the king's choices were in no way restricted by considerations of rank: in 1713, at the peace negotiations at Utrecht, France was represented by the nobleman Huxelles, the cleric Polignac, and the bourgeois Messager. Even the most determined enemies of France recognized the superiority of French diplomacy. William Temple, for example, concedes that no set of negotiations was ever "conducted with so much adroitness and skill" as those at Nymwegen "by the French. The conduct of the French in this whole matter has been admirable."

It was the chief task of this diplomacy, according to Louis XIV, to increase "the number of my friends and diminish that of my enemies." The foremost means to this end—one might almost say the only means—was money; to win supporters abroad, you had to pay them. The king lists in his *Mémoires* the expenses in this category for the year 1666: pensions paid to Dutch deputies, Polish lords, Irish Catholics, and English refugees. The King of Denmark was to receive 100,000 écus and his queen a necklace; the Elector of Brandenburg was to have 300,000 écus and his wife a necklace. According to Pompone, the senators of Sweden, having received one sum of money, "think about nothing but to await most impatiently the date of the next payment." In another year the Elector of Mainz is assured a payment of 90,000 livres, and Switzerland the dispatch of 300,000. As time went on, such expenses mounted. The Hungarian rebels, Charles II of England and some of his ministers, the cardinals in Rome—all demanded financial aid. There is only one ruler who proved modest in his demands: the Elector of Saxony wished a gratuity but left the matter up to "His Majesty's generosity."

Expenses mounted even more sharply when Louis XIV managed to win over a foreigner who placed himself in the service of France. The strangest of these persons on regular pensions was Count William Egon of Fürstenberg, "a clever lad and a good horseman." From 1661 on he was in contact with Lionne. Having become bishop of Metz in 1663, he was abducted in 1674 to Cologne at the orders of the Emperor who wished to have this German prince condemned to death as a traitor. Liberated by the Treaty of Nymwegen, he became bishop of Strasbourg in 1682, a cardinal in 1686, and archbishop of Cologne in 1688. When the war on the Rhine was going badly, he left for France, where he died in 1704. Despite his assurances to Lionne that he had relinquished all his benefices in the Empire in order to come to France, for ten years he never ceased demanding money from Pontchartrain. Of doubtful morals —he was completely dominated by his niece—he wound up obtaining pensions and sinecures bringing in more than 700,000 in annual income. He was frequently called into service, though Louvois disliked him and questioned, wrongly it seems, his abilities.

Beyond any doubt these enormous expenditures for diplomatic purposes were one of the causes of France's financial disequilibrium, but they did secure much support for France abroad, even if the motivation for this support was primarily financial interest, rather than sympathy.

A second means used by the government and its diplomats was

polemics. In order to defend his political conceptions and parry the attacks of his enemies Louis XIV resorted to practices that had been adopted not so much by Mazarin as by Richelieu. In the beginning he did not make extensive use of polemics, for at first he encountered only tactful treatment and general confidence. When he and his collaborators, especially Louvois, came under attack in Germany and Holland for wishing to dominate Europe, he made use of excellent polemicists like Eustache le Noble and Courtilz de Sandras, who were not always reliable, and especially toward the end, of La Chapelle and Legrand, who defended the French cause with remarkable logic and consistency, reinforced by a constant tone of moderation.

In conclusion, when we consider what would be called today "the department of foreign affairs" during the personal government of Louis XIV, we have the impression of an organ put together piece by piece according to the necessities of the moment, without a pre-conceived plan and operating outside a regular system. For that very reason we find it an extremely flexible instrument, perfectly suited to a regime in which foreign policy, like everything else, depended solely on the will of a prince who was determined to exercise his kingly calling in full liberty, consulting all those who he thought might give him useful advice, while reserving final decisions to himself alone. He had at his disposal a powerful navy, a superior army, an excellent diplomatic corps, and energetic polemicists. This organization may appear shapeless to us, but it allowed Louis XIV to pursue a foreign policy, in agreement with his ministers, which very quickly made him the most powerful monarch of Europe.

DUKE DE LA FORCE

The Daily Life of the Great King

WHAT WAS THE NATURE of an ordinary day in the life of Louis XIV? Saint-Simon furnishes us with a very detailed picture starting from 1694, the year in which he came to court as a young man of nineteen and began his almost uninterrupted residence there. "One needed merely to know the day and the hour to know exactly what the king was doing. . . . It is difficult to appreciate the extent to which this regularity benefited

---

Translated from Duke de La Force, *Louis XIV et sa cour* (Paris: Librairie Arthème Fayard, 1956), pp. 74–106. Used by permission of the publisher. Translation © 1972 by Hill and Wang, a division of Farrar, Straus and Giroux, Inc.

his service, the brilliance of his court, the ease of paying him
court and speaking with him. If each might speak but little with
him, each would have his turn and there would be opportunity for
intercourse with others, harmony in his household and efficiency
and dispatch in his business."

Sire, It Is Time

Seven A.M. In the king's bedchamber a man rises in the dim
glow of a lamp that has been burning all night. It is the first valet
of the chamber. He slips out quietly, dresses in the antechamber,
and returns no less quietly in a quarter of an hour. In the summer
a servant lights a fire in the fireplace; in the winter he puts on
more wood. In the meanwhile other servants open the shutters and
remove the silver lamp and candle; they clear away the collation
of the previous night and the first valet's bedding. About fifteen
minutes have elapsed. Alone once more, the first valet approaches
the king's bed and pronounces the ritual words: "Sire, it is time."
Then he goes and opens the door.

Even before the *grandes entrées,* or ceremonial admissions of the
most privileged courtiers, the first physician, the first surgeon, and
Perette Dufour, wife of Étienne Ancelin and former wet nurse to
the king, enter through the back door of the chamber. Until her
death in October, 1688, Dufour came every morning to kiss Louis
XIV "while the others rubbed him down and changed his night
shirt." The wife of a carter from Poissy, the good Dufour was
"the only nurse who had been able to bear the pain of suckling"
the dauphin, who, by the time that he was weaned at the age of
two "had chewed off the nipples of all his wet nurses." When
Louis XIV spent the night with Marie Thérèse, Dufour slept in
the queen's chamber in her capacity of first chambermaid. On
March 9, 1661, when Louis XIV and his mother, Anne of Austria,
had moved to the Château of Vincennes to be near the dying
Mazarin, Dufour stayed in their room and early the following
morning announced with a wink to her royal baby that he had just
lost his cardinal prime minister.

THE GRANDES ENTRÉES

And now come the *grandes entrées*. "Those who had entry and might see the king while he was still in bed were Monseigneur; the dukes of Burgundy, Berry, Orléans, and Bourbon; the Duke of Maine and the Count of Toulouse. These were members of the royal family. Similarly privileged by virtue of their office were the grand chamberlain, the four first gentlemen of the chamber, the grand master and masters of the robes, the four first valets of the chamber and the first valet of the wardrobe on duty, the first physician and the first surgeon (who were already present), and all who had held these offices in the past or who enjoyed the reversion of them." Saint-Simon asserts that "the *grandes entrées* are the mark of rare and signal favor, and deprivation of them is the greatest and most useful punishment." In 1712 only the Duke of Lauzan and the Maréchal de Boufflers were granted the *grandes entrées* without holding an office that would automatically confer this privilege.

The grand chamberlain or the first gentleman of the chamber draws aside the bed curtains. "While the king is still in bed," we read in the *État de la France,* the first valet, holding a flagon in his right hand and a silver-gilt basin in his left, pours spirits of wine over His Majesty's hands. The grand chamberlain or the first gentleman of the chamber presents the holy water font to His Majesty, who dips his hand and makes the sign of the cross." And Saint-Simon characteristically adds: "These gentlemen were there for a moment, and it was a good opportunity to speak with the king if one had something to tell him or something to ask of him; thereupon, the others would retreat."

Now "the person who has drawn aside the bed curtains and presented the holy water presents the prayer book with the office of the Holy Ghost and all retire to the council chamber. This office is one of the shortest. The king supplements it with a few prayers. At the end of a quarter of an hour he calls them back from the council chamber. Then the barber, Quentin, appears; he holds two or more wigs of different lengths in his hand." Louis XIV began to wear a wig only in 1672. "The king chooses the one that best suits his plans for the day." He then gets up from his bed, slipping his feet into mules presented by the first valet. The grand chamberlain wraps His Majesty in his dressing gown. Every year the king orders two of these sumptuous robes, one for summer and one for winter, personally supervising the choice of the cloth. At the end of the year these dressing gowns, together with the mules, will be given to the first gentleman of the chamber or the first valet as they leave office.

So it was that on June 10, 1663, during the *petit coucher* at the Louvre while the king was at stool, Dubois, Sire of Poirier, related the following incident in the presence of the Count of Lude, the first gentleman of the chamber, concerning the count's visit to his château in the course of a journey from Lude to Paris: "Sire, Monsieur le Comte paid me the honor of his visit during a spell of very cold weather and was without his retinue. Shame prevented me from serving him in my own vile dressing gown, and I asked him for one of Your Majesty's old ones."

Let us return however to Versailles. Louis XIV is now seated beyond the balustrade in an armchair by the fire. This is what is termed the *petit lever:* the king's day is about to begin. The grand chamberlain has removed "the nightcap from His Majesty's head," and one of the barbers is combing the king's hair, for the king did not always have his own hair shaven.

The Secondes Entrées

Now the secondary entrances begin: four secretaries of the dressing room, the first valets of the wardrobe off-duty, the two lectors of the chamber, the two major-domos and wardens of the plate, those who enjoy the reversion of these offices or have occupied them in the past, the ordinary physician and surgeon on duty, the chief apothecary, and lastly those who hold the *brevet d'affaires.* A strange privilege, this royal patent "that bestows permission to enter the king's chamber when the others have withdrawn and the king is seated on his *chaise d'affaires* or closestool." Dangeau had

had the honor of receiving one of these patents. By 1712 there were only five still in force.

When the king's hair has been combed he dons the periwig of his *lever,* which is shorter than the one which he will wear during the remainder of the day. As the officers of the robes approach to dress him, he calls for his chamber. The ushers of the chamber thereupon take their places at the door and admit the valets, the cloak bearers, the harquebus bearers, and other officers of the chamber.

THE ENTRANCE OF PEOPLE OF QUALITY

One of the ushers "whispers the names of the people of quality waiting at the door to the first gentleman" (cardinals, archbishops, bishops, the nuncio, ambassadors, dukes and peers, marshals, governors of provinces, generals, presiding judges of the high courts, and others). The first gentleman repeats these names to the king, and the king "orders them to be shown in." A second, later usher marshals the crowd and clears a path for those who are to enter. Finally, all of the nobility present themselves: the usher at the door asks for the names and titles of those persons he fails to recognize. It is their duty to accept this "without taking offense."

Meanwhile the king's toilette continues. Now it is the slippers and the garters, the "breeches to which are attached silk stockings," the "pumps, which usually have diamond buckles." Every second day he is shaven in the presence of his courtiers, a practice that astonished Spanheim, the envoy from Brandenburg.

A French crowd cannot keep silent for long. The ushers raise their voices to impose silence, or at the very least to make the crowd lower its tone.

THE KING'S BREAKFAST AND TOILETTE

When the king asks for his breakfast, he is brought two cups of sage and angelica tea, but is not permitted to drink them until the formalities of tasting have been completed. Originally he took a bit of bread with wine and water. For four months in 1696 coffee replaced wine. Louis XIV never drank chocolate or tea.

After breakfast the king takes off his dressing gown and his nightshirt. He lays aside the holy relics that he wears day and night. The first valet takes them to His Majesty's dressing room together with his watch and guards them until the king returns to the room.

A shirt faced with white taffeta is brought by a valet of the wardrobe. The dauphin or, in the absence of the dauphin, the Duke of Berry or the Duke of Orléans gives it to the king. While his shirt is being changed, two valets hold up the dressing gown to conceal His Majesty, who remains seated in his chair.

"The valets of the wardrobe bring the sword, the jacket, and the Cordon Bleu. The grand master of the robes attaches the sword to the king's side, helps him into the jacket, and slips the Cordon Bleu over it like a sash. The diamond-studded cross of the Order of the Holy Ghost is attached to the end of it and hangs to the same side as the sword together with the Order of Saint Louis, which is tied with a small red ribbon. Now dressed further in his jerkin, the king picks out one of several neckties brought to him in a basket and knots it himself." As he dresses he empties the pockets of the clothing that he has taken off into the pockets of the clothing that he puts on. Finally, from an oval tray offered by the grand master of the robes on which lie three handkerchiefs "of different sorts of lace" the king takes two. The master of the robes hands him his hat, his gloves, and his stick. While the king is dressing, the watchmaker winds and adjusts the clocks of the apartments and the king's personal timepiece.

THE KING'S PRAYER

Fully dressed, the king goes directly to the side of his bed and kneels down on two cushions that a valet has placed upon the floor, one above the other. The king takes holy water and prays. When he has finished praying, the grand almoner softly recites the prayer "*Quaesumus, omnipotens Deus, ut famulus tuus Ludovicus, Rex noster . . .*" "All of the clergy present in the chamber, including the cardinals, fall to their knees. The laity remains standing, and the captain of the guards takes up his station at the balustrade."

Now the king goes into his dressing room and dons his ordinary wig. He is followed into the room by those whose offices entitle them to do this. "To each he gives the orders of the day. All subsequently leave except the bastards and their former tutors, Monsieur de Monchevreuil and Monsieur d'O, who have come in through the back entrance of the dressing room, and the valets. They spend a pleasant moment together talking of plans for the buildings and the gardens. . . . The entire court waits in the gallery, and the captain of the guards waits alone in the bedchamber, seated by the door leading to the dressing room. He is notified when the king wishes to go to Mass and then goes into the dressing room."

THE KING AT MASS

At ten o'clock the king is already in the Grande Galerie and will pass through all the rooms of his apartments before he reaches the gallery of the chapel. He is often dressed in brown, his favorite color, and he comports himself with utmost respect, rosary in hand. He requires that all remain kneeling from the *Sanctus* until the end of the priest's Communion. The choir never fails to intone a motet and the *"Domine salvum fac Regem"* follows the last Gospel. The king will not suffer the least whisper or noise during the Mass. This was demonstrated by the incident that befell the Maréchal de Boufflers, the captain of the guards.

One day during the Mass someone whispered the words of a satirical song about the Montsoreaus into Boufflers's ear, and the marshal was unable to hold back laughter. "He was the gravest and most serious man in France, a slave to appearances; the king turned around in astonishment, which increased greatly when he caught sight of the marshal convulsed with laughter, with tears streaming down his cheeks. When he returned to his dressing room, he sent for Boufflers and demanded to know what it was that had reduced him to such a condition, particularly at Mass. The marshal told him the words of the song. The king laughed even harder than the marshal and for two weeks thereafter could not refrain from laughing every time he happened to notice the provost marshal or one of his children."

On his way back to the dressing room the king allows anyone to approach him for a word, provided that he has expressed his intention in advance to the captain of the guards. He finds his ministers waiting in the dressing room. Having met with no delay on his return from the chapel, he also finds "distinguished people" who take advantage of his absence to confer with his ministers. These now withdraw. The king calls his council to order. The personal preparations are over.

THE COUNCILS

Councils are held in the dressing room or occasionally in the king's chamber. On Sundays, and frequently on Mondays also, there is the council of state; on Tuesdays, the council of finance; on Wednesdays, the council of state; on Fridays, the council of finance. Once or twice a month on a Monday morning there is a council of dispatches, which deals with affairs "within the realm." Saint-Simon describes "all the ministers seated according to rank behind the chancellor and the Duke of Beauvillier," the head of the council of finance, "except at the council of dispatches, during which all stood" except "the Sons of France, if any were present, the chancellor and the Duke of Beauvillier." "Thursday mornings," Saint-Simon notes, "were almost always free. This was the day for unannounced audiences through the back entrance; it was also the day of the bastards, the buildings, and the valets because the king was idle. On Fridays after Mass the king met with his confessor. These meetings had no set duration and might last until noon. The distribution of ecclesiastical benefices and religious questions were discussed in this "Council of Conscience." At Fontainebleau "no councils were held on those mornings," Saint-Simon tells us. "The king usually went straight from Mass to Madame de Maintenon's apartments, and he usually did the same at Trianon and Marly as well, if she had not left in the morning for Saint-Cyr. It was their opportunity for a tête-à-tête without any ministers or interruptions until dinner."

DINNER

By one o'clock, and sometimes even later, the king is ready to dine. If the council is still in session, dinner waits. Louis XIV eats alone in his chamber "at a table facing the middle window on the marble court." Saint-Simon does not indicate the menu but does confide that "the king ate so prodigiously and so substantially morning and evening that no one could grow accustomed to witnessing it." The Palatinate princess was no less astonished at the appetite of her brother-in-law: "I have often seen the king consume four full plates of different kinds of soup, an entire pheasant, a partridge, a large dish of salad, two large slices of ham, mutton with gravy and garlic, a whole tray of pastries, and then fruit and hard-boiled eggs." Until 1694 dinner was washed down with champagne, but after that year old burgundies were served. "The king and the late Monsieur were very fond of hard-boiled eggs."

Saint-Simon has described the ceremony of dinner in minute detail: "In the morning the king ordered either a simple or a very simple meal, but even the latter consisted of three courses, without counting the fruit and numerous dishes. When the table had been set, the principal courtiers entered (they themselves had dined earlier, at noon), followed by all who were recognized at court. The first gentleman of the chamber notified the king; he waited on him if the grand chamberlain was not there. . . . I have seen, but only on very infrequent occasions, Monseigneur [the grand dauphin] and Messeigneurs his sons at the simple dinner, but the king never once proposed that they be seated.

"I have seen Monsieur there rather often, on the occasion of his visits to the king from Saint-Cloud or after the council of dispatches, the only council in which he took part: he would serve the napkin (moistened at one end, dry at the other, so that the king might wash and dry his hands) between two vermeil plates and would then hesitate for a moment. The king, seeing that he did not withdraw, would ask if he might not wish to be seated. He bowed, and the king ordered a chair to be brought; a taboret would be placed behind him. A few moments later the king would say: 'Sit down, brother.' Monsieur would bow and sit down until the end of the dinner, when he would again serve the napkin.

"On other occasions, when Monsieur came in from Saint-Cloud, the king might order a place to be set for him as soon as he came to table, or else might inquire whether he wished to dine. If he declined this invitation, he left a few minutes later and there was no question of a chair; if he accepted, the king asked for an additional place to be set for him. Monsieur sat at the end of the table with his back toward the king's dressing room. His presence greatly increased and enlivened the conversation. . . . Ordinarily, the king spoke but little during his dinner unless some of his intimates were present with whom he chatted a bit more, just as he did at his *lever*."

It was not until January 11, 1712 that the king began to have his simple dinners on a regular basis in the apartments of Madame de Maintenon. Ladies were never present at the simple dinners, with the exception of the Maréchale de La Motte, who, being a duchess in her own right, would find a seat offered to her. Her appearances were extremely rare. Still rarer were the grand dinners.

When Louis XIV had a grand dinner, that is, a public one, there was more elaborate ceremony. An ordinance of 1681 determined the procedure for serving the meat that waited in the pantry. "The gentleman who is serving carries the first dish; the second is carried by the warden; the officers of the pantry bring the others. In this order they advance in a procession toward the table, with the major-domo at their head carrying his staff in his hand. The usher of the table, carrying a stick—and in the evening a torch—marches a few paces ahead of them. When the meat arrives accompanied by three bodyguards with muskets on their shoulders, the major-domo bows to the *nef* (the hexagonal salver on which are arranged the king's plate and cutlery). The gentleman who is serving places his dish on the table, next to the *nef*."

Let us note that this ceremony was already in use during the reign of Charles X. The Prince of Joinville, who was good at drawing, illustrated his *Reminiscences* with an amusing sketch of bodyguards escorting His Majesty's meat up the grand staircase of the Château des Tuileries.

The ceremony of the wine was no less complicated. "When the king called for something to drink, the gentleman who was acting as cupbearer immediately shouted, 'Drink for the king!' Bowing to His Majesty, he went to the sideboard to receive from the hands of the chief butler a golden saucer fitted with a glass cover and two crystal decanters filled with wine and water. He then returned to the table preceded by the chief butler and followed by an assistant butler."

In the time of Louis XIV decanters were not placed on the table, even in the most bourgeois houses. This is the reason for Chrysale's complaint in Molière's *Les Femmes savantes* about the discipline of his domestics, who have become as smitten with literature and science as his wife, Philaminte:

> One burns my roast, reading a story,
> Another dreams of verse when I am thirsty.

A grand dinner was an extremely rare event: it took place only on certain feasts, or when the court was at Fontainebleau, in the presence of Maria of Modena, the dethroned Queen of England.

Many people have imagined that Louis XIV, as an admirer of Molière's great plays, had once invited the poet to sit at his table. Three nineteenth-century artists have painted Molière seated at the king's table: Ingres, Gérôme, and Wetter. Gustave Larroumet has commented on the absurdity of these pictures in his *Comédie de Molière:*

> All three depict Louis XIV in a historic pose lecturing to his humiliated courtiers, while Molière looks on with stupefaction or resignation. In one the poet sits timidly on the edge of his chair; in another he strikes the serious pose of a man receiving a decoration; in the third he plays the Genius, like an actor in a prologue. Each artist strives to characterize the nature of the scene by stressing some obvious detail. One, misled by the title of valet, which he knew Molière to have received, drapes him in the striped cloak of Ruy Blas; moreover, he places a very tall and ugly bishop with a clenched fist in the highlight at the left of his composition. A later painter, eager to demonstrate his powers of invention while still clinging to the idea of the bishop, places him at the far right, in a much more significant attitude: contrite, half hidden, as if

trying to avoid the scandalous spectacle, he beseeches God in His
mercy to enlighten the king's blindness.

These artists were not particularly careful about the documenta-
tion of their scene. Doubtless, they were unaware that Madame
Campan had fabricated the anecdote that they proposed to illustrate. A reader to Louis XV's daughters and subsequently, around
1770, first chambermaid to Marie Antoinette, Madame Campan
was most happy to insert this detail in her memoirs, which were
published in 1822. She claimed to have heard this story from her
father-in-law, who asserted that it had been recounted to him by
an elderly man named La Fosse, who had been physician to Louis
XIV and "a man of honor, incapable of inventing such a story."
Incapable of inventing the story perhaps, but quite capable of
credulity. "He said," Madame Campan relates, "that Louis XIV
was distressed to learn of the scorn with which the officers of his
chamber had greeted the new valet when he presented himself at
their table and still more distressed to learn that the famous playwright had refrained for this reason from eating at court. Wishing
to put an end to this outrageous offense to one of the great geniuses
of the age, Louis XIV remarked one morning at his *petit lever:*
'We hear that you have been poorly received, Molière; that officers
of my chamber do not think you fit to dine with them. You are
perhaps hungry; I myself awaken with a great appetite; sit down
at this table and let them serve me my nightly snack.'

"Having invited Molière to be seated, the king began to carve
the fowl. He gave Molière one wing, and himself the other. Then
he ordered that some of the most distinguished and favored personages of the court be admitted to the chamber.

" 'You see me,' said the king, 'much occupied with having
Molière eat. My valets do not think him good enough company.'

"From that very moment, Molière had no further need to present himself at the table of the officers of the chamber. The entire
court showered him with invitations."

The anecdote is not without piquancy, but it is entirely false.
Let us return, however, to Versailles. Louis XIV rises from the
table after wiping his hands with the moistened napkin held by

the grand chamberlain. He heads for his dressing room, pausing for a moment to listen to the distinguished people who wish to speak to him. One frequently asks permission to follow him. Both would step into the embrasure of the window "just inside the dressing room door." The door closes, then opens again a few moments later when the man who was speaking to the king leaves.

Louis XIV does not forget his bitches. They are led into a room adjoining the cabinet, and the king feeds them dainties from his dessert and "many biscuits" that he has just stuffed into his pockets. These bitches as well as his greyhounds, setters, and small dogs are placed under the charge of a captain and four guards. The female setters that greet the king were gifts of Monsieur de Contades and Monsieur d'Effiat. The Louvre still houses the portraits of two of them, Diane and Blonde, painted by Desportes.

HUNTING

At about 2:30 the king prepares to go hunting. Sometimes he does this immediately after Mass, if the weather is particularly favorable. One February 25, for example, he found the day so tempting that he decided not to hold his council. When Louis XIV hunts stag, nothing can approach the size and opulence of the hunting party. In the saddle he is the admiration of his court. On September 2, 1684, however, his horse stumbled in the park at Fontainebleau, causing him to fall and dislocate his elbow. Although this mishap had no serious consequences, after that he rode in a barouche with a roof that "folded back like bellows." Until 1700 he invited ladies to ride with him; afterward he rode alone in a lighter carriage drawn by four small horses with postilions of from nine to fifteen years of age. Saint-Simon observes: "He drove at full speed with a skill and address that exceeded that of the finest coachmen." The Palatinate princess wrote on May 16, 1702, "With him you almost never fall behind in the hunt." And Dangeau noted on December 31, 1700, after a hunt in the park at Marly: "Trying to cut the turn a bit too sharply, he tipped over without hurting himself. He had never overturned the carriage before, for he was the most skillful of drivers." Another mishap for which Louis XIV was in no way responsible occurred in the

same park: a stag at bay charged the king's carriage, and the
king struck him with the whip. The animal "leapt into the space
between rear horses and the carriage, pulling the reins from His
Majesty's hands."

Louis XIV "did not wish people to come on the hunt if they did
not enjoy it," if we are to believe Saint-Simon; he found this
ridiculous and "bore no ill will toward those who never came."

His skill in shooting was no less remarkable. On occasion he
bagged as many as fifty and sixty birds within the space of two
or three hours. Neither age nor gout could hold him back. The
attacks of gout from which he suffered in 1686 and 1687 prompted
him to devise a special sedan chair, from which he continued to
prove himself the best shot in the realm. On January 19, 1687, he
climbed into this chair and, without setting foot on the ground,
shot several pheasants. Dangeau noted in his diary that Louis was
"quite pleased with this little contrivance." On November 18 the
king was again at Versailles shooting much game from his carriage. The Duchess of Burgundy and a number of other ladies
followed on horseback. One of them, the Marquise de Listenois,
was thrown from her mount but was not hurt. When the hunt was
over the king distributed the game that he shot among the ladies.
The ladies hung the birds on their belts and galloped back to the
château in triumph.

Outings and Picnics with the Ladies

At Marly and Fontainebleau stag hunts take place at least once
a week and fowl shooting at least twice a week. On other days the
king goes to inspect work on the château: he walks "through the
gardens and the buildings." On occasion there are outings and
picnics with the ladies in the forest.

Madame de Maintenon marveled at the cavalcade that took place
at Fontainebleau in October, 1707. On October 17 she described
it to the Princess of Ursins: "We counted twenty-four carriages
driving around the canal. The young people rode on horseback
near the doors of the king's carriage. The Queen of England and
all our princesses were seated inside." It was not like this at the

other châteaux. There the king was accompanied only by "those who held the most important posts and were closest to his person."

Still, the king's entourage was numerous on those rather rare occasions when he took walks in his gardens at Versailles, during which "he alone wore a hat." And Saint-Simon adds: "When he stayed at Marly, all who had accompanied him there were free to follow him into the gardens, to join him there, to go away from him—in short, to do as they pleased. This place had a privilege that existed in no other. When the king was going out for a walk, he would say in a loud voice: 'Hats, gentlemen.' Immediately all the courtiers and officers of the guards would don their hats in front of him, behind him, and beside him, and he would have been most displeased not only if someone had failed to put his hat on but even if he had hesitated to do this. Hats were worn during the entire outing." If the Duchess of Burgundy was with him, the formula was a bit different: "Put your hats on, gentlemen. Her Grace approves."

At Versailles, when he returned from his outing and dismounted from his carriage in the marble court, he allowed himself to be accosted by whomever so wished; back in his apartments, he changed his coat, shirt, wig, and hat. Then he would sign letters of friendship and courtesy that had been drafted and copied by four secretaries charged with imitating his hand (Picon d'Andrezel, Caillieres, Duret de Chevry, and Hennequint de Charmont). Mademoiselle d'Aumale, who came from an ancient family of Picardy and had studied at Saint-Cyr before becoming the secretary of Madame de Maintenon, took up the pen on more than one occasion for the king, when he did not wish to entrust something to one of the official scribes. "The king was an hour or more in his dressing room; then he went to Madame de Maintenon, and on the way spoke again with anyone who wished."

Quite often he organized a lottery for the ladies of the palace. All the numbers were lucky ones and the prizes were "items for their personal use such as cloth, silver or jewelry. . . . Madame de Maintenon took a number just like the others and almost always gave her prize away."

THE LOTTERY OF MAY, 1681

These intimate lotteries could not match the magnificence of
the lottery the king organized in May, 1681. *Le Mercure galant*
celebrated that event in the following terms:

> It may be said that it has served as the entertainment and diversion
> of all of France during the winter and has occasioned an infinite
> number of pleasant gatherings. Indeed, the majority of those who
> took part in it had pooled their resources in such a way that each
> wagered only three or four louis, forming diverse groups holding
> tickets in common. There were high hopes on all sides and each
> opening of a box [of tickets] brought new delight. The source of
> this delight was that each hoped to win the grand prize; each
> imagined spending the hundred thousand francs in the way that
> he most fondly desired. Some surrendered so completely to their
> imaginations that a young woman who was about to marry de-
> cided to wait until after the drawing, thinking that she would
> make a more advantageous match if she had won the grand prize.

On the day of the drawing Louis XIV was seated at a large
covered table parallel to the walls of the chamber within which
it had been placed. "One may be confident," stated the editor of
Le Mercure, "that the presence of such an august witness not only
precludes the occurrence of any irregularities, but even the very
idea of such a thing." Who is the man seated opposite the king
on a low stool in the rectangular space enclosed by the four sections
of the table? Who is the lady of such stately mien seated on the
folding chair at the right of the man on the stool? Who is the
handsome lord at his left, so gallant, so winsome, so like the king?
The man is one of the king's valets; the lady is the Marquise de
Croisy, Colbert's sister-in-law; the lord is the Marquis de Dangeau.

The valet "held a sack containing the lottery tickets." He counted
them and gave them to Madame de Croisy and to Dangeau, who
recounted them and passed them to other lords and ladies seated
about the table. Like the king, they were at the outer side, with
their backs toward the walls. These lords and ladies were "all that
is most illustrious." Each had a box and placed as many tickets

within as was indicated on the lid. Each had a candle with which to seal the box and a small silver plate to cool the seal.

The boxes were passed to a bishop sitting at the far end of the table. His countenance radiated nobility, intelligence, and kindness. By his fiery eye he could be recognized as the former tutor of Monseigneur le Dauphin, Bossuet, "presently bishop of Meaux." Just two years earlier he had published his *Discours sur l'histoire universelle*. On each box he set a second seal, surveying this realm of chance with the same serenity with which he had written of Divine Providence only a few months earlier: "He alone holds all in His hands, knows the names of what is and of what is yet to be; He alone is present to all ages and informs all counsel." A bit farther off the austere Duke of Montausier, the former tutor of the dauphin, "placed the boxes in a basket which from time to time was emptied into sacks hanging on the wall."

Le Mercure gave no further explanation of the manner in which the drawing was conducted, but it did give the names of the winners. The king, who had purchased a large block of tickets, won the grand prize of one hundred thousand francs, but he lost no time in returning this money to the lottery for the benefit of those who had not won. A prize of ten thousand écus went to a gentleman of Monsieur le Cardinal de Bouillon; a prize of twenty thousand francs went to Monsieur de La Coste, a captain of the Piedmontese regiment; Monseigneur le Dauphin, Madame de Bouillon, Madame l'Abbesse de l'Abbaye-aux-bois, and the clerks of Monsieur Picon won prizes of ten thousand francs each; the wife of the president of Larche, Monsieur de Grandmaison, Monsieur de Beauregard, and a valet in the service of Monsieur Le Nôtre won prizes of five thousand livres; Madame de La Vieuville, Abbé de Marcillac, a manservant of a judge of the court at Châtelet, and the porter of Madame de Saintou won four hundred pistoles; le Maréchal de Schomberg, Monsieur Pellerin Bertho, and the domestics of Monsieur l'Intendant Desmarets won four hundred louis d'or. Purses of one hundred louis went to the following: the queen, Monsieur le Prince de Conti, Madame de Fontanges, Mademoiselle de Scudéry, Monsieur de Furstenberg, the Marquis de Chavigny, the Marquis de Charencey, Made-

moiselle de Gargan, a clerk of Monsieur Picon, the commissaries
of Les Invalides, the porter of Monsieur Colbert, the head butler
of Monsieur de La Feuillade, the house steward of Monsieur
Pussort, a valet of Madame de Sanguin, a valet of Monsieur de
Langres, Monsieur Drochant (draper), Madame Bigot (seam-
stress), and the domestics of Monsieur de Saint-Vallier.

The spectacle of all this good fortune drove the losers to despair.
In 1700, in the drawing that was held for the Duchess of Burgundy's lottery from which forty-six thousand livres had been
deducted in advance to be used for the benefit of the poor, a second
prize of three thousand louis d'or went to a hatter (who had been
born with a caul). But a carrier and his wife, unable to reconcile
themselves to losing, took their own lives.

No such grim turn of events was to be feared at the intimate
lotteries, which were merely an expression of "the king's gallantry
in making presents to the ladies."

THE APPARTEMENT

At the end of the day came the *"appartement,"* the gathering
of the whole court that took place every Monday, Wednesday, and
Friday from October to Palm Sunday "between seven and ten
o'clock, when the king sat down to table" in the state apartments
stretching across the garden side of the château, from the vestibule
of the chapel to the Hall of Mirrors. The salons with their orna-
ments of gold and marble; the chairs, taborets, and draperies of
green or flame velvet trimmed with gold fringes and braiding
that lent warmth and gaiety to the rooms; the silver tubs planted
with orange trees in the billiard room; the silver statues of the
concert hall; the silver balustrade and the great silver chandelier
of the bedchamber; the pictures by Domenichino, Rubens, Car-
racci, Veronese, and Van Dyke; the splendid frescoes of the ceilings—all were bathed in light. The court amused itself, and because respect required that no one raise his voice, "the sounds that
one heard were not at all disagreeable."

At times there would be music in one of the salons and dancing
to the strains of the violin or the oboe. In another salon the queen

(it is December 1682, the last autumn of her life) would be deeply engrossed in a game of *reversi*. In yet another, tables draped with magnificent cloths awaited and while the dauphine played cards with her ladies at one of these tables; the dauphin, Monsieur, and Madame engaged in other games at different tables. "Each played the game he liked best, and all were served by a great number of domestics," dressed in coats decorated with gold and silver braid, "whose only thought," the Marquis de Sources complacently explained, "was to anticipate the slightest wish of the players."

The third salon, with its billiard table, was much appreciated by many a nobleman of the court. No less attractive was the second salon—with its lavish spread of fruits, pastries, and preserves —and the first, with its bars dispensing coffee, tea, chocolate, wine, liquors, ices, and "all sorts of fruit drinks." A delightful relaxation prevailed over the atmosphere of ceremony. The king did not wish the players to rise at his approach. Escorted only by the captain of the guards, he strolled among his guests with the graciousness of an obliging host.

Dangeau and Sources found all this quite enchanting, and to us it seems very pleasant, much like a ball or the opera of our own day. At the time, however, it was not to everyone's taste. The German Madame, the second wife of Monsieur, stated her own, rather harsh opinion:

> The *appartement* is something quite unbearable. We all tramp to the billiard room and lean on our bellies without uttering a word until the king has finished his game. Then we all straighten up and go into the concert hall, where they perform an act from some old opera that we have all heard a hundred times. Next we are off to the ball, which lasts from eight until ten o'clock, and those of us, like myself, who do not dance sit without budging for two hours; we see and hear nothing but an interminable minuet. At a quarter to ten all do the contradance one after the other, like children reciting their catechism lesson, and then the ball is over.

More Trouble Than Fun

Toward the end of his life, Louis XIV no longer put in an appearance at the *appartement;* he would spend the evening at work in Madame de Maintenon's quarters. At ten o'clock, accompanied by his family, he comes to that antechamber of the Great Hall that is called the Oeil-de-boeuf, or else to the antechamber that precedes it. There he sups in public, unless he is ill, in full mourning, or eating meat on a fast day. The table is set on a dais, and the ceremonial is the same as if it were a dinner.

Let us listen to Saint-Simon as he describes the strange scene that took place at such a supper on June 26, 1691. On the previous day an unknown person or persons had removed all the gold fringe from the red and green velvet furnishings of the king's state apartments. This theft was the despair of Bontemps, first valet of the chamber, and the talk of the entire court. One may well imagine that the duchesses who sat behind the guests at table and the courtiers and their ladies who stood in front watching the king eat could think only of the daring theft that had been carried out in a place that was filled with people during the day and tightly locked at night, and closely watched at all times.

Saint-Simon was surely not the least interested of those present. "Only d'Aquin, the king's first physician, stood between myself and the table. As dessert was being served, I caught sight of a large, dark object hurtling through the air toward the table. It fell so fast I had no time to make out what it was or even point to it, and it came to rest on the table at a point just in front of the places usually occupied by Monsieur and Madame, who were in Paris at the time and who always sat at the end of the table to the king's left, with their backs to the windows looking out on the main courtyard. The noise that it made when it landed and the very weight of it made us think that it would go right through the table; the dishes bounced but none were upset: by chance it fell on the cloth and not on them.

"As it came crashing down, the king turned his head slightly but did not betray the least alarm: 'I think,' said he, 'that that must be my fringe.' The package was as wide as a broad-brimmed priest's hat and about two feet high, roughly in the shape of a pyramid. It had been thrown from some distance behind me, and a small piece of fringe that had come loose from it in mid-air had fallen on top of the king's periwig. Livry, who was standing at his left, noticed this and removed it. He then approached the package as all continued to stare at it, murmuring back and forth to one another. When he started to lift it, he discovered that there was a note attached. He picked up the note and left the package.

"The king stretched out his hand and said 'Let me see that.' Livry was unwilling to do this, and rightly so. Stepping back he read the note silently and handed it behind the king's back to d'Aquin, who allowed me to read it with him. On it, in a disguised hand, rather like a woman's, were the following words: 'Take back your fringes, Bontemps, they are more trouble than fun. I kiss the king's hand.' The note had been rolled and not sealed. The king still wished to take it from d'Aquin's hand, but d'Aquin drew back, sniffed the paper, rubbed it, turned it over and over, and only then showed it to the king without letting him touch it."

No doubt, the physician feared that the paper had been poisoned. Two centuries later, given the great advances in explosives and revolutionary ardor, there would have been fear that the package held a bomb. "The king instructed d'Aquin to read the message aloud, although he himself was perusing it simultaneously. 'This is a fine piece of insolence,' said the king in a calm and, as it were, historic tone. He spoke after they had removed the package. Livry found it so heavy that he was scarcely able to raise it from the table. He handed it to a blue footman (one of the six footmen of the chamber) who came to his assistance."

If we are to believe the Marquis de Sourches, the king immediately ordered the doors to be barred. If we can believe Saint-Simon, the captain of the guards on duty, the Duke of Gesvres, didn't execute this order until three-quarters of an hour later. Only one person was arrested, a gentleman from Saintonge who was on visit to Versailles. He was just going to bed when they summoned him, but the Duke of Uzes, the Governor of Saintonge, was able to vouch for him and he was released "with apologies." On the king's orders the investigation was closed, for, according to His Majesty, "only a madman could have done it."

Let us now observe the king bowing to the ladies in his chamber, his back toward the balustrade. He goes to his dressing room, then returns to his chamber. At the door they take his hat, his stick, and his sword. Then taking holy water, he kneels on a waiting cushion and begins to say his prayers. The first almoner holds a candle for him and recites in a low voice the prayer *"Quaesumus, omnipotens Deus, ut famulus tuus Ludovicus, Rex noster . . ."*

The king undresses sitting, puts on his nightshirt and dressing gown, then stands. At the fireplace he bows to his courtiers and gives the order to the colonel of the French guards. The *grand coucher* is at an end. It would take the strength of an ox to go through this exhausting ritual twice a day. One can readily understand Saint-Simon's addition to Dangeau's diary for December 20, 1705: "The king's protracted attack of gout gave rise to the practice of omitting the *grand coucher;* this proved so comfortable that he did not reinstate it."

When the *grand coucher* was over, the *petit coucher* began. "Those who enjoyed grand or second *entrées* or possessed the *brevet d'affaires* remained in the chamber." "This was short," Saint-Simon observes. "These courtiers withdrew only when the king was actually getting into bed. It was another good moment to have a word with the king, and all the others withdrew when they saw one of their number approaching the king for this purpose."

OTHER RELIGIOUS ACTIVITIES

At the beginning of this chapter we described Louis XIV at his daily Mass. But there were other religious exercises that lent pomp to the celebration of the great feasts.

On Christmas Eve, 1711, the king was about to receive Communion. At ten o'clock in the morning he entered the chapel—not the gallery that he normally occupied—but the nave below. The Duke of Saint-Simon explains the intricacies of the ceremony:

"After the Elevation of the Mass a folding table is pushed to the place where the priest begins to distribute Communion. A large tablecloth is spread over it, trailing to the floor in front and back. At the *Pater Noster,* the chaplain of the day rises and then proceeds to kneel, without rug or cushion, behind this table. Two specially appointed dukes and the captain of the guards rise from their kneeling cushions and escort the king to the table, the senior duke at his right, the junior at his left, the captain of the guards behind. All three kneel and each duke lifts one corner of the cloth while two almoners support the other two corners of the cloth on the side toward the altar.

When he has received Communion and taken the ablution, the king pauses for a few moments, then returns to his place, followed by the captain of the guards and the two dukes, who also return to their places. The king appoints these dukes himself to show that he alone is master when it comes to making a choice among them and is not bound by seniority (within the peerage). It has never happened, however, that he preferred less senior. I remember walking before him one day when he was on his way to chapel to receive Communion. The presence of the Duke de La Force came to his attention, and I saw him begin to speak in a low voice to the Maréchal de Noailles (the captain of the guards). A moment later the marshal came over to me to ask which of us had seniority, Monsieur de La Force or I." (La Force had received his title in 1637; Saint-Simon had received his in 1635. The king wished to know this in order to avoid a mistake.)

At his Mass on December 24, 1711, the king received the oaths of fidelity of the bishops of Grasse and Saintes; after a second Mass he touched people afflicted with scrofula. Sometimes three thousand were assembled in the marble court or in the orangery expecting the miracle that would take place when Louis XIV pronounced the ritual blessing: "The king touches thee; God heal thee."

Now, after dinner, the king goes again to the chapel and attends vespers celebrated by the Bishop of Riez. Afterward he returns to his apartments and assigns the vacant benefices: the Bishop of Belley is appointed to the see of Chalon-sur-Saone, the Abbot of

Ecquevilly is appointed to the abbacy of Mezières, Abbé Colbert to the abbacy of Aumale, Dom Fitz-Herbert to the abbacy of La Piété, Madame de Bussy-Rabutin to the abbacy of Praslong, Madame de Carbonnel to the abbacy of Notre-Dame de Coutances, and Madame de Bernis was appointed abbess-coadjutrix.

On certain occasions the king's supper is moved forward to nine o'clock. At ten the king goes down to chapel, entering the nave. "On these occasions the chapel is thronged, all the bays of the gallery are crowded with ladies of the court in dishabille. All ears are charmed by the orchestra, which is far superior to that of the Opéra or any other orchestra in Europe, while all eyes are entranced by the beauty of the spectacle."

The three Masses the king hears will not keep him from attending the High Mass to be sung a few hours later by the Bishop of Riez, nor vespers after dinner, at which the Jesuit Father Gaillard will address him "a splendid compliment entirely drawn from his sermon," the last sermon of Advent, which he has just preached to the court.

Louis XIV went to Communion only five times a year: "on Holy Saturday at the parish church of Versailles, the other days at the chapel, which days being the Vigil of Pentecost, the Feast of the Assumption, the Feast of All Saints, and Christmas Eve."

If Louis XIV did not attend all the sermons of Advent, he did attend all the sermons of Lent. Saint-Simon asserts that he sometimes "issues a public statement a few days before Lent at his *lever* that he disapproves of serving meat under any pretext whatsoever and has instructed the Grand Provost, the Marquis de Sourche, to keep him informed of any infractions." He maintained a strict observance of the regulations of the church. Toward 1700, however, he ceased to observe the Lenten regulations and merely fasted for four days, and later three, in addition to fasting during the last four days of Holy Week.

He did not allow those who broke the fast to eat in company and permitted them only "boiled or roasted meat." He was no less severe on his own account on those days on which he himself was dispensed from fasting. Dangeau noted on February 9, 1684:

"The king dined and supped privately in his apartments because he is eating meat and does not wish to be seen eating it in public, even though he is ill." On these occasions the king would deprive himself of the pleasure of having his dinner brought to Madame de Maintenon's because he "did not wish to eat meat in company and the menu was considerably simplified."

On Wednesday of Holy Week the king never missed the service of Tenebrae, celebrated in the afternoon. On Holy Thursday he attended the High Mass and presided over the rite of the Maundy. He assisted again at Tenebrae and returned later to the gallery of the chapel to kneel in adoration before the Blessed Sacrament before he retired for the night. On Good Friday he heard the Mass of the Presanctified and venerated the cross; after Tenebrae the Passion was read to him. That day there was a grand dinner consisting only of vegetables, for "not even fish was served." This was all that was served at the table of those who dined *"bouche à cour,"* that is, those who were fed at the king's expense, such as the major-domo, the first gentlemen of the chamber, the butlers, the valets, and others.

Louis XIV took part in the two processions of Corpus Christi. Dangeau wrote on June 23, 1701: "The king and the entire royal family left the château at half-past nine and drove to the parish church, whence they accompanied the Blessed Sacrament on foot to the chapel of the château (which in 1710 became the vestibule of the new chapel) and thence, despite the great heat, back to the parish church where they attended the High Mass."

Louis XIV was very devoted to another procession instituted on February 10, 1638, in commemoration of the vow of Louis XIII. He did not forget that his father's vow had preceded his own birth by several months. This procession was falling into disuse. On June 10, 1700, he wrote to the bishops and archbishops of his realm asking that it be observed with full solemnities. The king describes how he fulfilled the conditions of the jubilee in 1661: "I walked publicly with all the members of my household to the stations of the jubilee, wishing for all to see and know the respect that I rendered unto God, for it was by His grace and protection rather than my own conduct that I proposed to achieve the accomplishment of my projects and the happiness of my subjects."

One of the last religious ceremonies of Louis XIV's life took place on Holy Thursday, April 18, 1715. The day before, during the service of Tenebrae, the king's first chaplain and first physician, assisted by surgeons and barbers, picked out thirteen poor children, choosing "the most pleasing ones." "On Thursday at six o'clock in the morning," a historian of the time explains, "these thirteen children were brought to the servants' quarters of the château, where the barber of the king's domestics shaved their hair and cut their toenails; they were warmed by the fire and given breakfast while servants washed their feet with warm water and sweet-smelling herbs."

At half-past nine, the king, accompanied by Monsieur le Dauphin (the future Louis XV, then five years old), entered the Hall of the Guards, where a pulpit had been erected for the preacher. Attended by the Duke of Orléans (the future regent) and all the princes of the blood, he encountered the thirteen children who had just been led in by their parents. Dressed in red robes and white linen gowns that enveloped them from head to foot, the children were seated on a long bench facing the pulpit with their backs toward the table at which the king would serve them. Cardinal de Rohan was there in full pontifical garb.

After a sermon by the Reverend Foissard, vicar-general of Evreux, who did not fail to pay His Majesty the usual compliment, the cardinal mounted the pulpit with the miter on his head and the crozier in his hand. The choir intoned the antiphon: *"Intret oratio mea in conspectu tuo, Domine."* When the grand almoner finished the prayers and pronounced absolution, the king approached the children and knelt, while the grand almoner presented a silver-gilt basin and one of the chaplains held the first child's foot. The king washed the foot, dried it, and kissed it. The ceremony was repeated for the twelve other children. After this the children took their places at the far side of the table, at which Louis XIV would serve them.

The readers of *Le Mercure galant* were treated to a full and detailed account of this rite:

The poor were served in the following order: First came Monsieur Desgranges, the Master of Ceremonies, preceded by an usher and followed by Monsieur le Marquis de Dreux, the grand master of ceremonies, then thirteen chief stewards, carrying their staves of office, the first chief steward, the Marquis de Livry, also carrying his staff, and Monsieur le Duc carrying a staff studded with gold fleurs-de-lys and topped with a crown. Each bowed as he passed before the king. Then came Monsieur le Dauphin carrying a wooden tray with three rolls and a flat-cake, Monsieur le Duc d'Orléans carrying a similar tray with a jug of wine and a cup, all of wood, Monsieur le Compte de Charolais, Monsieur le Prince de Comti, Monsieur le Prince de Dombes, Monsieur le Compte d'Eu, each carrying a plate of fish, vegetables, preserves or fruit, followed by the grand butler, the grand pantler, and gentlemen-servers to the number of thirteen, all carrying wooden dishes decorated with flowers. As each in turn approached the king, he bowed and presented the dish, which the king then gave to one of the poor children. This ceremony was repeated thirteen times in the same sequence, because thirteen dishes were served to each child.

There were also purses of red leather containing thirteen écus—no trifling gift—which the king hung around the neck of each child. Full of admiration for him who was to become, much sooner than one thought, King Louis XV, the editor of *Le Mercure* added: "It should be noted that they had to fetch the plates from a rather distant room, and Monsieur le Dauphin made this trip thirteen times, as did the other princes, marching resolutely and carrying his tray with much skill, always followed by Madame de Ventadour, his governess."

Fénelon did not permit himself to be impressed by these externals. In 1710, some two years before the victory of Denain, he wrote a letter of exceptional asperity that was ostensibly addressed to the Duke of Chevreuse but was really intended for the king, although the king most surely never saw it.

You will tell me that God will support France. I ask you, however, where is the assurance of this. Do you merit miracles in a time when your approaching ruin is unable to correct you, when you are cruel, proud, given to ostentation, unreachable, unfeeling, and ever willing to accept flattery? Will God be appeased seeing you humbled without humility, confounded by your own faults but unwilling to acknowledge them and ready to repeat them if you are able to go on living for two more years? Will God be satisfied with devotions that consist of gilding a chapel, saying a rosary, listening to a choir, being easily scandalized, and flushing out an occasional Jansenist? It is not only a question of putting an end to the war abroad; it is a question of giving bread to the starving at home . . . of recalling the true nature of the kingship and of tempering despotism, the source of all our misfortunes.

However just this criticism may have been, Louis XIV had far too much sense to fail to wish for peace, but only for a peace that would be consonant with the dignity and security of France.

PIERRE GAXOTTE

Religious Strife and the Revocation of the Edict of Nantes

THE MOST FAMOUS of the religious quarrels, the Jansenist controversy, dated back a quarter of a century. Cornelius Jansen, called Jansenius, Bishop of Ypres, had died in 1638, leaving in manuscript a large theological work in which he had attempted to restate and condense St. Augustine's doctrine concerning grace and election. After the Fall, is man capable of desiring and doing good unaided? Is grace given to all Christians because they have

Reprinted with permission of The Macmillan Company from Pierre Gaxotte, *The Age of Louis XIV*, trans. Michael Shaw (New York: The Macmillan Company, 1970), pp. 189–200, 204–217. Copyright © 1970 by The Macmillan Company. The original edition of this book was published in France in 1958 under the title *La France de Louis XIV*, © 1958 by Librairie Hachette.

been redeemed by the blood of Christ? Can they cooperate to obtain such grace? No, Jansenius answered. If man could do good unaided, if Adam's sin had not made him incapable of it, what would be the point of the redemption? And if man could cooperate with the action of grace, what would become of divine omnipotence? While man is incapable of good, he is capable of evil. This is a mystery that reason wonders at, because it cannot conceive how man may be responsible for evil without being equally responsible for good. Nor does reason grasp how one pan of a balance may descend and the other fail to rise. But for the Jansenists, reason was pride. Man must convince himself that unaided he is capable only of sin, but that he is saved by grace. Because he never knows whether he is in a state of grace, he must constantly crave it by practicing the most rigorous Christian morality: the life of a Christian is a perpetual act of penitence. This is the resolution of the apparent contradiction between a theology which crushes man and a morality which raises him up.

Jansenius' doctrine conquered Port-Royal, thanks to the work of one of its directors, Duvergier de Hauranne, Abbé de Saint-Cyran. Port-Royal was transformed by this encounter. In its beginnings, this was merely one of the numerous movements of the Catholic revival, such as were in the making everywhere. As the center of Jansenism, Port-Royal stirred up the religious life of France up to the time of the revolution. Although so many years had passed, its prestige was still so considerable that Sainte-Beuve could say without stretching the point too much that all the great literary figures of the period had had more or less intimate connections with it. As much as anyone else, the Jansenists experienced the genuine Christian sense of the emptiness of grandeur, the equality of men in their misery and sin. They introduced depth and a new spirit of reflection into religion, but they were not the only ones to do so. Their defining characteristic is pride, and they were a powerful example of what the human spirit is capable of once man is convinced that he possesses the truth. They felt theirs was a superior form of moral authority, they lived with a great deal of austerity and virtue, an unswerving firmness but also obstinacy, a passion for disputes and polemics, a certain taste for secrecy and clandestine action.

The real head of the Jansenist group was Antoine Arnauld, doctor of theology from the Sorbonne, whom his friends called "the great Arnauld." He was a small, dark, and ugly man, a jurist, dialectician, geometrician, grammarian, a person with a liking for legal procedures, a walking syllogism, bristling and vehement, who feared no one, always thought in opposition to someone, and was bent on repeating himself and convincing others. The Abbé Henri Brémond called him a militant theologian. Under his influence the preoccupation with asceticism and mysticism that had formed the basis of Port-Royal assumed a place of secondary importance. Henceforth the essential thing became to define the doctrine, to be in the right, to show that one was right, to make others admit it, and to make full use of all the resources of discussion and procedure to crush the adversary and emerge victorious. When the theological faculty obtained from Rome, in 1653 and 1656, a condemnation of the five propositions which, according to the syndic Cornet, were the very heart of the *Augustinus,* Arnauld submitted like everyone else. He recognized that legally there was no possibility of further wrangling since the pope had spoken. The propositions were really heretical and scandalous, but, Arnauld added, they were not contained in the *Augustinus.* They did not sum up its contents. Jansenius had never advanced anything of the kind; he had simply stuck to the doctrine of St. Augustine himself, and the condemnation was therefore not relevant to Jansenius himself or to his disciples.

This distinction between fact and law dominated the entire quarrel. Rome ordered all clerics to sign a document by means of which they condemned with heart and mouth the five propositions. The Jansenists agreed to this only with more or less subtle reservations and did not commit themselves on the question of fact. The bishops and the vicars-general who administered the diocese of Paris in the absence of Cardinal de Retz backed them. Louis XIV, who wanted to bring the matter to a close because he feared both the political clique and the religious sect that Jansenism repre-

sented, had his council annul the orders of the acting bishops of
the diocese of Paris. All persons, including the novices, living at
Port-Royal-des-Champs were expelled and the small schools
wrecked. Arnauld went into hiding, and finally, when Péréfixe had
taken over the see at Paris, the most obstinate nuns were taken
away by the police and placed in various other convents.

But the bishops still had to be dealt with. Because there was danger of a schism, Pavillon, bishop of Alet, agreed to sign the document of condemnation, but after having taken steps to confirm
the doctrine in a mandate of his diocese and to preserve his own
spiritual authority in a letter of remonstrance to the king. In 1667,
at the death of Alexander VII and the election of Clement IX
(Rospigliosi), four bishops were still in rebellion, and several others
took an interest in their cause. Nineteen of them signed two letters,
one of which was addressed to the king, the other to the pope.
They wrote to the pope that it was a "new and unheard-of dogma"
to "establish the infallibility of the church in human affairs not
revealed by God," that is, that he did not have the right to decide
the *fact* that the propositions were actually contained in the book
by Jansenius. They told the king that this doctrine was "pernicious,
contrary to the interests and the safety of his state" and that the
liberties of the Gallican church had been violated by the pope's
appointment of a commission to judge the bishops. According to
the customs prevailing in France, every one of the accused men
would have to appear before a court of first instance made up of
his metropolitan and twelve bishops of his or neighboring provinces.

The letter to the king was condemned by *parlement* as being
the work of a clique. But the ministers themselves said that the
matter was "off to a bad start." Nor did the king readily address
himself to the Curia, for it made it apparent that to be obeyed,
he required help. Persuaded that the church would be the first
victim of the struggles, Clement IX accepted a plan worked out
by Le Tellier and negotiated by Lionne. The four signed a declaration, adding an involved commentary to it. The pope praised them
for having signed with a sincere heart. Arnauld was received with
distinction by the papal nuncio and the king. Port-Royal-des-
Champs reopened its doors to the nuns, the *Messieurs* installed

themselves again in their solitude at the gates of the convent, and
piety flourished once more in the valley. Such was the Peace of
the Church; it was celebrated as a major event of Louis's reign.
But apparently no one was deceived: it was a peace of weariness
and had been concluded for fear that something irreparable might
happen.

Throughout the crisis, the chief adversaries of Port-Royal, the
men who had been most active and persistent, had been the
Jesuits, and it is against them that Port-Royal had directed its
counterblows. Twelve of the eighteen *Provincial Letters* attacked
their morality and their theologians. Quoting abundantly, Pascal
denounced their would-be spiritual advisers whose ingenious doctrine consisted in excusing and permitting everything, including
lies, theft, calumny, duels, and homicide. He thus raised innumera-
ble suspicions and created strong hostility against the company.
While it had not succeeded as dogma, Jansenism had made a splash
as polemics. The *Provincial Letters* were placed on the Index at
Rome and burned at Paris. But this had no effect whatever. The
conclusions advanced in them triumphed irresistibly. The maxims
of the Jesuit casuists were reproved by all priests, censured by the
Sorbonne, condemned by several popes, taken by Bossuet to the
assembly of the clergy in 1682 and stigmatized by it unanimously.

There was too much rancor for any permanent lull to set in. The
Jesuits had not laid down their arms, and their power at court
grew stronger. The king felt that Port-Royal was attracting too
many people; and there was too much ado about the *Messieurs*.
Something of the atmosphere of a victorious Fronde hung over
the valley. In April of 1679 the Duchess of Longueville died; in
her Jansenism lost a powerful supporter. At the end of that same
year Pomponne, the nephew of Arnauld, was discharged. Soon
thereafter the Duke of Estrées, Ambassador at Rome, began an
anti-Jansenist campaign. But the popes, who were wiser and more
prudent, did not want to reopen the affair. The nuns were merely
forbidden to admit novices at Port-Royal, and the convent had to
put up with only intermittent acts of brutality. Considering the
period, it was not very much that four or five persons were thrown
into prison during the course of fifteen years. Yet Arnauld, who

had been ordered to discontinue the meetings on the Faubourg
Saint-Jacques, believed it prudent to go to Flanders.

In August, 1695, the archdiocese in Paris became vacant. Madame
de Maintenon saw to it that the Bishop of Châlons, Louis-Antoine
de Noailles, was nominated to the post. Noailles was austere, he
loved St. Augustine, and one day, in a conversation with Bourdaloue, who had been sounding him out on his feelings toward
the Jesuits, he had said: "My Father, I always want to be their
friend, but never their servant." Everyone now called on him to
take sides. The furor raised in connection with a case of conscience
that had been submitted to the doctors of the Sorbonne in 1701
refused to subside. There was a storm of orders, censures, instructions, scurrilous satires, replies, briefs fulminating from Rome, and
decisions of the council, fulminating from Versailles. At the center
of the debate was a book, *Moral Reflections* by Father Quesnel,
and the exegesis of this book was still more difficult than that of
the *Augustinus,* because its title, its format, its appearance, and
part of its contents had changed several times.

But by this time the second generation of Port-Royal had disappeared. Arnauld, his sister, Mother Agnès, his brother, the bishop
of Angers, Pavillon, Caulet, the Bishop of Pamiers, Le Maître de
Sacy, Hamon, Lancelot, and Nicole were all dead. The spirit of
Jansenism had undergone a further evolution. It was no longer a
question of a group of stubborn, erudite, and religious men who
obstinately defended a doctrine they believed to be true. It was
now a sect, a party. These newcomers exhausted the sympathy of
the bishops, who would have liked to save what was essential in
Jansenism, its morality. But now a persecution set in which hardly
encountered any resistance, and the name of Jansenism became "a
hopeless tangle most useful for destroying whomever one pleases."

On the order of Louis XIV, Father Quesnel was arrested in
Brussels and his documents taken to Paris. Here they were examined by Father La Chaise, "deciphered, rearranged, deliberately
misinterpreted, examined with the most minute care in a kind of
black cabinet. They were excerpted and classified, turned over to
the king sections at a time, read, reread, and hashed over at Madame de Maintenon's every evening over a six-year period." What

was discovered here was proof of considerable clandestine activity and a widespread correspondence. Louis XIV demanded that the pope condemn in plain language the "respectful silence" as to the question of *fact*. A new document was drafted. All members of the church, including those who did not know Latin and had not read the *Augustinus,* were ordered to acknowledge that the five propositions were contained in it. Father Quesnel was condemned by the Inquisition, Port-Royal-des-Champs abolished, the sisters dispersed by the police (1709), the buildings and the cemetery destroyed, the skeletons of the recluses and nuns exhumed, thrown on carts, and taken to the Cemetery Saint-Lambert (1710). Finally, on September 8, 1713, Clement XI condemned in the bull *Unigenitus Dei Filius* one hundred and one propositions culled from the *Moral Reflections* as false, captious, reckless, injurious, impious, blasphemous, erroneous, or heretical. But not only did this bull utterly fail to put a stop to the agitation, it marked the beginnings of an even noisier, more serious, and more vast prolonged rebellion, which lasted up to the end of the *ancien régime* and even longer. Deprived of its doctrinal content, Jansenism was now no more than an expression of Gallicanism, or, more precisely, it fused with it and revived it thereby. Jansenism had produced one of those solemn situations where the rights of the pope, of the king, and of the church of France met head on.

The church of France was closely tied to the king and was almost one with the state. During the last two days of Lent in 1662, Louis XIV had made Pierre de Marca archbishop of Paris. This man died some weeks later but remained for a long time the posthumous doctor of the clergy of France and of the throne. His voluminous dissertations on *The Concord of the Priesthood and the Empire* were the charter of Gallicanism during the last century of the *ancien régime*. It was an extremely erudite charter, based on thousands of extracts from the canons of councils, from pontifical decrees, from capitularies, edicts, and ordinances of a number of kings, and from judgments by ecclesiastical and lay tribunals. In a small manual that constantly went through new editions, Counselor of State Le Vayer de Boutigny popularized all of this material

and thus explained the authority of the sovereign. God had turned
the guidance of the church over to a pilot, who is in charge of
navigation, and a captain, who supervises the safety and the defense of the vessel. "It is up to the captain to defend the ship
against outside enemies. He must see to it that the crew obeys the
pilot, that peace and discipline are preserved. He must prevent
those who act, including the pilot, from becoming careless." The
pilot is the pope, the captain the king. The captain judges any
slackening of discipline on the part of the pilot. By virtue of the
concordat which had entrusted him with guiding the destiny of
the church, he owns, theoretically at least, everything on board
ship. He chooses the bishops and distributes the abbeys, and no
intermediary exists between him and God.

On the other hand, the church of France believed that if the
pope had superior authority *within* the church, he did not have it
over it. While his power extended over any single church, it did not
extend over the church universal. While the bishops, like the pope,
were successors of the apostles and subject to the authority of
Rome, this was true only in the manner defined in the old canons
and, as Bossuet put it, within the limits "established by our fathers." Yet all this did not prevent the French church from glorying
more than any other in its indefectible attachment to the papacy.
Nor did it ever forget that it was an order within the state. It was
even the only one which was organized and had regular assemblies.

Yet within the clergy, interests and positions did not always har-
monize. Among the bishops, the Jesuits, the theologians at the Sorbonne, the members of the various religious orders, the priests in
Paris and the other major towns, disagreements did occur. De-
pending upon the nature of the questions and the manner in which
they were brought forward, attitudes varied a great deal. The
Gallicanism of the bishops and that of the magistrates refused the
pope the right to define the faith without the consent of the church
universal, but certain magistrates, going back to the first centuries
of Christianity, would readily have transferred this right to the
prince, in virtue of the "royal priesthood."

The court of Rome and the court of France were constantly
negotiating about all kinds of litigation. More often than not, the

tone in which the negotiations were conducted was quite sharp. And yet, whether they wanted to or not, the king and the bishops had to invoke the doctrinal authority of the pope. Generally speaking, the policy of Louis XIV with respect to Rome oscillated between brutality and submissiveness, had no true grandeur, no coherence, and was ultimately futile. In 1663 the Sorbonne had censured writings in which the doctrine of infallibility had been upheld, and the first conflict was about to break out. The king squelched the matter at once. He had too much good sense not to know how difficult it would be to undertake a precise definition of papal power. Yet in 1673 he took up this enterprise himself when the question of the *régale* came up, and one readily imagines that he did not do so altogether willingly. But there is no sphere in which the pressure exerted on him was greater.

In every bishopric, property and revenues were allotted to the bishop. They constituted his temporality. The bishop also had at his disposal benefices whose income furnished a living to archdeacons, archpriests, priests, and others charged with the care of souls. The *régale* was the right of the king to collect the temporalities and to bestow the episcopal benefits as he saw fit upon the death of a bishop and up to the moment his successor had been appointed and consecrated and had his oath registered with the chamber of accounts. But the *régale* was not in use in all dioceses. The declaration of 1673 extended it to the entire kingdom and ordered the bishops of dioceses that had been exempt up to that time to have their oaths registered. As long as they failed to do so, their see would be considered vacant. Although fifty-nine bishops came under this ruling, only two protested: the Bishop of Pamiers and the Bishop of Alet. The assembly of the clergy convened in 1675 said nothing about this matter. Pavillon d'Alet died in 1677; the last opponent, Caulet, appealed to Rome against the confiscation of his revenues. A great change had occurred. The Jansenists turned to the pope, while the Jesuits, who kept the accounts of available benefices, ranged themselves on the side of the king.

Innocent XI (Odescalchi), elected in 1676, had a vivid imagination and a conqueror's soul. Austere, very devout, and tormented by sickness, he was haunted by the memories of the great days of the papacy. He would have liked to unite all Christian princes in a crusade against the Infidel. He offered Louis XIV the kingdom of Constantinople and thrones for all his children. When the affair of the *régale* was brought before him, he pounced on it. For two years the king turned a deaf ear, did not answer his briefs, and refused to discuss the matter. In 1680 the assembly of the clergy assured him of the extreme displeasure which the papal letters had caused it. "We are so bound to Your Majesty, that nothing can separate us." The declaration was serious, and Rome was perplexed for several months. But at Pamiers the situation deteriorated. Since the bishop had died, the chapter, consisting entirely of Jansenists, had elected as its vicar one of the canons dispossessed by the recently extended *régale*. The king had him and his successor removed from office. The archbishop designated a third vicar, whom the intendant forced on the chapter. The chapter then appointed a fourth, whom the tribunals sentenced to death in his absence. The king would have liked to make the pope understand that "the affair was not easy to decide," but Innocent XI said that "the *régale* is God's business" and that he counted on the support of the Bishop of Pamiers, "who is in heaven."

The tactics of the king always consisted in placing the clergy of France between himself and Rome. The next quinquennial assembly was not scheduled to convene until 1685. By convoking the bishops who were at court or in the neighboring provinces, a first restricted assembly was brought together, but it did nothing decisive. A "General extraordinary assembly representing the synod" was therefore called in November, 1681. Bossuet, recently promoted from Condom to Méaux, played the most conspicuous role. Harlay maneuvered silently. It was like a *parlement* dressed in cassocks. The deputies discussed, and presented their reservations of a spiritual nature concerning the application of the *régale,* the legitimacy of which, however, they did not dispute. In spite of the intransigence of the council, the king made those concessions which good church discipline demanded: henceforth, no one would receive benefices involving the care of souls unless he had the age, the degree, and other qualifications required. The priests in possession of benefices first had to request "canonical approbation and mission" either from the vicar if the bishopric was still vacant, or from the bishop if one had been appointed. But Colbert and the magistrates demanded more. Fearing the irreparable, Bossuet resigned himself to the inevitable.

On March 19, 1682, he drafted a declaration comprising four articles. The first states that "God gave no power to any ecclesiastical authority over kings and sovereigns in temporal matters" and that "they cannot be deposed either directly or indirectly by the authority of the heads of the church." The second article is less straightforward: without quoting them, it alludes to the decrees of the Council of Constance which subordinate the pope to the authority of a council. It states that the church of France "does not approve the opinion of those who tamper with these decrees." The third article, which was general and vague, stated that "the rules, customs, and constitutions which are traditional in the kingdom must be adhered to." The fourth, finally, is almost unintelligible: "Although the pope has the principal role in questions of faith and although all his decrees concern all churches and every church in particular, his judgment is not immutable unless the consent of the church is given."

Bossuet had wanted to do what was best, but on the eleventh of April, the assembly received a letter from the pope addressed to his venerable brothers and beloved sons of the Gallican church in which he practically told them that they were cowards. Besides, he disapproved and declared null and void everything they had undertaken in the matter of the *régale*. Not a word was said about the four articles. But this was merely a question of prudence, for in a bull that was kept secret, and whose contents were not revealed until 1691 by Alexander VIII, Innocent XI was to write a short time thereafter that "all the acts of the clergy of France in 1682 and all the articles laid down by it concerning ecclesiastical power are void, invalid, and a dead letter." But at the time, and while the assembly protested very loudly that "the Gallican Church governs itself by its own laws" and that it would continue to consider them inviolate, everybody—court, bishops, the Curia—was negotiating backstage. Upon learning that Monsieur de Montespan was talking of seeking the annulment of his marriage in Rome, the pope himself declared that idea to be "ridiculous and impertinent." Suddenly, the king adjourned the assembly. It did not reconvene.

But peace had not been concluded. The four articles, which had been registered with *parlement,* had become laws of the state. They had to be taught in schools, seminaries, and universities. Licentiates and doctors of theology were obliged to subscribe to them. The pope's answer was to refuse the bulls demanded by the bishops the king had appointed. Soon there were thirty-five dioceses without a pastor. Louis XIV was upset, and he let it be known. He repeated in his dispatches to Rome that a bishopric without a bishop was a terrible scandal and a horrible confusion. He still did not know that Innocent XI had secretly excommunicated him. Occasionally he thought of frightening him. In 1687 the pope had deprived the foreign ministers accredited with him of certain privileges. The Marquis de Lavardin moved into Rome as a conqueror, and Louvois was getting ready to send troops to Civitavecchia. The agents of France—ambassadors, legal personnel, magistrates—showed the kind of hatred for the papacy that seemed to be leading toward a schism. But this was precisely the word Louis XIV did not want to hear. While the number of manifestos, decrees, insulating speeches, and pointless vexations increased at Paris and Versailles, the Curia waited patiently, absolutely certain that the king would be restrained by his religious sentiments and not undertake anything extreme.

In 1689 Innocent XI died. This death was merely an incident. Louis XIV pretended to see in it a solution and affected the belief that the disharmony between France and Rome was entirely due to the person of Innocent XI. He courted the conclave and contributed to the election of Ottoboni. But once he had acceded to the throne of St. Peter under the name of Alexander VIII, Ottoboni showed himself as intransigent as his predecessor had been. His pontificate was short (1689–91). Upon his death, the cardinals of the French party went about trying to get a pope who "could issue bulls to the bishops who had been present at the assembly of 1682 without demanding a disavowal, retraction, or disapprobation." Pignatelli agreed, or appeared to agree, to the obligations stipulated. He was elected and took the name of Innocent XII. He offered the bulls, but on condition that every bishop named would henceforth make a profession of his faith to the papal nuncio and condemn "the things done by the assembly of 1682." The king had already made too many concessions to draw back at this point. On September 14, 1693, he ordered that the declaration containing the four articles should no longer be observed, so that this "special sign" might manifest to all his veneration for the Holy See. This was a defeat and an act of penitence. . . .

The history of Jansenism and quietism obliges us to state that the church of Louis XIV utterly fails to present that quality of spontaneous, peaceful, and perfect unity which has often been taken to define the whole of his reign. Yet these divisions did not prevent it from pursuing obstinately the great dream of crushing Protestantism. And here again we are confronted with a disappointing and cruel chapter, because the contrast between the immensity of the task and the pettiness of the means is so striking.

At the moment Louis XIV took over the government, the Huguenots no longer wished to form a faction within the state. They were still very numerous. There were a million or perhaps even a million and a half of them, with 630 churches and 736 pastors, but the great families that had sought adventure and profit during the struggles had deserted the cause as soon as they had seen it fail. Once they had been rid of their turbulent chiefs, the Protestants had kept very quiet during the Fronde, and in 1652 the King had accorded them a general *satisfecit*. Many among them were serving in the army and the magistrature. Turenne, the prop of the throne and the state, was not yet converted. Polemics between Catholic doctors and Protestant ministers were less acrid. While a reunion of the churches, as Leibnitz would have wished, was too much to hope for, a religious peace, that is, a rivalry of merit, knowledge, and piety, did seem a possibility.

But it was obvious that hatred had not died. Where the Protestants were in the majority, as in certain cantons of Normandy, Poitou, and Languedoc, they annoyed the Catholics as much as they were able and deliberately and openly defied the church. The majority of the Catholics, on the other hand, felt that the Edict of Nantes had been an expedient, a provisional evil, and they had not surrendered the hope of crushing heresy and winning the heretics back. Their aversion to Protestantism was inspired not only by religious beliefs, but also by political convictions. It seemed scandalous that a nation should be divided into two distinct confessions, for this meant that the country was disunited. Everywhere it was the rule that the subjects' religion was the same as the sovereign's, so that the two forms of obedience—religious and political—might be fused and give each other reciprocal support.

The Catholics also held that the conversion of the Protestants would be a very easy matter and that the mere desire to bring it about sufficed. Without a hierarchy, without pomp, and without an official place in the monarchy, Protestantism seemed fragile because it was not the religion of the king. The state of Huguenot integrity, the personal adherence to a freely chosen belief, the passion for the Scriptures, the biblical enthusiasm, all this strength of resistance in the soul of the Protestants was unsuspected.

The king was too representative of his times not to have the feelings, opinions, and illusions of Catholic France. Yet he felt neither anger nor bitterness toward his loyal subjects. His faith was calm, and he did not have the temperament of a persecutor. "I believed, my son," he wrote in his memoirs, "that the best way gradually to reduce the number of Protestants in my kingdom would be, first, to abstain from bringing any pressure to bear upon them. The concessions made by my predecessors were to be observed, but nothing was to be granted beyond them, and even their implementation would be confined to the narrowest bounds justice and propriety might allow. . . . As for favors that depended upon myself alone, I decided . . . not to bestow any . . . in order to oblige them to reconsider from time to time . . . whether they had some good reason for depriving themselves voluntarily of those benefits which they might share with the rest of my subjects."

The *strict* interpretation of the Edict of Nantes defined royal procedure until 1679. This was also the line taken by the clergy. At the general assembly of 1655, and after having painted the activities of the Protestants in the blackest colors, the Archbishop of

Reims, Henri de Gondrin, had exclaimed: "The Church would derive some consolation if things did not go beyond the observation of the Edict of Nantes." But how was this to be done? It was a long, obscure, and painstaking piece of labor. The Company of the Holy Sacrament did most of it by investigating, writing commentaries, and making denunciations. The results of its labors found their way into two books which appeared in 1662 and 1666: the *Execution of the Edict of Nantes in Bas-Languedoc,* written by the Jesuit Meynier, and the *Explication of the Edict of Nantes,* by Bernard, counselor of the tribunal at Béziers. Meynier then wrote two other works: one, entitled *Truths,* which dealt with Poitou; a second, the *Edict of Nantes Executed According to the Intentions of Henry the Great,* which lists all the techniques for an interpretation of the texts that would allow the suppression of the rights of the Protestants. It is from this arsenal that judges, bishops, and intendants drew their weapons, some occasionally and listlessly, others with a kind of hatred.

For example, the Edict of Nantes nowhere stated explicitly that a member of the so-called Protestant church might be buried during the day. The burial must therefore take place at night. In 1662 the corresponding edict came out. Article 28 permitted members of the Protestant church to open schools in all the places where their form of worship was authorized. But it fixed neither what was to be taught nor the number of teachers nor the size of classes in any given community. The children would therefore be taught merely to read, write, and count; there would be only one teacher per school and one school per town. The result was that at Marennes the six hundred Protestant children, sons of sailors, had only a single teacher, a devious way of forcing the parents to use Catholic schools. Article 9 permitted Protestant worship in those towns where several differing faiths had been practiced in 1595 and 1597. It is certain that in many spots in Languedoc the Protestants had gained ground. The assembly of the clergy of 1660 to 1661 demanded that an inquiry be held. An edict published in April, 1661, specified that the inquiry would be conducted in every province by two commissioners, one Protestant, the other Catholic. But care was taken to choose the Protestant commissioner from among the lukewarm and those who were sensitive to favors that might be granted by the king. In Poitou seventy-four Protestant churches were "challenged" and sixty-four destroyed. In Gex all were condemned except two. Because this area had been reunited with the crown in 1661, the Protestants there could not lay claim to the benefits of the edict of 1598. Everywhere they were hindered in the pursuit of their various professions. In Paris the Protestant master embroiderers were forbidden to take on apprentices. In Calais, where the only two inns of any importance were run by Protestants, one of the two innkeepers was forced to sell his property to a Catholic. In Languedoc it was decided that half of the master craftsmen should always be Catholics. Later this was increased to two-thirds. The Protestant communities were administered by consistories, councils, and provincial synods and, at a higher level, by a national synod. The twenty-ninth of these synods had been held at Loudon during the winter of 1659–60; it was to be the last. Problems were raised in an effort to prevent provincial synods and conferences. The organization was to be destroyed in order to isolate the individual members more completely.

At every session the assembly of the clergy repeated the same complaints. After the *don gratuit* had been voted and as the sessions terminated, an agenda would be sent to the king, and this agenda became ever more pressing. Between sessions the two general agents followed matters at meetings of the council. As the next session approached, inquiries and denunciations began again and the king was told once more that he should emulate the heroes of Christianity such as Valentinian, Theodosius, and Charles if he wished to crown his glory. "Are you not indebted to God," the coadjutor of Arles asked in 1675, "for these glorious benefits [the military victories]? Yes, sire, without a doubt. And now you should show the full extent of your gratitude by employing your authority for the complete extirpation of heresy." And the assembly specified: "Freedom of conscience is looked upon by all Catholics as an abyss yawning at their feet, a trap set to catch them in their ingenuousness, and an open door to libertinism. We call upon you most urgently, sire, to deprive them of this baleful freedom."

The Peace of Nymwegen permitted Louis to apply himself more fully to the eradication of heresy. The assembly of 1680 recognized that while the war had lasted, considerations of state might have interfered with the good intentions of His Majesty. But now the path was clear. Because the assembly had been brought into conflict with the papacy over the question of the *régale,* it was anxious to manifest its zeal. In 1682 the king and the church acted jointly. The assembly addressed to the Protestants a *Pastoral Admonition.* After effusions of paternal tenderness, the document ended with this threat: "You must expect incomparably more terrible and fatal misfortunes than all those your rebellion and your schism have brought upon you in the past." The king promised to contribute to the projects worked out by his bishops. And indeed, the compilation by Pilatte, which lists only twelve royal acts concerning the so-called Reformed Religion between 1661 and 1679, lists eighty-five for the period between 1679 and October, 1685. In rapid succession the Protestants were excluded from all posts and offices. They were forbidden to be judges, notaries, attorneys, bailiffs, and secretaries to the king. They could no longer become advocates, booksellers, printers, or physicians. They were discharged from their positions at court or in connection with the administration and collection of taxes. In order to assure equal justice to all subjects of the king "without any suspicion, hatred, or favor," the Edict of Nantes had set aside special courts for the Protestants. These were discontinued. Being now permanently suspect, the members of the Reformed Religion were watched by priests and churchwardens, whose responsibility it became to inform the judges of the locality.

The persecution was extended to Protestant families. Mixed marriages were forbidden, and children of such unions were considered illegitimate and excluded from any inheritance. In his role as father of all his subjects, the king ordered that the bastards of both sexes, regardless of their ages, be instructed in the Catholic religion. One case has been cited where a bastard twenty-four years old was called upon to convert. Article 18 of the Edict of Nantes had forbidden the taking away "by force or persuasion" of Protestant children for the purpose of baptism and instruction. But a lawyer named Bernard had pointed out that without being persuaded or suborned by anyone whatever, the children could rejoin the Catholic religion, "for reunion with that religion is natural, and to be separated from it is a violent condition." The age of decision, which had been set at fourteen for boys and twelve for girls in 1669, was lowered to seven. The newly converted had the choice of either remaining with their parents and being maintained and provided for there or going elsewhere and demanding a pension corresponding to their social condition. Protestants were of course forbidden to send their children abroad or to leave the kingdom themselves. It was their conversion which was demanded and which was going to be forced upon them by making life impossible for them.

These large-scale conversions were essential to convince the king that the Edict of Nantes, which had been declared "firm and inviolable," "permanent and irrevocable" by his grandfather, could be revoked without committing an act of perjury. If no Protestants were left, what was the point of an edict designed to protect them? A fund had already been created to reward recantation. The price to be paid was low: 6 livres for a commoner, 20 for an infantry soldier, 30 for a cavalryman, 40 for a sergeant, and 60 for a sergeant-major. In the case of noblemen, pensions of up to 2000 and 3000 livres were paid. There were those who had their names put down in a number of parishes in order to collect more than once. The newly converted also benefited from tax exemptions; those who remained obstinate paid in their place. But the really efficient method was the quartering of troops, a technique called *dragonnades*. It is not known who conceived this idea. The intendant of Poitou, Marillac, was in any case the first to practice it systematically, as early as 1680. He was imitated by Foucault in Béarn and by Basville in Languedoc. The soldiers quartered in the houses of Protestants could conduct themselves like brigands, and with complete impunity. They committed the worst horrors: pillaging, rape, torture. Men and children had their feet burned, women were dragged over the ground by their hair, old men tied to their chairs and mercilessly beaten in the presence of their children. When the victims had come to the end of their strength, they were taken to church and declared Catholics. In January, 1685, the Protestants sent the king a "Final Request" drafted by Pastor Claude. "We live," they stated, "under the sacred pledge of the kings, your predecessors, which has not been buried with them in their tombs." They invoked the sanctity of the laws, and they concluded: "Compulsion can only turn people into atheists or hypocrites, or promote in men of good faith a resolution and a perseverance which triumph over tortures." Cardinal Le Camus at Grenoble and Cardinal de Coislin at Orléans opposed the persecutions and even managed to get the troops withdrawn from their dioceses. But though Louvois disapproved of disorders that might jeopardize military discipline, he insisted that the generals perform miracles: the terror practiced by the soldiers precipitated conversions.

In the autumn of 1685 the king, who knew nothing of the abominations perpetrated upon his subjects, received the most comforting news. He must have believed that heaven was rewarding his piety by special acts of kindness. As he rose in the morning, he announced the marvels which he had been informed of the evening before: that on the first of September, 1685, all the Huguenots of Montauban had converted to Catholicism, having previously deliberated at the town hall; that on the sixth, the greater part of Bordeaux had returned to the fold; that on the twenty-ninth, the dioceses of Embrun and Gap and the valleys belonging to the abbey of Pignerol had accepted Catholicism before the dragoons had even arrived. On the second of October, it was Castres; on the fifth, Montpellier; on the ninth, Uzès; on the thirteenth, all of Poitou. And finally, on the eighteenth of October, at Fontainebleau, the king signed the Edict of Revocation, drafted by Le Tellier.

In the preamble Louis adopts the theory that the Edict of Nantes was merely a provisional measure intended to prepare for the reestablishment of unity. "Since the better and larger part of our subjects belonging to the so-called Reformed Religion has been converted to Catholicism, the implementation the Edict of Nantes has become pointless." Article 1 orders the demolition of Protestant churches. Articles 2 and 3 forbid assemblies to be held for reasons of Protestant worship in any place whatever, castle or private house. Articles 4, 5, and 6 order the Protestant pastors to leave the kingdom within two weeks and promise various benefits to those who will convert. Article 8 stipulates that children of Protestant parents will be brought up as Catholics. Articles 10 and 11 forbid Protestants to leave the kingdom, threatening male offenders with the galleys and female offenders with life imprisonment. Those who have already left must return; otherwise their possessions will be confiscated. Article 12 suggests a feeling of remorse. Provided they will not gather together and do not engage in Protestant worship, "our subjects of the so-called Reformed Religion may remain in the kingdom without recanting, until such a time as it may please God to enlighten them. . . ." The Edict of Fontainebleau did not apply to Alsace, whose religious status had been defined in the treaties of Westphalia, which had stated that matters would remain as they had been on January 1, 1624, the decretory year. Yet the declarations registered with the Supreme Council of Colmar introduced in the provinces some of the provisions of the revocation: mixed marriages were prohibited, Protestants were forbidden to have their children brought up abroad, and fiscal advantages were accorded to new converts. Other vexations were added in order to deprive the Lutherans of part of their churches or force them to share them.

The kingdom had thus once again become a state where the religion of the sovereign was law. Intolerance was the rule almost everywhere: Louis XIV lowered himself to the level of the rest. This regression was enthusiastically hailed by all of France. But the revocation settled nothing; on the contrary, it unsettled things. The king forbade emigration, but emigration got under way. At first no attempt was made to stop it, and there was even a show of satisfaction. But as the movement grew, extensive measures were taken along the borders and in places of embarkation. Skirmishes took place; fugitives were killed and others wounded, captured, sent to the galleys. The exodus was then more carefully planned and became methodical. Guides, ferrymen, relays, disguises came to be used; agencies sprang up where false passports could be obtained, and secret intineraries were worked out.

How many emigrated? Estimates vary considerably, ranging

between sixty thousand and two million. Speaking of his own time, Vauban put the figure at 100,000. But the exodus did not occur in a single year. It proceeded irregularly and over a fifty-year span. During the reign of Louis XV, when persecutions recurred, in 1720 and 1750, people were still leaving. Here is the number of yearly arrivals in Magdeburg, the most important place of refuge in Prussia, after Berlin, during the early years: 18 in 1685; 84 in 1686; 118 in 1687; 109 in 1688; 43 in 1689; 31 in 1690; 74 in 1691; 119 in 1692; 72 in 1693; 44 in 1694; 22 in 1695; 13 in 1696; 39 in 1697; 109 in 1698; 155 in 1699, etc. All in all, 125,798 refugees passed through Frankfurt am Main, and about 150,000 emigrated via Switzerland. The number of emigrants in one century must have exceeded half a million. It was not a fatal loss, but a serious one.

The *émigrés* were good craftsmen, sailors, soldiers, professors, all energetic, hard-working men of tested convictions. The Protestant princes fought over this human material by advertising cleverly and holding out wonderful promises. The Great Elector said he would give his "unfortunate fellow believers" land and subsidies (Edict of Potsdam, November 8, 1685), but the French knew how advantageous their settlement would be to countries without industry or commerce. Some had managed to take along their capital. We know of the case of a wine merchant from Paris who arrived in Holland with 600,000 livres, of a bookseller from Lyon who brought along 1,000,000. Before they established themselves permanently, they stipulated conditions, bargained, and demanded regular contracts. Thus came into being an exiled France beyond the frontiers, which was hostile to Louis XIV but whose émigré population continued for a long time to be loyal to the French language, to their memories, and to their customs.

The largest and most active colonies were those in Holland. They had great schools and writers such as Bayle, Jurieu, and Claude. In Germany the French Huguenots went to live in a great many different localities. In Brandenburg alone they developed some forty communities. Berlin, which had between five and six thousand inhabitants at that time, attracted over four thousand *émigrés,* soldiers, jewelers, glovemakers, tobacco growers, manufacturers of hats and of cloth. They had their own schools, churches, pastors, and council. For Brandenburg this was like a new town and another kind of life. Many sailors and industrialists, papermakers among others, went to England. From there some continued on to America. Because it feared reprisals, Geneva admitted only a very small number. The largest group settled in Lausanne and in the country of Vaud.

In France more and more difficulties developed after the first moment of joy. What was going to be done about the possessions of the Huguenots? Should pillaging be permitted, or should they be sold for the benefit of the state? Should the property be sequestrated and turned over to a governmental agency? Should the *émigrés* be considered as deceased and their property passed on to those of their heirs who had become converts? Every one of these possibilities was tried. Considerable loss, disorder, fraud, and injustice was the result.

What happened to the Protestants who remained? Those who refused conversion quoted Article 12 for support. Those who had adopted Catholicism had done so in almost all cases out of fear. In order to save time, they had sometimes merely been asked to sign a vague formula which did not commit them to anything. Father Tixier, a worthy Benedictine and an acquaintance of the great Condé, stated that the priests in Normandy discovered that the new believers were more convinced Huguenots after their conversion than they had been before. And the Bishop of Grenoble wrote, "They don't want to hear anything about mass or the sacraments."

Although they were threatened with the death penalty, Protestant pastors returned. In spite of vicious repression, in spite of numbers of people killed, the gallows, prison, and the galleys, assemblies continued to be held in remote places. The government did not succeed in catching Claude Brousson, who traveled all over Normandy, Poitou, and especially Languedoc, preaching, writing, and reviving people's energies and hopes. And it was even more difficult to find a way of forcing the new converts to worship. Should they be taken to church and communion by soldiers? And if they were not compelled, how were the effects of their pernicious example to be combatted? The church of France had its theologians, its saints, its politicians, its intelligent and clever prelates. It had turned out major works of controversy. Bossuet published the *History of Variations* in 1688; the church had shown itself capable of sending missionaries of great prestige into rebellious territory, as for example Fénelon to Saintonge, Bourdaloue to Languedoc. But it did not have a popular, enlightened, patient clergy that could win people over gradually.

At the instigation of Cardinal de Noailles and of Pontchartrain, the council undertook an investigation in 1698. It was agreed that the converts were insubordinate. But opinions differed considerably on the question of possible remedies. Vauban, Chamlay, who was Louvois's best assistant, and Bégon, the intendant of La Rochelle, had emphasized that the entire set of rules and laws had something unjust and revolting about them. A citizen of Nérac, for example, had been burned for having spit on the host. But who was actually responsible for this crime? Had there been no revocation and had the man remained unmolested, he would not have committed this sacrilege. Among the intendants and the legal personnel consulted, Daguesseau, the predecessor of Basville in Languedoc, recommended mildness. Basville and Pinon (in Béarn) favored coercion and would even have enforced attendance at Mass. All the prelates of Languedoc shared this view, while six bishops and archbishops, in Paris, Reims, Châlons, Soissons, La Rochelle, and Saint-Pons, opposed them. Bossuet (in Méaux) took an intermediate position. He condemned with indignation the barbaric custom of dragging the bodies of Protestants into the refuse dump. But he approved compulsion in the education of children, although not forced attendance at mass. Bazas and Saintes concurred. The most intransigent of the extremists was Fléchier: "If all the subjects of the king are not held to a uniform worship as they are to the unity of the faith, there will always be different peoples who will fight each other within the bosom of the church and of the state itself and who will constitute two separate bodies."

The declaration of December 13, 1698, and the instructions of January 7, 1699, did not by any means confirm the complete victory of the "spirit of moderation and gentleness" advocated by Daguesseau. Yet they admitted that the conversion of heretics and the instruction of converts were first of all the task of the church. They consequently called upon prelates, priests, and the faithful themselves to perform zealously their duties of guidance, assistance, piety, and charity. They forbade any differentiation between recent converts and others, recommended that the practice of defiling the dead bodies of Protestants be discontinued (without, however, officially abrogating it), and, finally, deprived the intendants of their special police powers in religious matters.

But in order to cut down on useless persecution, it was not enough that the king recommend gentleness, he also had to be obeyed. And he was not obeyed very rigorously. In different localities commissioners, commandants, noblemen, priests, and administrative bodies continued the course of violence. "The priests of Languedoc," Villars wrote in 1704, "cannot rid themselves of their habit of frightening all their parishes." Basville, who did not take seriously an edict he had voted against, allowed his lay and ecclesiastical agents to go on as they had in the past. One of them in particular, the archpriest of the diocese of Mende, François du Chayla, was indefatigable in supplying the tribunals with victims. The country became exasperated. In July, 1702, when a small convoy of fugitives had been arrested by the archpriest and locked up in his house at Pont-de-Mauvert, the peasants got together, freed the prisoners, and killed du Chayla. During the next few days, they murdered two priests, burned down a church, and finally put fire to a castle after having massacred its inhabitants. As Protestant preachers such as Gédéon, Laporte, Pierre Esprit, Couderc, Séguier, Mazel, Esperandieu, and Ravanel spoke out, other groups were formed. They found their real leader in the person of Jean Cavalier, twenty years old, a butcher's helper by profession; and this time it was a regular insurrection.

It occurred in an extraordinary atmosphere of Biblical exaltation and nervous excitement. The Protestants called their assemblies "The Desert" by way of allusion to the Jews who had waited forty years in the desert of Sinai before entering the promised land. They had the mystical conviction that they were reliving the early history of the chosen people. Suffering, injustices, and the anxious expectation of even more terrible misfortunes produced fear, hopes, and hallucinations which spread and were sustained by impassioned writings originating in Holland. Prophecies had stirred up the people of the valley of the Drôme in 1688, of the mountains of Vivarais in 1689. They had occurred again in Uzès in the summer of 1700 and spread to the entire Cévennes region. The prophets, who were often children, had cataleptic fits, and when they regained their powers of movement and speech, one could hear exhortations, cries, shouts of pain and rapture, and sometimes orders and coherent speeches. One of these visionaries marched to the stake after his capture, singing the praises of God and exhorting the bystanders. Savoy sent some supplies to the "fanatics." Two or three ships bringing arms from Nice were sunk or captured along the coast of Languedoc. Money, satiric writings, and great promises came from Holland.

The authorities believed at first that it was a flash in the pan, but the situation soon got out of hand. Protestant bands formed and disappeared mysteriously. Because they could not lay their hands on the enemy, the generals in charge of putting down the revolt, Broglie and Montrevel, vented their fury on property: they burned down 466 villages. The war lasted more than three years, with calm periods alternating with unexpected resumptions of hostilities. In order to master the situation, it became necessary for the monarchy to send its most illustrious generals, Villars and Berwick, into Languedoc. Villars forced the court to make intelligent concessions and succeeded in winning over Cavalier by having him made a colonel (Cavalier later went to England, where he died in 1740, having been governor of the Isle of Wight). Other leaders were captured and executed, and a "network of military surveillance" was set up and kept in a state of permanent readiness. In 1710 the English landed at Cette (now Sète) in the hope of reviving the insurrection.

The fury of the conflict gradually died down, but Protestantism had rebuilt itself in the course of the persecution. In the sixteenth century, it had been most popular with the rural population and with workers, scholars, and the feudal nobility. During the lull following the Edict of Nantes, Protestantism had become an urban and middle-class movement. At that time, a large proportion of merchants, lawyers, officers, and courtiers became members of the Protestant church. Owing to the force of circumstance, the original nonconformism had been replaced by the psychology peculiar to the middle classes, the wealthy, and the functionaries and had turned into opportunism, timidity, and the love of order. The revocation dealt this lukewarm church a mortal blow. The fearful dropped out and either recanted or stooped to a superficial conformism which deprived them of all authority. The Protestant church recovered its power by once again becoming rural and popular, that is, by reassuming its original character. The apostle of this reorganization was Antoine Court, a preacher from Vivarais. On the twenty-first of August, 1715, ten days before the death of Louis XIV, he called the first provincial synod in a quarry near Nîmes. The synod decided to put an end to illuminism* and to reconstitute the religious communities with pastors and elders who would once again be the shepherds of the flock.

Considered as a whole, the church policy of Louis XIV had failed. He did not re-establish the unity of the faith. He did not abolish Jansenism; he neither suppressed nor organized Gallicanism. On the contrary, the spectacle of the disputes, the severity, and the persecutions profoundly troubled people and laid the groundwork for a transformation of ideas. "The libertines triumph," Bossuet wrote in his *Relation,* "and avail themselves of the opportunity by turning piety into hypocrisy and heaping ridicule on the business of the Church." While the controversies had been at their height, the disciples of St. Cyran had been told that the spirit was upright and the conscience enlightened, that the will judiciously loved its true good, and that man could come to God by relying only on his own powers. This was giving nature and reason a great deal of credit. While the theologians were quarreling among the ruins of the sects, scholars and scientists were already engaged in constructing an edifice of reason whose majestic proportions were beginning to be seen by ordinary men.

* Here illuminism refers to a religious sect or group that claimed to obtain inspiration directly from God—thereby bypassing the church. [ed.]

JOHN B. WOLF

The Cult of the King

I HAVE EVERY REASON to be satisfied since the very Christian king has treated me most civilly and others have done all that they can to give me pleasure. . . ." Thus wrote Crown Prince Frederick of Denmark to tell his father of his trip to the court of Louis XIV. His letters are a charmingly naïve account of the parties, balls, and court functions that seemed only slightly dampened by the war that raged in Flanders, the Rhineland, and Italy. He was extremely happy to have his princely rank recognized by the right to an armchair in the presence of the king

From John B. Wolf, *Louis XIV* (New York: W. W. Norton & Company, Inc., 1968), pp. 357–378. Reprinted by permission of W. W. Norton & Company, Inc. and Victor Gollancz Ltd. Copyright © 1968 by W. W. Norton & Company, Inc.

and the dauphin even though he was "incognito." He visited most of the châteaux of the royal family, including the Palais Royal, Marly, Versailles (for a *Mardi gras* ball), and on his departure Louis urged him to stop at the Condé château at Chantelly, "where the gardens and the waters merit a visit." He must have been well treated, indeed handsomely so, for in one of his letters he tells his father that he has enough money, and needs no more. Surely this has happened to few enough tourists in Paris.

What young Frederick saw was the court of France ensconced in the grandeur of the palaces built by its kings. When Louis came to the throne, the royal family had many châteaux both in the Paris area and down on the Loire. Some of them, like Fontainebleau and Vincennes, were old and had been remodeled many times; the most beautiful of them dated from the time of Francis I, particularly Chambord and Saint-Germain. There were palaces in Paris: the Louvre, the Tuileries, and the Palais Royal that Richelieu had built and willed to the crown, and, after the death of the dowager Duchess of Orléans (Gaston's wife), the Luxemburg Palace. At Compiègne and Versailles there were "hunting lodges"; the latter lodge dated from the period of Louis XIII and was a delightful structure. There were other châteaux belonging to the houses of Orléans, Condé, and Conti, but the king's government had nothing to do with their upkeep.

Mazarin had believed that the king should build inside the walls of the great fortress of Vincennes, and, indeed, the cardinal caused two pavilions to be constructed there and refurbished the chapel. But Louis's own first important construction was in Paris; in spite of his dislike for the city, he allowed Colbert to convince him that a great king should have an imposing palace in his capital city. The Palais Royal did not quite reach the specifications, nor did the "new Louvre" built by Catherine de Médicis, Henry IV, Marie, and Louis XIII. What was needed was an important addition to the Louvre opposite the church of Saint-Germain l'Auxerrois and along the front of the river. Bernini came from Italy to help with the plans, but the final designs accepted were drawn by a French architect, Claude Perrault. These pavilions built by Louis XIV are still impressive for their monumental style as well as their excellent taste, but Louis probably had very little to do with them beyond giving his approval and supplying the money. When Colbert urged further construction in the city, the king was not interested. The memories of the Fronde and his own love of the open countryside combined to make him distrust and dislike the big city; he avoided visiting it for years on end.

Versailles was Louis's favorite project. The site seems first to have appealed to him in 1664 at the time of the party of the Enchanted Island, but the really important remodeling of the château did not begin until 1669–70. During the Dutch War the construction languished, but after 1679 it moved forward with a great pace. By 1682 Madame de Maintenon could write that Versailles had an "incomparable beauty," by 1687–88 the greatest part of the construction was complete—only the chapel remained to be built. Despite Saint-Simon and the other critics of Versailles, the great château remains as one of the important artistic accomplishments of our civilization. Louis built it at Versailles rather than at Vincennes to show the world that the king of France could build in the open. His soldiers were his defense; he needed neither walls nor moat to guarantee his security. . . .

The emergence of Versailles can best be followed in the drawings of Sylvester and Edelnick, which give a pictorial history of the growth of this wonderful building. There were many details that were actually tried out in brick, stone, and plaster, only to be rejected as the characteristic forms of the château emerged. Le Vau and, above all, Mansard were the most important architects; Le Brun was responsible for the decoration; Le Nôtre, for the gardens and alleys and roads. These men were supported by the king and had plenty of time and money to work out the grand style of the palace. Versailles has to be seen to be appreciated; one can only say that the sumptuous public rooms, the apartments of the royal family, the halls and stairways, the rich baroque decoration all combined to make it a palace fit for a great monarch and worthy of a rich and powerful kingdom. It was at once a home for the king, a reception hall for state occasions, an office building for the king's government, and a dwelling for hundreds of courtiers and royal officials who somehow managed to find living space in the rabbit-warrens of the *petits appartements*. The château, as it finally emerged, completely surrounded the original little hunting lodge of Louis XIII.

The garden and fountains and alleys of Versailles are every bit as imposing as the château itself, and they set a standard and a style that the Western world will never forget. There were many fountains. One of the most charming was in the center of the Apollo-Diana garden circle depicting Latone with her children demanding the vengeance of Jupiter for the insolence of the peasants. As the god changes the peasants into frogs, the pool is filled with them in various stages of metamorphosis, each shooting water. The swamp fountain of the baths of Apollo, the fountain *renommée,* the dragon fountain with its grotesque fish and maidens, the three levels of fountains at the central stairs as well as dozens of smaller ones made the water play at Versailles a thing of wonder. Today it draws huge crowds who are enchanted by the magic qualities of the display. There was a zoo with animals from many lands. There were statues everywhere: Louis even dispatched warships to Italy to bring back the large blocks of marble for his garden statues. There was the rape of Proserpina, a series for Spring, Summer, Autumn, and Winter, Diana, Venus, and other Greek and Roman deities, a faun seven feet high, satyrs of all sizes, nymphs, dancers, and magnificent bronze and stone vases with bas-reliefs. Versailles represented the most conspicuous consumption of art since the great days of the Roman Empire.

Louis has been severely criticized for spending so much money on the palace, for building the water works that cost much both in blood and treasure simply to provide visual satisfaction, for surrounding himself with so much grandeur and luxury when his people were so poor. These criticisms are surely justified in light of the assumptions of the men who made them, but Louis would have had difficulty understanding what his critics were talking about. He loved to build, he enjoyed his gardens—according to his upbringing, this was quite enough to justify the spending of so much money and energy. It would never have occurred to him that his palaces should not be decorated and his gardens cared for just because his people were poor; Louis had none of the "humanitarian" democratic sentiments of later eras and little sense of "charity" embedded in the Christian thought of his own. If hard-pressed, he might have come upon the nineteenth-century "trickle down" theory to justify his work. After all, Versailles did give employment to many, many craftsmen and artists with all sorts of artistic talents. However, it is even doubtful that he would have bothered to use any such argument to justify his constructions.

He might answer some of the criticism by pointing out that he allowed properly dressed citizens of Paris to walk in the gardens of the Louvre and Tuileries, and that anyone who was "decently dressed" could visit Versailles or Vincennes or Saint-Germain. Colbert opposed allowing the public to use the royal gardens and, when Louis overrode his objections, decided somehow to profit from their presence. Indeed, the practice of selling the concession for renting chairs in public gardens dates from Colbert's decision to reap some benefit from these visitors. The public was often troublesome; visitors walked on the grass, broke limbs from the trees, and made trouble for the gardeners; the registers of the secretaries of state contain numerous letters dealing with these problems. It is surely true that the vast majority of the people of Louis's kingdom never saw Versailles, and yet before his death the palace was already a mecca for visitors from France as well as from foreign lands.

Versailles was both the residence of the king and the seat of his government. His ministers with their assistants, engineers, clerks, and agents, and the whole paraphernalia of government were housed in the château. Anyone who has visited Washington, D.C., with its miles of marble façades, its imposing office buildings, the Pentagon, and the palaces of government, who has seen the offices of a senator or a cabinet minister, will realize that Louis did not really house his government in the majestic style that twentieth-century men can afford. The king's apartments were adequate, and the state rooms sumptuous, but those of the courtiers and ministers were surely substandard. One would have to drop far down the ladder of hierarchy in Washington to find bureaucrats living under such conditions. Louvois would be astonished to see the Pentagon, of which his ministry was the prototype. On the other hand, it would be unfair to fail to say that Louvois, Colbert, and the other ministers of the crown did have sumptuous country châteaux and Parisian *hôtels* that were the result of the bounty of the king.

It is always a difficult question to discover how much the king himself actually knew about the work that was being done, how much he actually had to do with the plans. There can be little doubt that Louis loved to build. He took the same pleasure in the erection of handsome châteaux and beautiful gardens that other men take in the building of their houses and the care of their yards, but we do not know whether he took an active part in making the plans, merely approved plans presented to him, or in general outlined what he wanted, leaving the details to the architects of the Bâtiments. The Bâtiments was a bureau that supervised the royal châteaux, paid salaries of many kinds, prepared plans for rebuilding, new building, gardens, and many other such things.

Colbert, Louvois, Mansard (the only professional), and the Duke of Antin in turn ruled this department during the reign of Louis XIV. It was an important post because the superintendent of the Bâtiments always had ready access to the king. But we do not know what part the king actually took in this area. Mansard's *Register* for 1699–1701 has survived in part, but it does not really answer all the questions. Obviously, Louis was informed about much of the detailed work that needed to be done (cleaning statues with *eau forte,* repairing water systems, changes in the gardens at Marly and Versailles, and so forth) and he may possibly have taken an active part in the projection of this work. However, it is impossible to know just what Mansard's formula "His Majesty has ordered the pavement . . ." really means. Louis was probably merely ordering the Bâtiments to do what the superintendent proposed to do. One thing that the *Register* does indicate is the fact that Mansard had many interviews with the king. The Duke of Antin gives us further evidence that underlines the importance of the position of superintendent, because of the opportunities he had to talk to the king. He also tells us that the professional personnel at the Bâtiments were pleased to be administered by a "man of quality" who, unlike Mansard, did not interfere with their artistic plans and projects! The king was undoubtedly the kind of gardener who did not get his hands dirty or his nails black; he left that to the professionals who were expected to be "experts." But Louis was fond of his collaborators in the building of Versailles. There are touching stories. Many years after Versailles was completed, Louis, Mansard, and Le Nôtre—all old men—were being carried in chairs along the paths at Versailles, and Le Nôtre with tears in his eyes said, "Sire, truly my good father would have wide eyes if he saw me in a chair beside the greatest king in the world." Mansard: "One must say that Your Majesty treats his mason and his gardener very well." The words were probably never spoken, but they still seem to represent a truth about the relationship between the king and these two distinguished men. A further bit of evidence on Louis's love for his palace and gardens is the "Tour of Versailles," which he wrote in his own hand describing the "best way to see" the palace and gardens. It is an itinerary designed to show off the palace that a modern guide could still find useful. . . .

If the royal châteaux were evidence of the king's power and importance, so also was the organization of the royal households. The king, the queen, the dauphin and dauphine, the king's grandchildren, the king's brother and his family each had a "household." These households included hundreds of people ranging from the two grand masters of France (the Prince of Condé and the Duke of Bourbon) who were paid 3,600 livres a year, a grand chamberlain (also 3,600 livres), four first gentlemen (3,500 livres), grand masters of the wardrobe, of the pantry, of ceremonies, and so forth, masters of the hunt, the stable, and the kitchen, secretaries of the chamber (usually held by a secretary of state at a stipend of 1,200 livres). And below these people, hordes of lesser servants of nonnoble origin did all sorts of work around the palace. Many of these people would hold appointments in more than one royal household, so that a top professional person like a doctor or a surgeon might have an income of over 10,000 livres; a secretary of state would have many times this amount. Besides the civil "household," there were clerical and military ones, each having officers of varying degrees. The *Maison du Roi* were the elite troops of the royal army.

All of these offices, from the captains of the guards, the chaplains of the king, the grand masters of "this and that," down to the clockmakers and valets and cooks' assistants, were venal. It was usual for a son to inherit his father's position by securing from the king during his father's lifetime a brevet assuring his succession. If the king wished to appoint a new face to a position, the new appointee had to buy the office from his predecessor at a figure set by the king. This was as Louis wanted it. He inherited his position and would pass it on to his son; he liked to have the same people about him, men who knew that they were destined from birth to carry on the family position in the royal society. By staffing the royal households with "people of quality" and ambitious nobles on the make, Louis could also assure himself that the wealthy of the land would have something to do and to talk about besides rebellion, and that they would fulfill their métiers under his supervision. When one remembers that the king also held the power of appointment to the clerical benefices of the kingdom, to hundreds, indeed thousands, of military and civil commissions, and to all these "household" offices, the picture of the court, watching carefully the news of deaths and rushing to the king to ask the dead man's place for themselves or their friends, becomes credible, for there was a considerable turnover, in spite of the brevets of survival rights. To look at a three-month period at random, in the first quarter of 1686 there was a new maître d'hôtel and a new "ordinary" gentleman to the king, a new captain of the guards, a new lady and a maid of honor to the queen, a new chaplain to the dauphine, a new ensign in the queen's guards, a new ordinary gentleman to the dauphin. A cross check of the lists of household officers in 1673 with those of 1699 reveals that the total number of people remained about the same; so did their pensions. It was possible, however, for an individual to make some progress, for there were several grades of each rank or profession, and the higher grades were paid more generously. Sainctôt, for example, moved from master of ceremonies at 2,000 livres (his successor got only 1,500 livres) to grand master at 3,000 livres. . . .

The most important offices in the royal households were occupied by great noblemen and their wives. There were about 250 individuals—men, women, and children—who were classed as people of quality: the princes of the blood, the dukes and peers, the very wealthy noblemen of ancient lineage (usually with the title *"marquis"*), important clergymen, and soldiers with high rank in the king's army or navy. Some of these people had family histories as old as the royal family itself, for indeed the kings of France were of this stock; but the majority were of more recent creation. There were considerable gradations among them. The peers and dukes took their position from the date of the creation of the title, the simple persons of quality from positions in the household, the church, or the armed services. Louis assured these people the respect due to their status in society; in court functions, at the grand sessions of *parlement,* or simply in the social setting of the court, the dukes and peers shared the grandeur of the king. They were his "cousins"; they acted as if they were set apart from the rest of humanity. Under Louis XIV they acted out roles that helped to create the mystique necessary to justify the power that the king did, in fact, exercise. Their roles, however, were purely ceremonial, for they were excluded from the realities of power. As Saint-Simon contemplated this situation, he reached the conclusion that Louis XIV was deliberately attempting to destroy the dukes and the peers of the realm.

Most of these people of quality owed their positions to recent kings; only a very few of them could actually trace their lineage deep into the Middle Ages. The kings of France had long since been encroaching upon the traditional feudal orders. None of the lay peers still ruled their provinces as quasi-independent lords, for the crown had absorbed their powers. However, in the sixteenth and seventeenth centuries a new feudality struggled to establish itself out of the disorders of the "religious" war and the rebellions of the first half of the seventeenth century. As men with enormous wealth, with governorships of provinces made hereditary in their families, these "great ones" of the land had dangerously threatened the king's authority. Louis XIV was well aware of the problem through his own experiences during the Fronde. Like his father and grandfather, he strove to curb these "great ones." One of the most effective means was to cheapen their ranks by the creation of new peers, and by the encroachment upon their real powers as governors or as holders of great fiefs through the action of royal intendants dependent upon the king and directed by his ministers. In this way the new feudality could be curbed; at the same time, by bringing these great ones to court and domesticating them as servants of the royal households, Louis gradually weakened their will to rebel.

All of the bowing and scraping, the pretensions to grandeur, could not conceal the fact that Louis had separated real power from social prestige. Elizabeth-Charlotte saw this most clearly: "I am not ignorant to the point of not knowing what difference there is between the Elector of Brandenburg and Monsieur [her husband], but in order to prevent Monsieur from seeing that he is only in a way a slave of his brother, one gives him a huge idea of his grandeur, to which nothing can approach and which nonetheless is without any foundation, and is purely imagination." In another place she wrote, "I hold grandeur as purely chimerical when great power is not joined to it." But what was left to the great ones? They were offered social prestige, ceremonial importance, grandeur—if they would act out roles that would supply the mystique for their king's exercise of power. If they refused to accept the offer, they also gave up the royal favor that was translated into patronage, pensions, gratifications, and the divertissements of the court. . . .

All this emphasis upon grandeur, precedence, rank, and etiquette has led many historians to charge Louis with megalomania. At first glance the accusation seems quite correct, but a closer look will show that the king of France was really no different from the other monarchs of his age. They sought to fulfill their *gloire,* just as Louis did, and the contests over diplomatic rank were not single-sided affairs; other monarchs were just as desperately anxious to establish their places in the hierarchy. The squabbles over rank of the Diet of Ratisbon were notorious as one of the causes of the ineffectiveness of that institution. There can be no doubt about

Louis's pride for his family and his kingdom; and this in effect meant personal pride, since the kingdom of France was centered on its king. But to see the ceremonial life of the court and the demands of his diplomats for recognition of their master's grandeur as megalomania quite misses the point. As Louis's power grew to the point where his officers could really reach into the provinces of his kingdom, and his soldiers could actually assure his government against revolt and rebellions, the mystique that has to accompany power had also to grow; this is the most important fact about the elaborate setting for the king.

On another level, the grandeur of the king was reflected in the music, art, and drama presented for the amusement of the court. Louis was the first king to have musicians directed by a conductor in the modern manner. Lully not only wrote music for his master; he also directed the musicians who played it. Indeed, his death resulted from an accident that happened while he was directing the violins of the king. The drama at court was often acted by courtier amateurs who fancied their ability to interpret the pieces of the theater, but Molière's troupe and others also played before the king, as the charming "Impromptu at Versailles" so cleverly testifies. The plays of Corneille, Molière, and Racine, as well as of other dramatists whose work is no longer known in our theaters, were frequently produced at court, in spite of the grumbling of some of the clergy who feared the influence of the theater. Louis also supported a "stable" of artists who produced under the direction of the "first painter to the king." Throughout most of the reign, Le Brun occupied this post. He and his coworkers have been criticized for their slavish adulation of their patron by men who failed to realize that they, like the builders of the châteaux and the gardens, were promoting the mystique, the cult of royalty necessary to Louis's government. Anyone who has seen a representative selection of Le Brun's paintings will quickly admit that he was a master painter as well as a courtier to his master.

While music, art, and drama gave pleasure to the court as well as helped to make an imposing façade for the monarchy, the men of letters and of science also received the bounty of the king and responded by praising his reign. Voltaire long ago pointed out that

Louis's government stood like a shining light as the patron of art, literature, and science, in striking contrast to the government of his archfoe William of Orange, who became king of England. This is true. One has to wait until the establishment of the great American foundations like the Guggenheim, the Rockefeller, the Mellon, and others to see patronage of culture and science on the scale set by Louis XIV. Moreover the king's government was probably more important to the scientist and the artist than our contemporary foundations are. For today a man of letters can make a living from his royalties; a scientist, as a professor or an employee of a great corporation; and even an artist or a musician, as a teacher; whereas in the seventeenth century few such opportunities existed. Thus the king's bounty was very important. The list of the recipients of Louis's pensions and *gratifications* sounds like the roll call of the Guggenheim fellows: in one year there were three theologians, eight linguists, twenty-five French and three foreign "men of letters," five historians, one painter (most painters were employed by the Bâtiments on regular salaries), one lawyer, six students of physics, four surgeons and medical men, one botanist, one mathematician. Some of these men were to become famous, others soon sank into decent oblivion. In 1669 Racine, Molière, and Corneille were on the list; so were Perrault, Boileau, Tellement, and Godefroy. De la Croix never missed it, for his studies of oriental languages required money for travel. Many of these honored will be known only to specialists in their fields. For some of them royal patronage was onerous; Racine, for example, had to accompany Louis on his campaigns; his remark that he now understood that soldiers allowed themselves to be killed so freely because their lives were so bad was not as much of a joke as he imagined. He repaid Louis for taking him along by a *History of the War* that reads like a fairy tale, but properly adds to the stature of the king.

Louis also sponsored academies of the dance, of painting, of science, of letters; but one often suspects that he knew little or nothing about these organizations. For example, he made only one visit to the observatory that he "built and supported"; the tapestry commemorating that event does not tell of its uniqueness. Obviously, much of the king's sponsorship was the work of his ministers, but it does not really matter whether the inspiration came from the king, Colbert, one of the Le Telliers, or some other of Louis's creatures—it was done in his name and the intention was to bring prestige to the king and his regime. It was no accident that in the literary quarrel known as the "battle between the moderns and the ancients," men compared the age of Louis XIV with those of Pericles and of Augustus. Louis's efforts to support science and culture obviously paid off in terms of royal prestige, and as we shall see, his government needed his prestige as a mystique to cover the extensions of power that accompanied the creation of the military-police state. When the king's power grew to the point where another Fronde was simply out of the question, then also his prestige and grandeur, the mystique that justified power, had also to expand.

However, the doings at court and in the capitals of Europe were known to only a few. The *Gazette* printed stories of court functions, but it had a limited circulation. Thus, there was the problem of carrying the message to the people of the kingdom. They were feeling the imposition of power that came with the development of the bureaucratic, military-police state; they had also to accept the mystique that justified the king's assumption of this power over the kingdom. The solution lay in the profoundly royalist sentiments of the French. The clergy, the professors, the literate had long explained that God gave the power to govern to kings while He retained the authority to himself, and that He would hold the king responsible for his acts. The king was the "father of his country," the object of admiration—perhaps veneration—a consecrated figure with functions that made him godlike. Even the more violent pamphleteers during the Fronde professed loyalty and love for the king; he was the object of their desires. His role as a political agent, however, was not so clearly defined; there were many who believed that the centralizing tendencies of the royal governments were at least unfortunate and probably illegal. Since the last of the fourteenth century there had been a growing struggle in the kingdom between the decentralized sources of power (nobility, towns, guilds, and so forth) and the centralizing tendencies of the monarchy. By Louis XIV's time this contest within the inherited pluralistic structure of politics had reached a crisis, a crisis that tipped the balance of force in favor of the central authority. This new balance had to be spelled out both in political institutions like the new army and the bureaucracy, and in the symbols and ceremony that gave to the people a visual apperception of political order. A most important factor in this vision was the image of the king in the popular mind.

The lives of most seventeenth-century men were lived out in a dull routine of traditional activity broken only by some colorful religious festival, an occasional arrival of a stranger, a troop of minstrels or players, a military cavalcade, or some such event. Thus, the progressions of the court from one château to another that had long been the usual pattern of monarchy were "events" of importance in the lands through which the court moved. Anyone who has journeyed up the Nile on an excursion steamer, where he can see the seventeenth century juxtaposed to his own, will never forget the cries of the children and others who greet the weekly visit of the steamer as a contact with the outside world. How much more exciting must have been the cavalcade of soldiers and courtiers, the gay carriages, the wagons and mule trains, the fine gentlemen and bedecked ladies, with the person of the king as the center of attraction. A newsletter from the court in 1683 tells the story of the royal voyage toward Fontainebleau:

> On the road from Chambor[d] . . . the king was loaded with presents of fruit and flowers that the people brought to him and for which they were liberally recompensed. One person . . . threw in front of the king's carriage the most beautiful lamb that you have ever seen . . . but it fled so quickly that no one could catch it. . . .

It was a typical scene reflecting the popularity of the king—or perhaps the vacuum in the lives of the people. Kings were well advised to travel from place to place, to show themselves to the people, to allow the local clergy to tell their parishioners that this was the king that God had given them. It secured stability for their position and consent for their rule.

This was the age-old pattern. For centuries French kings had traveled through their lands, giving justice, receiving the blessings of the clergy and the cheers of the people. During the reign of

Louis XIV, in addition to this well-established relationship, new patterns developed—a new cult that associated the king more closely with the Godhead. This new cult foliated in the form of festivals, fireworks, statues, fountains, palaces, expositions, books, pamphlets, and religious services—all organized to glorify the king, to raise his throne to the steps of heaven, to remove his person from the ranks of ordinary human beings. Louis contributed to the process in numerous ways. For example, contrary to traditional custom, he refused to allow his queen, the dauphine, or his grand-daughters-in-law to kiss anyone outside of the senior blood lines of the Bourbon family; he spent millions to erect the magnificent palace of Versailles; he allowed his courtiers to heap adulations upon him beyond all reason; he tried never to appear in any role except that of the king. This last effort of his has created problems for historians, for he left hardly a scrap of paper from his pen that could be called intimate. He always wrote *en roi!* "In his writing and his works," writes Grouvelle, who edited them, "one always feels the presence of the diadem. We find almost no letters, no notes, not even to mistresses, nothing intimate, nothing friendly. He was always on parade, always the king." But Louis did not create this image of royalty all by himself. His soldiers, his ministers, his servants, his clergy, the magistrates, the Hôtel de Ville, the University all joined to give a new interpretation to the role of king.

This generation of princes and statesmen stood on the edge of a past that had been both difficult and disorderly; all over Europe the military and political pluralism inherited from a yesterday had led to civil wars, rebellions, violence, contempt for the processes of law. Cloaked by religious flags, by demands for the recognition of "liberties," or simply by a brutal urge for pillage and plunder, these disorders had endangered the tranquillity of the European world and the security of all men. The historian does not have to journey far in the years 1600–60 to understand why Hobbes decided that the Leviathan was the only hope for society; such disorder could be cured only by power. A Henry IV might try to govern the kingdom in the manner of a guerrilla chieftain, but he had to realize that he shared his power with the men whose backs he slapped.

Richelieu and Louis XIII could govern with erratic brutality, using picked panels of judges and the executioner to impose their will, but the headsman's sword cannot long replace the scepter if the king is not to appear a tyrant. This was the problem of the men around Louis XIV: they were willing to use force to give form to society, to break the will of rebellion, but they recognized that consent of the governed is most important for the ruler. Louis carefully explained to his son that it would be quite inconvenient to have to use force all the time to secure obedience. He had not read Machiavelli for nothing.

The vital forces of the kingdom seconded the royal will to restore order and break the political and military pluralism that had caused so much trouble in the past. The new army that Mazarin and his creatures were making was popular, for it could expel the "pillagers," as men called soldiers during the Fronde. The *Grand Jours* that invaded the provinces to bring malefactors to justice and peace to the land were welcome even though many of the criminals slipped through the nets. The intendants of police, justice, and taxation were well received when they began to inquire closely about the murders that passed as duels or accidents, the kidnapings that passed for elopements, and other acts of violence in the land. This was bringing order out of the melee and control over the pluralism that had created disorder. The new army and the bureaucracy were the agents of this action, but in addition there was needed a new image of royalty, a new mystique, and new sanctions for the power that it was exercising. This was the work of a propaganda that utilized all the vital forces of the kingdom.

A new image could be created only out of ideas that men already had or at least were in the process of acquiring. This was an age in which the literate of the population were familiar with classical antiquity and Byzantine practices. Ovid, Suetonius, and other Roman authors were widely read in excellent editions; in 1645 the publication of Byzantine antiquities provided insight into the practices of Roman emperors both east and west and added considerable underpinning to the basic assumptions of the supporters of monarchy from Luther to Hobbes and Bossuet. One has only to see the *feux d'artifice* to realize that this generation understood that

Caesar became a god in order to strengthen his position in society
and cure its disorders. Augustus in the Pantheon, Hadrian identified with Hercules, the deification of living emperors had become
the common property of the literate world. The idea had long been
established that kings ruled by divine right—this was the club that
had beaten down the papal pretensions. Now was the time to
identify this gift of God with the person of the king and thereby
endow him with the authority to curb the lawless forces of society.
This mystique seemed reasonable to a generation that willingly
accepted theological assumptions, that believed in providential notions of historical causation; they could not be expected to know
that their brothers, who were scanning the skies, who were studying the forces of nature, who were dissecting the human body, who
were exploring the non-Christian world both past and contemporary, were in the process of destroying this theological orientation
and of substituting for divine intervention a secular conception of
the world. It is so often forgotten that Louis's entourage had every
reason to believe in a theocentric world, and small reason to suspect
that the elite of the next century would have little use for gods and
would seek secular solutions and secular salvations for themselves
and society. This may be why the late seventeenth-century men
have so often been misunderstood. Let us listen to some of their
voices and try to understand them in the light of their religious—
rather than our secular—solutions to the questions before the world:

> God of Gods, Lord of Lords,
> > Save the king!
> God who established kings on the throne,
> > Save the king!
> God by whom kings rule,
> > Save the king!
> God who subjected people to kings,
> > Save the king!
> > > FROM *Litanies pour le roi*

. . .

Should anyone be astonished that God has blessed this regime
that was consecrated to Him . . . that He has sustained its counsels which He inspired, that He has favored its enterprises con-

ceived at the foot of His altars, that He has brought success to its projects of which He Himself was the author. . . ?

.   .   .

Kings are the visible image of their invisible creator, and outside of His divine rights which we owe to the latter, all honors belong to the former by a new indispensable right . . . the sovereignty of an absolute monarch comes from God rather than from men . . . a true subject can never be faithful and obedient enough. . . .

.   .   .

Yet while God has created all men according to His image . . . it is nonetheless true that it is in the person of kings that He has imprinted the most vivid colors, and it is there that He carved the most perfect characters of divinity. . . . There is only one God in the world, and in the kingdom there is only one king to whom alone one should render honor and duty . . . the power of kings is without limits. . . . God loves all His creatures, but not equally . . . one cannot doubt that, among all the mortal creatures, kings and monarchs are the most cherished by God. . . . [De Montmeran finds that God was also partial to France in giving the kingdom the most beautiful climate, landscape, and setting in the world and adds:] if God has poured so many benedictions on French soil, He has not been less liberal toward French kings. It is proper that a kingdom so favored of heaven should be ruled by kings filled with the grace and the gifts of heaven. . . .

.   .   .

These sons of our Alcide
Issue of the blood of Gods. . . .

.   .   .

Oh My God . . . Conserve for us this prince that you have given us through your love for us. Give him time to accomplish that which he plans for your glory. Cover him with grace as he covers us with his favors. . . .

.   .   .

It is the order of the world established by Providence that places inferior things in subordination to superior ones. Whoever interrupts this order resists Providence and who resists Providence works for his damnation [Paul]. . . . Good or bad, pagan or faithful, one must obey princes; we are their subjects, they our sovereigns. Happy, happy people whom God favors with a good king, who find their grandeur in his piety. . . . All men are the

image of God but His true portrait is in the person of the sover
eigns; their authority represents His power, their majesty, His
éclat, their goodness, His charity, their rigor, His justice. They
hold His place on their thrones, they speak in His name in their
edicts, they exercise His vengeance in their wars and present in
their persons the visible divinity. . . .

       .   .   .

Jupiter: This is the blood of Louis, victorious king under whom
all Europe trembles and who sees nothing under the skies that
equals him or resembles him. It is for him that I call you together.
Apollo: How many times have your fine verses not made Louis's
exploits live, you have astonished eyes and are sad not to be able to
follow [the king's activities]. . . .
[There follows a dialogue between Venus and Mars promising
great things for Louis's grandson; then:]
Jupiter: "How much is the happiness, how much the prosperity,
how much the *gloire,* how much the peace of peoples who live
under the august power of Louis, of his son, and the young hero
whose birth we celebrate [Duke of Burgundy]. Never has heaven
seen so long a course of happy success and beautiful days. . . .

All these people had a common need to identify the king with
divine power; they required this image to support the power that
the king was assuming over the land and the people. Louis accepted
this status, for he too needed the identification; as Madame de
Sévigné tells us, it was only when a misguided provincial published
a thesis comparing the king with God in such a manner that
"would indicate that God was only a copy" that Louis ordered the
work burned. This was going too far!
Many of these voices have been those of clerics; but judges, town
officials, university professors, and men of letters talked and wrote
in the same tone. For example, Professor Fejaco from Caen wrote
in 1685 that "the invincible, the magnanimous Louis gives happiness to France, destiny to Europe, and astonishment to the universe
[Angels]. The glory of his name will extend to the extremities of
the land. . . ." In this *panégyrique du roi* Louis emerges as a godlike figure whose achievements dwarf those of the heroes of antiquity. This was the slight effort compared with the anonymous
La Mémoire éternisée de Louis le Grand (Paris, 1683) in which

some three hundred pages are needed to prove that there had never been a ruler like Louis: a "surprising prodigy of wonder"; the most "magnanimous of heroes"; "the most incomparable of monarchs"; "compassionate and generous" as a conqueror, and equitable and just as a king: a combination of "wisdom and valor" unparalleled in the world, to whom both France and the church owe "immortal obligations." A poem of Bernard, Sieur de Hautmont, is of the same genre; a naïve and tiresome account, it praised military, political, even engineering (water to Versailles) triumphs. A member of the Royal Academy of Arles dedicated his book to the dauphin, but it was a chant of praise for the king whom he compared with other figures in history meriting the surname "the Great." Like the clerics, these men were picturing a king who could be associated with the deity, a king partaking of the qualities of God. Some critics have called these people Louis's literary valets; they certainly were the literary servants of a new image of the king that would clothe him with the authority to govern.

There was another type of propaganda that dramatized the identification of the king with God. When the court traveled through the land in former eras, it was usual for the king to be received and perhaps "harangued" by the local clergy; the royal family often spent the night in the bishop's palace. By the 1680s these local receptions often got completely out of hand. We know about many of them because local pride required that accounts of the reception of the king should be published and sold abroad and many of these pamphlets have survived to our day. In Louis XIII's time men were content with a speech, a poem, or a sermon, and perhaps a bonfire; now an extravagant *feu d'artifice* became the accepted pattern. In studying these elaborate designs we discover that the word "baroque" applies to them with the same appropriateness that it does to the settings for opera or theater during these years. There would be a stage, papier-mâché figures, inscriptions, fireworks, and of course descriptions explaining what the event was all about. On the trip north in 1680, one town after another welcomed Louis with a *feu d'artifice*. At Valenciennes the city magistrates begged pardon for failing to use the figures of Apollo and the Sun as the central theme; in their humble opinion, however, Hercules and his labors could epitomize the important works of the king. The elaborate tableau had a central figure of Hercules supporting the earth with the "labors of the god" on the four sides of the platform. They were, of course, the "labors of Louis XIV": fighting the hydra monster with three heads (Luther, Calvin, and Jansenius); cleansing the kingdom of revolt; giving peace to Europe. Lille was not to be outdone: its *feu d'artifice* showed the defeat of the giants (enemies of the king) and the granting of peace. When Louis reached Tournai he passed through an arch of triumph bearing inscriptions about "Louis the Great, the sun that gives light to the day . . . the sun that makes the birds sing." Marie Thérèse was "the moon brightened by the sun" along with the other stars of the sky. One could extend such examples indefinitely. It is not necessary, however, to cite more of them to indicate the process of development.

The person of the king was not even necessary for a celebration in his honor. After 1680 many occasions inspired townsmen to hold a pageant, to present a *feu d'artifice*. The birth of one of Louis's grandsons, the capture of Luxemburg, the occupation of Strasbourg, the revocation of the Edict of Nantes—all became occasions for the people to express their faith in the monarchy with oratory, music, and poetry. If the king could not be present in person, an account of the event could be printed and placed at the foot of the throne. These publications are interesting evidence of the loyalty of the kingdom; they are even more evidence of the pressure of the royal intendants and their subdelegates upon the people of importance in the towns to persuade them to pay for such festivities; they are also probably evidence of the need for entertainment, an occasion to display local talents of oratory or poetry or music, surely a welcome release from rough labor and bleak, colorless lives.

By the mid-1680s papier-mâché and *feux d'artifice* were no longer adequate to express the ritual of admiration and adulation of the king. It seems that the Maréchal de la Feuillade was the first to set a new pattern when he commissioned Sieur des Jordans to create a bronze statue of the king crowned with victory. It was an elaborate affair mounted on a pedestal surrounded by slaves and decorated by bas-reliefs that recounted the victories of the king's arms.

Apparently much touched by this gesture, the king and council issued an *arrêt* ordering that the statue be placed in the street of the Fosses Montmartre where it intersected the new street then under construction, the Rue des Petits Champs. All this called for a new square, and Mansard designed one causing the removal of houses belonging to Dame Hôtman, Sieur Perrault, and Sieur de Serre. The cost: 306,000 livres, paid by the Échevins and merchants of the Hôtel de Ville. Habitués of the Bibliothèque Nationale will recognize this as the Place des Victoires, but the present statue was put in place in the nineteenth century and, happily, is quite unlike the original.

When all was ready, a great celebration dedicated the statue and the *place* on March 16, 1686. It was marred a little by a squabble over precedence that broke out among the several sovereign courts, but all the important figures of Paris contributed to the celebration. Louis was ill; the dauphin took his father's place, reviewed the parades, listened to the oratory, and watched the show that included musket fire, drums, trumpets, and religious symbols. That evening there was a *feu d'artifice* at the Hôtel de Ville that represented Louis's victory over heresy (now a headless hydra), the bombardment of the Barbary pirates, the submission of the Doge of Genoa. Naturally there was more poetry and oratory.

Not to be outdone by the marshal and Paris, other communities also demanded the permission to erect statues to the king. At Caen the city fathers, stimulated by the intendant Monsieur de Morangis, hired a local artist to make the statue and managed to hold their celebration on Louis's birthday, September 15, 1685, a full six months before the Place des Victoires was completed. The statue was of dubious artistic value, but the celebration—with oratory and artillery from the château and a parade of monks, university professors, bourgeois militia, and local nobility—was a fine affair; the Bishop of Bayeux presided, while local talent had a field day in French and Latin verse. Undoubtedly the fete brought joy to Caen, and it may also have deepened the respect for the monarchy and its authority. The account of the celebration at Poitiers naïvely admits that the intendant "suggested" the erection of the statue in that city; that was probably the pattern everywhere.

At Ruel the Duke de Richelieu urged the erection of an equestrian statue of the king, and persuaded the merchants to pay for
it, since they had "just recompense from the favors that they receive every day through the protection that he [the king] affords
to commerce and the arts. . . ." How better could he say that the
new exercise of power warranted new symbols of its authority?
However, closer look would be needed to know whether the merchants paid for the statue as willingly as the account of the celebration seems to suggest. The city fathers at Paris, not content with
having made a contract with the University for an annual eulogy
to the king to celebrate the anniversary of his ascension to the
throne, erected another statue of Louis XIV in the temple of honor
at the Hôtel de Ville and dedicated it with an elaborate *feu
d'artifice*. It is interesting to note that this ceremony came on July
14, 1689, just one hundred years before another *feu* that has also
many times been celebrated with oratory, poetry, and artillery fire.
There were many other statues that, happily, have not survived:
one of the most elaborate celebrations came in 1699 when the
equestrian statue was erected in the Place Louis le Grand, to com-
memorate the "victory" of Ryswick. The inscription proclaimed
that the king "gave peace to Europe." It proclaimed that in spite
of his wishes he had taken up arms to "defend religion and justice"
and by those arms he had secured peace. The text must have
sounded a little hollow even to the men who wrote it, but it suited
the patriotic needs of the kingdom.

What was Louis's part in all this? We shall never really know
whether he encouraged this slavish adulation or merely tolerated
it. There is, however, one story that seems to cast doubt on the
picture of the king as an egotist seeking glory even when it is un-
deserved. When Pontchartrain proposed a plan for the reconstruction of the Place Vendôme at great expense, Louis remarked:

> Louvois did almost everything in spite of me. All these gentlemen,
> the ministers, want to do something that will bring them honor
> before posterity. They have found the secret of making me appear
> before Europe as a man who loves all these vanities. Madame de
> Maintenon is witness of the chagrin that Louvois and La Feuillade

caused me by these things. I wish henceforth to save myself from
them and I want no proposals . . . except that my people shall be
well nourished; I shall always be well-enough housed.

Before we leave these hymns of praise and celebrations, we
should note that a study of this literature will call to mind the
small-town, pre-motorized age of patriotic celebrations and ceremonies of July 4 or of July 14 (Bastille Day) and other such days
that men set aside to instill patriotism and love for the Republic.
The words in a society dedicated to popular sovereignty will be
different from those used by men who believe that authority comes
from God, but the impact is very similar. The orators who extolled
the glories of the Republic, the heroism of its soldiers, and the
faultless purity of its national policies were creating a secular deity
out of the state, and their hearers were thrilled by their words and
made more ready to obey the laws that were set above them. So
was it when the clergy, the poets, the local dignitaries, and the
chorus of singers from the cathedral gathered to honor the king
and the kingdom by the erection of a statue or a celebration to
thank God and the king for peace or some other blessing. The
festive air, the excitement of the music, and the parade all helped
to implant in the hearts of men the mystique that justified the
exercise of royal authority. Men like Colbert, Louvois, Richelieu,
La Feuillade, and others who inspired these events obviously did
not need to do so merely to inflate the ego of the king. They knew
that by involving the people of France in the cult of the king, the
people would more freely submit to his exercise of power.

As is so often the case with Louis XIV, there is little direct
evidence that will link the king as a person with the things that
were done in his name or the processes that developed under the
direction of his government. It is difficult to believe that Louis was
personally responsible for the development of the mystique that
raised the throne of the king to the foot of the throne of God and
endowed his person with divine attributes; it is more likely that
his creatures were responsible for this. By raising the throne far
above the older centers of power, by placing the king in a unique
and remote position instead of in the status of "first among equals"

that had been true of the medieval feudal monarch, and finally, by identifying the person of the king with the vital forces in the kingdom, these men were preparing for the future state that would be able to exercise truly great power over the lives of its people. It would be interesting to know how much Louis was the author of this drama; perhaps he was merely a clever actor who took his cues from the men who were giving characteristic form to the emerging bureaucratic military-police state of the West. Unfortunately we shall never really know which is the case.

LOUIS BERTRAND

The Political Philosopher

IT WAS NOT until the death of Mazarin that Louis XIV really understood what it meant to be king of France; at last he realized how vast was his authority, how unbounded the field that lay open to his passion for glory. He was exalted, his whole being felt this new stimulus; there was a new note of loftiness in his desire for power. In his *Mémoires* he tried to give words to this intoxicating and confused emotion, this realization, as it were, that he was more than human. "I realized," he writes, "that I was king; for that I had been born. A sweet exaltation permeated me

From Louis Bertrand, *Louis XIV* (New York and London: Longmans, Green & Company, 1928), pp. 309–317. Reprinted by permission of David McKay Company, Inc., New York.

that you will never understand until you experience it yourself."

When a king has such warmth and is so thrilled with pride and energy, it is not surprising that he should love his profession and devote himself conscientiously to it. It is difficult at a later period to analyze one's ideas and sensations at such a time, but Louis XIV resolved to do so. He did it, first of all, for his own satisfaction, to clarify his ideas; in the second place for the instruction of his son; and lastly for posterity, "in order to put historians upon the right path," he says, "if, as a result of misunderstanding my plans and the reasons for them they have strayed from the path of truth." These words apply especially to the many historians who have neglected his *Mémoires*. The *Mémoires* were never finished, but they are complete enough to give us the king's opinions on most subjects. By gathering up the disconnected references and ideas, we are able to piece together his exact theory of the monarchical power. He took the trouble to write down his ideas himself, or, to have them written down under his personal supervision and to reread and revise them. Thus, there is no danger of crediting him with opinions he never actually held. He sits at his desk and lectures to us on the French monarchy.

He begins by differentiating between spiritual and temporal powers. He is firmly convinced that he holds his own power directly from God, the source of all authority. In that he is merely following the theory of the Gallican theologians. He did not, as is frequently asserted, originate this idea himself; it was current in France long before his time and had always been combated by the church. The church admitted the divine right of kings only when they ruled with the sanction of popular approval.

Louis XIV agreed with the Gallican doctors and jurists in holding that the power of the king was directly delegated to him by God, without any intermediary whatsoever. He looked upon the unction administered to a king at his coronation as a proof and outward sign of this; he considered it, as it were, an eighth sacrament. He, like popes and bishops, was consecrated. Moreover, he knew, or thought he knew, within exactly what limits he might exercise this divinely delegated power. To the pope and the priests fell the obligation of caring for his subjects' souls; to him, the duty of safeguarding their material interests. Thus, at the very beginning he drew a sharp dividing line. Once the premise was admitted, there could be no misunderstanding of the practical application of the theory. The temporal and spiritual powers were to be developed side by side, as if the state could be and should be wholly secular. Louis XIV's Gallican advisers might urge him to pass upon spiritual questions; he himself may have felt tempted to do so; but in the end he always refused to do so and bowed in submission to the authority of the pope. He might question the limits of that authority; the authority itself, never.

The king was naturally anxious not to share this power. There was to be no division of it, no favorites, no prime ministers, no sovereign legislative assemblies. He scorned rulers who were "at the mercy of rash popular assemblies." To the best of his ability, he safeguarded his sovereignty, his absolute freedom to do as he saw fit. France encouraged him to do so; such a course corresponded with his ideal of sovereignty, and, to a certain extent, the dictates of his conscience. He so distrusted ministers, acquaintances, and favorites that one who wished to suggest a decision to him, or to induce him to make an appointment, had to go about it in the most indirect and subtle manner. Even Madame de Maintenon, with all her craft and cleverness, never dared propose what she wished directly. She feigned indifference to the one she favored, for had she so much as allowed the king to guess her desires, he would have reacted unfavorably to her candidate.

Thus, he was determined to accept no limitations upon his sovereign power, save those of justice and reason. Again and again he identified the authority of the prince with reason. This theory was in perfect accord with the Cartesian philosophy; in propounding it the king was at one with the important currents of thought of his age. And it was this rational quality that, according to him, distinguished the authority of the monarch from all others. He writes:

> There is no governor who does not usurp privileges to which he has no title, no army that does not impose on civilians, no gentleman who doesn't oppress the peasants, no tax collector, public

servant or constable who, within his own sphere, has not been guilty of criminal insolence. . . . Instead of having one sovereign power as they should, nations are subject to the whims of a thousand tyrants. Moreover, the orders of a Prince are invariably reasonable and moderate, because they are based upon reason, while those of usurpers, based as they are upon undisciplined human passions, are always immoderate and unfair.

Thus, the king was governed by reason, but reason tempered by common sense derived from wide practical experience. One might almost say that in Louis XIV common sense reached the heights of inspiration. It was this perfectly balanced judgment that permitted him to counteract the tendencies of such ministers as Colbert and Louvois to overemphasize and overorganize their own departments and thus impair the efficient working of the rest of the government, to carry their programs to logical but immoderate conclusions. His unerring common sense kept his aims and ambitions within the range of the practical; his broad comprehension of the various conflicting interests of different governmental departments allowed him to correlate them so that the actions of one would never interfere with those of another.

Lastly, he considered that he alone was competent to decide what was best for the state; his functions included all branches of the government, whereas each minister concentrated upon his own specialty alone. His reasons coincided with reasons of state. "It is always," he writes, "worse for the public to control the government than to support even a bad government that is directed by kings *whom God alone can judge*. . . . Those acts of kings that are in seeming violation of the rights of their subjects are based upon reasons of state—the most fundamental of all motives, as everyone will admit, but one often misunderstood by those who do not rule."

What terrifying words those—"kings, whom God alone can judge!" But Louis XIV realized full well the appalling responsibility that rested upon a man endowed with such power.

To do his duty, to govern personally and in accordance with the dictates of reason and justice, he knew that he must not only take constant and unremitting pains, but he must also surround himself with the best possible assistants, so that the royal decisions should be based upon a thorough knowledge of the facts.

It was for this reason that Louis XIV worked so industriously and even in his old age put in eight or nine hours a day upon the problems of state. He wished personally to see to everything, to know everything, to pass judgment on everything, and to decide every question. His conception of the perfect ruler was one who could say: *"I know everything."*

His first duty, then, was to have a thorough and minute knowledge of his kingdom; he must know his subjects and the national institutions; he must have exact information upon the fertility of the soil, the variety and location of all natural resources, the income to be derived from all forms of taxes—and he must know the personal characteristics of his administrators, the mood of the nation at large, what people were thinking and saying and plotting, not merely at court and in the large towns but in the remotest provinces. A ruler could no more live a separate and shut-in existence than could his subjects; he must know what was happening in other countries in order to defend himself against them, if for no other reason; he must know their resources, the nature and degree of development of their commerce and industries, the size of their armies, their political plans and court secrets. He must be accurately informed upon all such matters by diplomats, agents, or special emissaries. "A man who is well informed upon all that takes place," he writes, "will not make mistakes. Thus a ruler's most obvious duty is *to take every possible precaution to know everything that is happening in his age.*"

The sovereign must know not merely what is going on about him but also what has happened in the past; he must have a knowledge of history, especially military and political history. "I believe that an acquaintance with these great events, through the writings of men of sound judgment, helps one to arrive at important decisions. One can recieve valuable hints both in military and in political tactics from a study of the illustrious men and the notable events of antiquity. . . . The only difficulty is to find time enough for such study." Louis XIV found a way: "I resolved to set aside a definite time for this study, *just as I should have done for important problems of my own."*

Yet, however steadily and intently he may work, a ruler can gain only a fraction of the information necessary for the conducting of a government. He must rely upon his ministers to enlighten him on all points to which he cannot give his personal attention. Not only must he hear them and receive their recommendations, but on some pretext or other he must talk with all who seem competent, seeking to inform himself and to balance the opinions of one against another and so to enlarge his point of view. For this he must be armed with great patience. "He should," writes Louis XIV, *"be able to listen even to nonsense."*

To govern, one must not merely *know* what is happening; one must foresee what will happen and act accordingly. Everything must be carefully organized to bring this to pass; a ruler must use every means that the industry and science of the nation put at his disposal; he must rely on money, on his subordinates, and on his own unremitting energy. In this, one sees the genius of Colbert's schemes. Louis XIV shared his minister's views on most subjects and supported him vigorously. His government was a model of organization and system unsurpassed in Europe.

Too much stress cannot be placed upon the fact that the state, as Louis XIV conceived it, was a practical, scientific organization. And yet practical and reasonable though it was, it must be *just*. Louis XIV wrote extensively upon the justice of kings. He looked upon justice, mercy, and generosity as the three most important royal virtues. A prince should vigorously suppress any temptation to be arrogant and should, upon occasion, know how to be humble. Those who think of Louis XIV as insufferably arrogant should read and ponder this magnificent advice to the dauphin:

> Although it is proper for us to take pride in the dignity of our office, a certain modesty and humility is no less becoming. Do not think, my son, that such virtues are not for us. On the contrary, they are more appropriate in us than in the rest of mankind. If one has not achieved a position of preeminence, either by birth or by natural ability, then, no matter how little he may think of himself, he can never be humble or modest. These virtues pre-

suppose on the part of him who practices them an importance
sufficient to justify a certain vanity. But when those about you
wish only to fill you with a sense of your own importance, do
not, my son, compare yourself with lesser princes. Think rather
of those in past centuries who are most to be envied and admired.
. . . Reflect upon your own shortcomings. In so doing you will
learn to be humble. But when you act as a king, and not as an
individual, when it is a question of your rights and of the privileges of your crown, boldly assume the loftiness of mind and of
spirit of which you will find yourself capable. Do not betray your
glorious predecessors or jeopardize the interests of those who are
to follow you, *for you hold your office in trust.* In such a case
humility is despicable.

Thus, a king should be proud not of himself but of his crown;
he should only be haughty when it is to the interest of the state
for him to be so. Louis XIV returns to this a hundred times in his
Journal and his *Mémoires*. He repeats that a prince's one reason
for existence is to serve the state, and that to this he should sacrifice
his time, his pleasure, his desired personal wishes, and, if need be,
his life. The good of the state should be his only consideration.
And when he says the state he means France, that France which
he studied so profoundly and knew so thoroughly, the real and
living France that he saw before him composed of laborers, artisans,
nobles, magistrates, priests, and soldiers.

Thinking of his subjects, each in his allotted place performing
his special function, he wrote in his *Journal,* under the date of
March, 1666: "Love them all. *Remember that they are all in our
service. Never take sides, but be father and judge all alike."* Among
these subjects, all of whom are contributing to "the glory and support of the monarchy," he places the common laborer in the first
rank: "Laborers are even more useful than soldiers, for neither
civilians nor soldiers would be able to get along without the product of their toil."

Thus, this government, based upon and organized in accordance
with reason, is tempered and humanized by the prince's sense of
justice and by his paternal generosity. Having emphasized the
human quality in monarchy as Louis XIV conceived it, we may

now define it exactly: It is a state free from ecclesiastical interference and essentially democratic. It is democratic in that birth counts for less than personal merit. It is organized rationally and scientifically with the purpose of exploiting as intensively as possible all national resources.

LOUIS BERTRAND

The World of Ideas

IN THE DEPARTMENT of foreign affairs and of the interior, Louis XIV encountered almost insurmountable obstacles, but in the world of ideas his triumph was complete. Not only did he draw to his court writers and artists worthy of his great reign, as talented in their field as his generals and his ministers, but through him French culture, heretofore unknown, gained such prestige that for fifty years it was unrivaled in the world.

One could disregard the wars of Louis XIV and reconstruct the history of his reign entirely from its literature and science. Nothing

From Louis Bertrand, *Louis XIV* (New York and London: Longmans, Green & Company, 1928), pp. 330–341. Reprinted by permission of David McKay Company, Inc., New York.

is more fascinating than to study history in this way, for triumphs in the intellectual field are more quickly recognized and more easily achieved than in the world of events. But it would be superficial not to see that the wars of Louis XIV were his most important contribution both to France and to his own glory. Without them and without the leadership and inspiration of the king, French culture would not have attained such prestige nor would French letters have had the assurance, the tone, and the style, which were reflected from the royal mind.

We must assert clearly—for the fact has been questioned—that Louis XIV loved intelligence, that he was interested in and friendly to literature and literary men—at least, those who were socially gifted—and, in a general way, he cared for scientists and philosophers.

Even in love, he demanded intelligence. He admired the ugly Marie Mancini because of her brilliant and flashing mind; in the end he deserted the affectionate La Vallière because she was less intelligent than Madame de Montespan. And if the latter, ugly, rolling in fat, irascible to an extreme, could still triumph over the youthful charms of a Fontanges, it was because Mademoiselle Fontanges was "as stupid as a dunce." At the age of forty, when he was still in the prime of life, the king fell in love with and married the prudish Madame Scarron, largely because she was intelligent and witty.

Louis XIV's intellectual awakening began when he was still a boy. He and Marie Mancini would often read aloud to each other; novels attracted them especially. He himself tried his hand at prose, and even at verse, although unsuccessful in the latter. He had an instinctive feeling for the French language and a natural style of his own. The reader ought not to judge him by the fragmentary *Mémoires,* which were edited by Pellisson and President de Périgny, and which so often have an air of self-consciousness and condescending grandeur. The real Louis XIV had more wit and charm, and, even more important, a feeling for style, a gift for hitting on the happy phrase and the right word; he was one who, as a leader, could make himself understood without discussion and, as a diplomat, could with complete assurance draw up a treaty. Even more than Boileau, he showed the nation the importance of using the exact word necessary, the *mot juste*. Benserade, when he received President de Mesmes into the Academy, praised "the sure taste of the king in his use of words. "His Majesty," he said, "has as little patience with a word misplaced as with a soldier out of line."

His natural literary gifts were supplemented by a strict course of training that has been ignored by subsequent writers. Saint-Simon painted Louis XIV as uneducated, illiterate, and lacking in any form of culture; most historians have been content to repeat his calumnies without verifying the facts.

It would be silly, for instance, to accept at its face value such a statement as the following by Primi Visconti: "The very sight of a book wearied him—even those dedicated to him, much as he liked to have that done. Marshal de la Feuillade told me confidentially that the king had made a unique exception in my case when he read a few pages of my *History of the Dutch War."* That first sentence, taken without regard to the content, would lead one to suppose, as Saint-Simon did, that Louis XIV hated to read. But continuing, it is easy to see that Primi Visconti is merely trying to impress the reader with the magnitude of the honor paid him by the king.

In a sense, one might say that Louis XIV did have his reading done for him—and by the best minds of his day. So extensively was this done that Visconti is forced to admit a little further on that Louis XIV became fatigued from listening to sermons, poetry, speeches, and from reading books dedicated to him.

Forced to spend hours on end every day plodding through endless reports, letters, and despatches, why should the king have thought it a relaxation to do still more reading?

Whether he wished it or not, he was read to continuously. He used the eyes of others to save his eyesight, overtaxed by the almost daily cabinet meetings. We are too prone to forget that, partly because he felt it his duty to listen, partly because to do so gave him pleasure, he listened patiently to practically every literary work of any importance whatsoever that was produced during his age.

Much of that literature has not survived, and the ephemeral part was, of course, much more extensive than the other.

Plays, sermons, funeral orations, poems, discourses had their first hearing before him. Bossuet and Bourdaloue preached before him. It was before him that Molière's plays were produced, and for him that they were written. *Esther* and *Athalie* were written for his pleasure and edification. Racine read aloud and interpreted for him. Who today has received such a literary education as this, so broad and connected, superintended by men of such genius! Fancy hearing Racine read his plays and comment upon them! It is not too much to claim that no one knew the literature of the century as well as Louis XIV himself.

Louis XIV never lost an opportunity of giving evidence of the esteem in which he held the arts and literature. No other ruler treated the French Academy with such consideration as he. After the death of Chancellor Séguier, he took it upon himself to be its official patron. There is no question but that there were political motives behind this act. But the king avoided the appearance of applying pressure, and urbanely allowed the offer to come from the academicians themselves. He installed the Academy in his own palace, the Louvre, although Colbert suggested the Royal Library as more convenient. In the margin of Colbert's letter, the king noted in his own hand: "The Academy ought to meet at the Louvre; that seems to me the better plan, even if a little inconvenient."

The king emphasized his connection with the Academy by receiving it formally at Versailles. Pellisson in his *Histoire de l'Académie française* remarks that the king wished the dauphin to be present "upon an occasion so complimentary to letters." The king learned the names of all the academicians he had not previously known and said to Colbert, "You must let me know what I can do for these gentlemen." He ordered six places reserved for academicians at each performance at the Court Theater. The Versailles meeting was further commemorated by the striking of a medal inscribed:

APOLLO PALATINUS
ACADEMIA GALLICA INTRA REGIAM EXCERPTA
MDCLXXII

Finally, above the great stairway of the ambassadors, he placed a relief representing the king's reception of the French Academy. This was grouped with the *Passage of the Rhine* and *Spain Humbled,* thus indicating that Louis XIV put the professions of arms and letters on an equal footing.

When the Academy completed the new edition of its dictionary, the king again received the members with full honors at Fontainebleau. "Monsieur de Toureil," wrote Racine to his friend Boileau, "came here to present the dictionary of the Academy to the king, the Queen of England, to Monseigneur, and to the ministers. . . ."

At times the academicians were invited to court. [Bussy-Rabutin described one reception]:

> After the king's Mass a dozen members of the Academy were informally present at the dinner of His Majesty, who was served at a small table. Monsieur le Duc was there, Monsieur le Prince de Conti, Monsieur de Vendôme, the Duke of Roquelaure, the Count of Gramont, the archbishop. The king said to Monsieur de Vendôme: "You, sir, who are a man of parts, should belong to the Academy." "I have no merit, sire, but perhaps they might overlook that, since no great intelligence is necessary." "What!" exclaimed the king. "Not necessary? Look at Monsieur the archbishop, Monsieur de Bussy and all these other gentlemen, if you consider intelligence not necessary." Then they spoke of the difficulties of effective oratory. The discussion lasted throughout the king's dinner; after this, the archbishop, the ten Academicians and I went to dine with the Chamberlain. The king had commanded Livry to serve us well. *We were six hours at table,* where the health of the Protector of the Academy was not forgotten. . . .

This royal protection was not a condescension accorded an official group; the king took a deep and lively interest in men of letters, and enjoyed their company if they chanced to be sociable. He did not like old fogies like Corneille and La Fontaine, both of whom were untidy and neither one of whom opened his mouth. But his warm friendship for the greatest writers of his reign—Molière, Racine, Boileau, Bossuet—was well known. Of these, Bossuet was a loyal monarchist while Molière was a radical, perhaps a free thinker. Racine and Boileau were Jansenists and belonged to the opposition party, as we would say today. Despite this they were favorites with the king. He treated them as personal friends; he was interested not only in their work but in their success and their health. When Boileau was taking the cure at Bourbon, Racine wrote him from Paris: "Three days ago the king inquired at dinner about your throat trouble. I told him you were at Bourbon. Monsieur continued to talk about you, as did Madame, and you were the subject of conversation through half the dinner. I ran across Monsieur de Louvois the next day; he also inquired for you and said how sorry he was that your malady was lasting so long."

Unquestionably, it was generous of the king to show such warm friendship for two plain men of letters who did not hide their partisanship for Port-Royal and who freely and frankly praised such exiles as Arnauld.

It has been claimed that Racine fell from grace because of his connection with Port-Royal; another story has it that it was because of a petition he wrote concerning "the misery of the people." Today it has been proved not only that this petition was never written but that Racine was never disgraced. At most there was only a slight coolness on the part of the king when Racine toward the end of his life was somewhat indiscreet in championing the Jansenists. Racine, a simple gentleman in waiting, was never banished at all. To the very end, he attended the parties at Marly. During his last illness, the king sought news of him with the greatest solicitude. When Racine died, His Majesty said to the aged Boileau, then feeble and deaf as a post, "We have both suffered a great loss, in the death of poor Racine."

Perhaps never, except at the death of his mother, did the habitually restrained and reticent Louis XIV express such deep grief at the loss of a dear friend as is found in those few simple words about Racine. The remark was not just a casual and graceful way of dismissing the subject of Racine's death. A friend of Boileau records that the conversation "lasted more than an hour."

This royal recognition of letters and literary men was a new note at court; it displeased many important personages there. Through his patronage, Louis XIV exemplified the modern attitude toward art.

Primi Visconti was frankly indignant at the attitude of most French courtiers toward men of letters. "In France they honor only military titles. Literary and professional men are treated with contempt; a nobleman who writes well is considered as having lost caste. I know that the Urfé family think it a disgrace that their grandfather, Honoré d'Urfé, wrote the poem (sic) 'Astrée.'" Bussy-Rabutin, himself a fine type of cavalry officer, had only scorn for nonentities like Racine and Boileau. "People like that," he said, "whom the king allows at Versailles." Once Bussy-Rabutin came near caning Boileau for a facetious remark made at his expense.

In another passage Bussy-Rabutin discloses his attitude toward erudition and literature with delicious naïveté: "It is true that the nobility is well represented in the Academy. However, it is always a good plan to include a number of literary men among the members, because they are industrious and will complete the work on the dictionary; for, of course, persons of our class could hardly be expected to devote ourselves to such an occupation." How delightful! Louis XIV was not so scornfully aristocratic.

Louis XIV not only respected but actually liked literature and men of letters, but he did so as a king—as a man of the seventeenth century and not as a twentieth-century æsthete and dilettante. He did not believe in "art for art's sake"—neither did he understand science or foresee the importance it was to assume toward the end of the nineteenth century. Judged by contemporary standards, he may seem backward; in his own age he was almost radical.

Louis XIV was thoroughly convinced that intelligence was a force—a great force—and this being so, it was his obvious duty to make this force serve the state and to prevent its being used against it.

Louis XIV also realized the power of public opinion and began to press that, as well as literature, into the service of the state. He organized an elaborate system of propaganda long before the Germans had even conceived of such an idea. To prepare for his wars and to carry them on, he had to sway European opinion by what amounted to newspaper campaigns. To increase the prestige of France he distributed pensions and gifts to writers and scholars throughout Europe—in Holland, Germany, England, Italy. This proselyting was done with perfect taste and discretion. Nothing was required of those favored except that they think well of His Most Christian Majesty and upon occasion say as much.

The foreigners themselves responded eagerly to the flattery. At the Villa Medici in Rome there is still a statue—the work of an Italian sculptor—a contemporary of Bernini—that represents Louis XIV as a Roman emperor trampling under foot the globe of the world. The French would never have ventured such fulsome flattery.

We could have learned much on the eve of World War I from Louis XIV's system of propaganda.

Literature and art, he held, should serve the state. The French language should become an instrument of conquest. In early annexed territories, such as Roussillon, Franche-Comté, Flanders, and Alsace, his first act was to open schools and to teach French to his new subjects. Cooperating fully with him, the Jesuits proved marvellously adept at imbuing French ideals in these new subjects. At Strasbourg, Perpignan, Gray, Salins, Béthune, Arras, and elsewhere Jesuit institutions became outposts of French culture.

Neither did the king wish foreign languages to be neglected in France. Never were Italian and Spanish more generally studied in France than during his reign. After the advance toward the Rhine in 1670, there was widespread interest in German. Racine had his eldest son, who was attached to [the French] embassy at The Hague, study it vigorously.

Thus, he made language serve both king and country. This new attitude is reflected in Racine's speech before the French Academy, which deserves serious thought. In it the great creator of *Phèdre* and *Athalie* remarked that "every syllable, every word, of our language is precious, for it is one more instrument with which to serve the glory of our august protector."

Most of the writers of that period accepted this discipline with pride and with patriotic joy. Like Louis XIV, they felt themselves born to serve the state. Their personal and private feelings were of slight importance; only the public welfare mattered. The glory of the king was the glory of France and was necessary for the prosperity of the kingdom. What the king felt and thought was what was felt and thought by the best of his subjects; he was the constant and universal hero of poems, discourses, tragedies, comedies, romances—the hero type of the classic period.

Writers and artists, far from being degraded, gained personal distinction from this service. Louis XIV made Racine a gentleman in waiting—a signal honor—and gave him an apartment at Versailles, a still greater honor. In conversation, the king called him "the great poet"; Madame de Maintenon referred to him as "the sublime poet." In the list of pensions for 1663, Pierre Corneille is described as the "first dramatic writer of the world"—just as Louis XIV, in the eyes of his subjects as well as of foreigners, was "the greatest king in the world."

But too much stress should not be placed upon this connection between literature and the service of the state. Louis XIV himself did not do so. He cared genuinely for literature and loved it for itself, deeply and simply, like any other cultivated man of the time.

He was passionately fond of the theater. He was interested in the production of a play, the stage setting, the grouping, with the zeal and enthusiasm of an impresario. He was a good critic of music and the opera. In the midst of his many tasks he kept track of the latest trends in oratory, poetry, tragedy, and comedy. "My father," said Louis Racine, "read the king the last three epistles of Boileau; the latter had been in the habit of reading his own writings to His Majesty."

What sovereign, what president, what prime minister has ever shown a more flattering interest in a writer? For fifty years Louis XIV was the official "protector" of the French Academy. He should have the honor of remaining in the eyes of posterity the great patron of French letters.

G. P. GOOCH

The Legacy of Louis XIV

THE PRINCIPAL LEGACY of Louis XIV was a powerful and centralized France. Though *le Roi Soleil* was no superman in the sense that he would have fought his way to the front had he not been of royal descent, he gave his name to the greatest era in French history, and his rays penetrated to every corner of Europe. He owed his success to the combination of his political heritage and his personal qualities. Frederick the Great saluted the French of the age of Louis XIV as the Romans of the modern world. The founder of dynastic autocracy was Richelieu, who broke

From G. P. Gooch, *Louis XV: The Monarchy in Decline* (London: Longmans, Green & Company, 1956), pp. 1–29. Reprinted by permission of the publisher.

the power of the feudal nobility and the Protestants and, by the creation of intendants, asserted the authority of the crown over the whole country. So decisive was his achievement that the Fronde was little more than a straw fire, and Condé was the last of the *noblesse de l'Épée* to draw his sword against the throne. The most sordid episode in the history of seventeenth-century France left the monarchy stronger than it found it, for the angry disgust it aroused led to a national demand for the curbing of anarchy by a firm hand at the helm. The *noblesse* and the *parlements* had discredited themselves, and Mazarin steered the ship of state into calmer waters without shedding blood. *Le Grand Siècle* had begun.

If Richelieu's edifice was to outlive its architect, it demanded rulers of ability and industry. Louis XIII, the most colorless of the Bourbon monarchs, preferred hunting to politics and left the management of the state to the mighty cardinal. There was no need for Anne of Austria to anticipate the injunction of another royal widow a century later, "George, be a King." Though but a child during the hectic years of the Fronde, Louis XIV never forgot the humiliations of the royal family during the dark days of the Fronde, the early morning flight from the Palais Royal, and the thunder of Condé's cannon in the Faubourg St. Antoine. Even before the death of Mazarin he had resolved to be his own master, to allow no minister and no favorite, male or female, to shape his course, to make the nobility the ornament instead of the rival of the throne. His veto on the duel, which had taken heavy toll of the aristocracy during the reign of his father, embodied his desire to preserve the *noblesse* while abolishing its power. Its chief function, as he saw it, was to contribute to the splendor of the court and the prestige of the crown. Landowners of limited means who vegetated on their estates, called *noblesse de province,* were disapproved, and when their names came up in conversation he curtly remarked: *"C'est un homme que je ne connais pas."* "I intend to be my own First Minister," he announced, and he kept his word. Court posts naturally went to the *noblesse de cour,* but the business of state was largely transacted by lawyers and other capable *roturiers* who owed everything to the sovereign. The king demanded from his people obedience, not collaboration. Never for a moment did he question his capacity to fulfill the task allotted to him by providence, and the incense by which he was surrounded confirmed his massive self-assurance. His ability was above the average, his industry unique in the annals of the Bourbon dynasty. Even under the shock of military disaster or domestic sorrow he remained calm and dignified, though at times when alone with Madame de Maintenon tears came to his eyes. He was the first and last demi-god to occupy the throne of France.

"There was nothing to be compared to him at reviews, fetes, every occasion on which the presence of ladies created a tone of gallantry, a gallantry always majestic," testifies Saint-Simon, a rather unfriendly observer, saluted by Sainte-Beuve as the Tacitus of France.

> Sometimes there was gaiety, but never anything misplaced or in-discreet. His slightest gesture, his walk, his bearing, his coun-tenance—all was measured, appropriate, noble, majestic, but quite natural. Thus, in serious matters such as the audiences of am-bassadors and other ceremonies no one was ever so imposing. One had to get used to him in order to avoid embarrassment when speaking to him. His replies on these occasions were always brief and to the point, rarely without some obliging or even flattering remark when the occasion demanded. In every company his pres-ence imposed silence and even fear.

Never was any human being more obviously born to be king. Nothing suggests more vividly the awe he inspired than the suicide of the unhappy cook when the fish for dinner on a royal visit to Condé at Chantilly failed to arrive, and the confession of one of his generals on entering the royal presence: "I never trembled like this before your Majesty's enemies." Like other autocrats, he made costly mistakes, but his devotion to his task is beyond challenge. He believed in the system bequeathed by Richelieu as implicitly as he believed in himself. If Henry IV was the most popular of the Bourbon rulers, his grandson earned the maximum prestige. That the longest reign in French history was also the most illustrious is the conviction of Frenchmen who agree in little else. It was a glit-tering vision, the splendor and strength of which aroused the envi-ous admiration of the world. With such a monarch there seemed no need for the States-General. The army was without a rival in Europe, and the navy, the most enduring of his creations, was double the size of the British fleet. Under the fostering hand of Colbert industry and commerce grew apace. The master of twenty million Frenchmen was the richest and most powerful prince in Europe, and scarcely anything seemed beyond his grasp. Since Charles II of Spain was childless, he reflected, perhaps a Bourbon might soon replace a Hapsburg at Madrid. In the technique of kingship he was not only unrivaled but unapproached. "He was born prudent, moderate, friendly, and just," testifies Saint-Simon; "God had given him enough to make him a good king and perhaps a fairly great king. All the evil came from elsewhere." The ceremonies of the *lever* and *coucher* recalled the solemnity of a religious cult.

The essence of Richelieu's system was the concentration of authority. It was said of the Hohenzollern Empire after the fall of Bismarck that in the most elaborately organized of European states there was anarchy at the top. The young Louis XIV was resolved that there should be no flicker of anarchy, no thought of challenge to his will, no division of power. The cardinal's *Testament politique,* published in 1687, uttered a solemn warning against nerveless rule: better too much severity than too much lenity, for weakness was the ruin of the state. The *Mémoires* of Louis XIV, first published in full in 1860, were at once a summary of the first decade of his personal rule and a manual of political instruction for his son. He portrays himself as the effective ruler of his kingdom and a jealous guardian of the prestige of the crown, while fully realizing how much is expected from an absolute sovereign. Here are a few of his precepts:

> It is essential for princes to master their resentments. In scheming to injure someone who has caused us trouble we may injure ourselves. Exercising as we do a divinely appointed function, we must appear incapable of the agitations that might lower the standard. If it is true that our heart, knowing its frailty, is conscious of the emotions of the common herd, our reason ought to conceal them directly they threaten the public weal for which alone we are born. A king must hold the balance between the many people who strive

to tilt it to their side. So many pay court to us for personal reasons
under specious phrases. You cannot satisfy everyone. Do not assess
the justice of a claim by the vigor with which it is pressed. The
result of the decision is more important than the merits of the
claimants: the greatest of rulers would soon be ruined if he granted
everything to deserving cases. Since those of our rank are never
forgiven, we must weigh our words. Kings are absolute lords and
have full authority over all people, secular and ecclesiastical; use
it according to the needs of the state. Never hurry. Take long
views. The king must know everything. Empires are only preserved by the same means by which they are created, namely,
vigor, vigilance, and hard work.

So far we seem to have been listening to the calm accents of the
father of the gods on the summit of Olympus, but the young ruler
goes on to admit the temptations of the flesh. Princes, he declares,
can never live too prudent and innocent a life. To reign happily
and gloriously it is not enough to issue orders if they do not regu-
late their own conduct. He had felt it right to recognize his daughter by Mademoiselle La Vallière by granting a title to her mother:

> I could have passed over this attachment as a bad example, but
> after drawing lessons from the failings of others I could not de-
> prive you of those you could learn from mine. The prince should
> always be a perfect model of virtue, all the more since he lives in
> a glass house. If, however, we yield in spite of ourselves, we must
> observe two precautions, as I have always done. First, that the
> time allotted to a liaison should never prejudice our affairs, since
> our first object should always be the preservation of our glory and
> authority, which can only be achieved by steady toil. Secondly—
> and more difficult to practice—that in giving our heart we must
> remain absolute master of our mind, separating the endearments
> of the lover from the resolution of the sovereign, since the in-
> fluence of a mistress is much more dangerous than that of a
> favorite.

Despite this frank admission of human frailty, the whole of this
Testament politique breathes the robust conviction that absolute
monarchy is the best form of government and that the author is
a blessing to his country and a pattern to the world.

Never for a moment after the death of Mazarin left him a free hand did Louis XIV allow a minister or a mistress to deprive him of a fraction of his authority. The chancellor, who kept the royal seal, the controller general of finance, the ministers of state without portfolio, and the departmental secretaries of state were merely executants of his will. The three successive *maîtresses en titre*— La Vallière, Montespan, and Fontanges—possessed no political influence, and there is no ground for the belief that the course of events in the closing decades was deflected by the virtuous Madame de Maintenon. The concentration of power that formed the core of his political faith involved unlimited responsibility before his subjects and posterity. When a minister apologized for referring decisions to the king on the ground that he was still new to his job, he was informed that he would never have to decide about anything and that his only duty would be to obey orders. Business was transacted by four principal councils, three of which he regularly attended. The small *conseil d'état,* the nearest equivalent to a cabinet, discussed and decided the great issues of national policy. The *conseil des dépêches* dealt with internal affairs, the *conseil des finances* with taxation. The *conseil privé,* consisting of lawyers and rarely attended by the king, was the highest judicial court in France. None of the councils possessed any statutory rights, and they were regarded as purely advisory bodies. When Colbert and Louvois were gone, the era of supermen was over, and during the closing phase he had no one on whose judgment he was inclined to lean. Never did he attempt to shield himself behind a subordinate when things went wrong; that would have been beneath his dignity. Like Mazarin, he imposed his authority without shedding blood. *L'état c'est moi* was his slogan, even if he never coined the phrase. Of all the princes in modern Europe Louis XIV and Frederick the Great came nearest to the ideal of father of the country, the first servant as well as the master of the state.

Every potential focus of opposition to the royal will was neutralized if not removed. The *parlement* of Paris, which had roughly challenged the court during the turmoil of the Fronde, was paralyzed by a veto on its traditional privilege of recording remonstrances against the decisions of the crown, and no further trouble arose while Louis XIV was on the throne. It was a highhanded proceeding, for the magistrates regarded themselves—and were widely regarded—as guardians of the fundamental laws. The *parlement,* an offshoot from the old Curia Regis, could boast of centuries of service as the supreme court of justice, dealing especially with appeals from lower courts. At its foundation by Philippe le Bel the president and councillors were appointed yearly, but they were usually reappointed. As business increased it was divided into the *chambre des enquêtes,* dealing with most of the appeals, the *chambre des requêtes,* with petitions on points of law, and a third chamber with criminal cases. The most important decisions were reserved for the *grand chambre.* Twelve provincial *parlements* were instituted during the following centuries. In addition to its judicial functions the *parlement* of Paris was required to register the royal edicts, but under Louis XI it claimed the power of remonstrance and delay, and the claim grew into a recognized right. The ruler, however, could override opposition by a *lit de justice,* and Louis XIV was determined to keep the magistrates strictly to their legal duties. The Estates still met occasionally in various provinces but were allowed little power, and the provincial governors, the French equivalent of the English Lords Lieutenant, were merely ornamental nominees of the king. The work of administration was carried on by the thirty intendants, usually chosen from the bourgeoisie, who took orders from and reported to the king and his councils at Versailles.

In 1692 Louis XIV abolished the right of the towns to elect their functionaries and further reduced their prestige by the sale of municipal offices in order to raise money for his wars. The local tribunals were no less dependent, for their decisions could be overruled by the king. The intendants could prevent cases coming into court and could sentence to the galleys or imprisonment. What Richelieu had begun was completed by *le Grand Monarque,* who had no scruples about using his power to the full. Blackstone bracketed France and Turkey as the countries where civil rights were most unreservedly at the mercy of the crown, for in the absence of habeas corpus or trial by jury an innocent citizen had little chance of securing his rights.

With equal determination Louis XIV clipped the wings of the church by reaffirming the principles of Gallicanism first formulated by Francis I, the essence of which was the supremacy of the crown except in matters of belief. The celebrated Four Articles of 1682, drafted by Bossuet, threw down a ringing challenge to the pope and the Jesuits. "Kings and princes," declared the first article, "are not by the law of God subject to any ecclesiastical power or to the keys of the church with respect to their temporal government. Their subjects cannot be released from the duty of obeying them or absolved from the oath of allegiance." Even in the field of doctrine the power of the Vatican is strictly circumscribed. "The pope has the principal place in deciding questions of faith," runs the fourth article, "but his judgment is not irreversible until confirmed by the consent of the church." The declaration, signed by thirty-four bishops and thirty-four lesser clergy, was registered by the *parlement* at the command of the king. An edict was issued prescribing that the Four Articles should be taught in all universities and accepted by all professors of theology, and the archbishops and bishops were summoned to enforce the decree. Though the angry pontiff considered the issue of a formal censure of the articles, no action was taken against Gallicanism, for the king, with the nation behind him, was too powerful to be coerced. Such influence as the church retained could only become operative with the consent of the crown.

His ideal was a homogeneous nation, looking up with pride, affection, and gratitude to its head. This monolithic conception of the state left no place for religious minorities, and when he turned *dévot* under the influence of his Jesuit confessor and Madame de Maintenon, his zeal for uniformity became an obsession. The revocation of the Edict of Nantes was as much an assertion of the principle of national unity as an affirmation of the Catholic faith. Richelieu had been content to destroy what little political influence the Huguenots retained after the Wars of Religion, and at the opening of his reign Louis XIV paid public tribute to their loyalty during the Fronde. That these orderly and industrious citizens asked only for a quiet life was recognized by all. The clergy had always detested the Edict, and their quinquennial assemblies demanded its abrogation or at any rate its drastic modifica-tion. Twenty years of mounting persecution, including the closing of churches and schools and the nightmare of the *dragonnades,* led thousands of Huguenots to seek shelter abroad and thousands more to avoid almost intolerable suffering by nominal conversion.

Declaring that it was his duty to convert all his subjects and extirpate heresy, and encouraged to take the final plunge by his confessor Père La Chaise, Harlay, archbishop of Paris, and Lou-vois, the ruthless minister of war, he revoked in 1685 the Edict of his grandfather. In a frenzy of fanaticism he exclaimed that he would complete the conversion of the Huguenots even at the cost of his right hand, and the greatest of French ecclesiastics piled incense on his altar. "Let us make known the miracle of our times," exclaimed Bossuet; "let us make known what we feel about the piety of Louis; let us raise our acclamations to the skies; let us say to this new Theodosius, this new Charlemagne: Here is the supreme achievement of your reign. It is this which gives it its true character. By your deed heresy exists no longer. God alone has wrought this miracle."

Huguenot ministers were ordered to leave France within ten days or go to the galleys, but laymen were forbidden to cross the frontier. Churches were demolished, services in private houses for-bidden, meetings held in the mountains; children were to be baptized by Catholic priests and brought up as Catholics. Hun-dreds of thousands defied the fury of their persecutors until the Revolution established equality before the law. The greatest crime of the reign was also the gravest blunder, for the thousands of skilled artisans who streamed across the frontiers before and after the revocation weakened France as much as they strengthened England, Holland, Prussia, and other Protestant states in which they found a new and happy home. A few even sought refuge in South Africa. The ferocious onslaught transformed the bolder spirits into rebels, and during the War of the Spanish Succession the bloody guerrilla struggle in the Cevennes added to the anxieties of the crown.

The king's detestation of the Jansenists was scarcely less vehe-ment than that which he entertained for the Huguenots, though the repression was less severe. The precise nature of their doctrinal deviation was beyond him, for he was no theologian. What stirred his anger was the thought that so many of his subjects, including a section of the clergy, continued to hold Augustinian ideas on grace proclaimed by Jansen, Bishop of Ypres, and popularized in France by Saint-Cyran and Antoine Arnauld. Five propositions concerning predestination in Jansen's *Augustinus* were declared heretical by Innocent X in 1653; and the Jansenist hostility to the Jesuits, which inspired Pascal's flaming *Lettres provinciales,* increased the determination of the king to enforce uniformity. It was no easy task since the Jansenists were widely respected for their piety and austerity. Their attitude was restated in Quesnel's *Réflexions morales sur le Nouveau Testament,* which enjoyed immense popularity and led to new measures of repression, culminating in the expulsion of the inmates of Port-Royal des Champs, the demolition of the convent buildings, and the issue of the Bull *"Unigenitus"* in 1713. It was not the end of the struggle, but the old king died in the belief that another focus of opposition had been removed.

Compared to the fierce battles against Huguenots and Jansenists, the Quietist controversy was a storm in a teacup. An extravagant variety of mysticism taught by Molinos, a Spanish priest, and commonly described as Molinism, was embraced with fervor by Madame Guyon and with greater circumspection by Fénelon. The aim of Quietism was to rise above ceremonies, sacraments, and dogmas into a rapturous vision of the Divine Essence by the *via negationis*—self-annihilation, an emptying of the soul from all thought, feeling, and will. That such a rejection of external authority and direct moral responsibility might degenerate into antinomianism was obvious, but Fénelon believed that much could be learned from this gospel of renunciation. His attitude was defined in his *Maxims of the Saints,* a devotional treatise saturated with mystical theology. Like all the great mystics from Saint Theresa and Saint John of the Cross to Molinos, his goal was complete surrender of self: all that mattered was to love God. At this stage Bossuet, the nation champion of orthodoxy and authority, entered the lists and fulminated against the new heretics.

When Fénelon appealed to Rome, the pope condemned his book, and the author submitted. Regarding himself as the guardian of orthodoxy, the king deprived him of his post as Preceptor to the Duke of Burgundy and excluded him from the court. Madame de Maintenon, who counted him and Madame Guyon among her intimate friends, bowed as usual to the royal will. In one of his temperamental outbursts Saint-Simon complained that the court vomited hypocrisy. In his later years the king was a gloomy fanatic, but hypocrisy could no longer be laid to his charge. The last of his Jesuit confessors, Le Tellier, incarnated the spirit of intolerance, which contributed to the growth of anticlericalism at least as much as the shafts of Bayle and Voltaire. Even during the later years of the *Grand Monarque* there was a good deal of unbelief in high circles. In 1699 the Duchess of Orléans reported to her German relatives that faith was extinct and that every youngster wanted to be an atheist. Doubtless she was thinking of her son, the future regent, who made no pretence of sharing the beliefs of the royal family. Regarding the church as a pillar of the throne, Louis XIV never worried about anything except an open challenge to its authority, which he regarded as an indirect challenge to his own.

II

The political ideology of Louis XIV was formulated by the most eloquent preacher of the age. In his massive treatise *La Politique tirée de l'Écriture Sainte* Bossuet spoke for France with the same authority as Locke and Halifax interpreted the England of 1688. As in his better-known *Discours sur l'histoire universelle,* compiled for his pupil the dauphin, the Bishop of Meaux draws his arguments from scripture, history, and reason in support of the system of dynastic autocracy. The Bible, he argues, is the touchstone of truth in the political no less than in the religious sphere. Sharing the conviction of Hobbes that by nature men are wolves to one another, he reaches the same conclusion that absolute power, preferably exercised by hereditary monarchy, is needed to keep them in order. He rejects the Aristotelian maxim that man is a political animal, and attributes the creation of so-

ciety to the instinctive physical need for self-preservation. To fulfill his duty of securing the public welfare the sovereign must
possess unfettered authority; his right once established, all other
rights fade away. *"O rois, vous êtes des dieux."* Private rights are
valid only if recognized by the law that the ruler decrees. Having
entrusted all their power to a single person, the people can do
nothing against him: even their lives are in his hands and in case
of disobedience he may take them. Bad princes, even tyrants, possess the same right to obedience as good ones, and the early Christians performed their duty in praying for Nero. If opposition is
permitted for any purpose, the state is in peril, for public order is
threatened. The ruler is no less under an obligation to maintain
his authority unimpaired than his subjects to obey his commands,
for its diminution would paralyze his capacity to keep the peace:
the best government is that which is furthest removed from anarchy. All benefits should derive from him alone. It is right that he
should be loved but he should also be feared. Caring nothing for
political or religious liberty, Bossuet denies both the need and the
value of constitutional guarantees, for it is as easy to sign a scrap of
paper as to tear it up. Hereditary monarchy has proved the best
system, for in working for his state the monarch is working for his
own children.

So far Bossuet's premises and conclusions are pure Hobbes, but
as the argument develops vital differences emerge. While the free-
thinking publicist is an incurable pessimist about human nature,
the pious bishop sees the stars shining in the heavens, since Christian ethics point the way to a better life. Though subject to no
terrestrial authority, the ruler is under the moral law, and is in
duty bound to maintain ancient institutions, fundamental laws,
and inherited privileges. Tradition, which meant as little to Hobbes
as it was later to weigh with Bentham, possessed for Bossuet an
authority that he dared not and had no wish to ignore. He believed in the wisdom of our ancestors, and in his eyes the passage
of time gradually legitimized conquest. If, however, the ruler
neglects his duties—even if he openly flouts the laws of God and
orders his subjects to do the same—he could be neither punished
nor resisted: like the early Christians, they must if necessary suffer

and die. While the system of Hobbes rested on the fear of punishment, the political edifice of Bossuet was theoretically cemented by love. He was too fine a spirit to flatter, and his paean to the ruler breathes genuine devotion.

A good subject loves his prince as the embodiment of the public weal and the safety of the state, as the air he breathes, as the light of his eyes, as his life and more than his life. He is more than the head of the state and the fatherland incarnate. Next to the love of God comes love for the prince, and how greatly must he love his people in order to retain their love! All men are brothers and should love each other like brothers. If he fears the people, all is lost. If he fears the great nobles, the state is weak. He must fear God alone. The more exalted the office, the greater the severity of the divine judge: mercy is for the little man, torments for the mighty. Without the divine judgment-seat absolute authority degenerates into arbitrary despotism.

Both as a believer in an all-powerful executive and as a pillar of the Catholic church, Bossuet rejects liberty of conscience as a challenge to the true faith and a threat to the spiritual solidarity of the state. As an embodiment of the mystique of absolute monarchy on a Christian basis in seventeenth-century France Bossuet's treatise ranks with the writings of James I and the divine-right teachings of High-Church theologians in the reign of Charles I. Its purpose was to convince the heir to the throne that a Christian prince was the representative of God on earth with all the powers, privileges, and obligations appertaining to the post. Written when *le Roi Soleil* was at the height of his glory, it breathed boundless confidence in the strength and stability of the Bourbon monarchy. As, however, the reign moved toward its close, an atmospheric change, arising from the almost unceasing wars and the ever-increasing frustration and resentment, stimulated a search for alternatives.

The critical spirit of a younger generation found its most eloquent expression in Fénelon, who, like Bossuet, was appointed to train an heir to the throne, though he was allotted a more promising pupil. No preceptor could have struck sparks from the indolent and mindless dauphin, but the qualities of his son, the

Duke of Bourgogne, seemed to authorize the highest hopes. Saint-
Simon's portrait of Fénelon is one of the gems in his gallery:

> This prelate was tall and thin, well proportioned, with a big nose,
> eyes from which fire and intelligence poured like a torrent, and
> a face unlike any I ever saw and which, once seen, could never
> be forgotten. It was full of contradictions, yet they always har-
> monized. There were gallantry and gravity, earnestness and gaiety;
> there were in equal proportions the teacher, the bishop, and the
> *grand seigneur*. His whole personality breathed thought, intelli-
> gence, grace, measure, above all nobility. It was difficult to turn
> one's eyes away.

For Saint-Simon, the Archbishop of Cambrai was the most dazzling ornament of the court. No French ecclesiastic except Richelieu has left such a legend of personal distinction; no Frenchman
of his time looked so far ahead and gave his contemporaries such
sound advice. In Acton's words, he was the first who saw through
the majestic hypocrisy of the court and knew that France was on
the road to ruin. A century before the Revolution he proclaimed
that the pyramid must rest not on its apex but on its base, and
two centuries before the League of Nations he pleaded for an
interdependent world. It was characteristic of this practical idealist
that his earliest publication was a plea for the higher education of
women.

Télémaque, like *Gulliver's Travels,* is a *roman à thèse,* a political
tract in fictional form: everyone realized that it was a broadside
against autocracy in general and Versailles in particular. Translated
into many languages, it was read with delight by the king's enemies, including the persecuted Huguenots at home and abroad.
Mentor is the oracle, Télémaque, the son of Ulysses, the eager
pupil. Every incident contains a moral or implies a criticism. "Love
your people, Telemachus," declares Mentor, "as if they were your
own children. A good king is all-powerful over his people, but
the laws are all-powerful over him. His power to do good is absolute, but his hands are tied when he would do ill. The laws give
him the people in trust as the most precious thing they can bestow
on condition that he looks on himself as their father. He should

live more soberly, less luxuriously, and with less outward magnificence and pride than others."

Mentor's sharpest arrows are aimed at the craving for fame and the wars of conquest to which it led. Though he scarcely ranks with his contemporaries William Penn and the Abbé Saint-Pierre among the pioneers of a league of nations, he denounced the slogans of arrogant nationalism with equal vigor: "The whole race is one family. All men are brothers. Say not, O ye kings, that war is the path to glory. Whoever puts his own glory before the dictates of humanity is a monster of pride, not a man." A meeting of kings should be held every three years to renew their alliance by a fresh oath and take counsel together. Not merely wars but the trade barriers of Colbert's mercantilist system were an offense against the unity of mankind. War was the costliest of royal follies, but the building mania was not far behind. Believing that all people and all nations are brothers, he paints a picture of the Elysian fields, a Christian utopia, a land of peace and joy. *"Peu sérieux,"* commented Bossuet, *"et peu digne d'un prêtre."* Though the Eagle of Meaux had powerful wings, he lacked originality and never soared into the upper regions of the sky. He was the greatest of conservatives before Joseph de Maistre; Fénelon, the greatest liberal of his age.

The attack on the principle and practice of autocracy was developed in an unpublished *Lettre à Louis XIV* so vehement in tone that its authenticity might be challenged but for the survival of the autograph manuscript, doubtless a first draft. "All your ministers," begins Fénelon, "have abandoned all the old maxims in order to glorify your authority. People no longer speak of the state, only of the king and his good pleasure. They have raised you to the skies; but absolute power is only a sham, for real power resides with the ministers, who have been harsh, arrogant, unjust, violent, false." The king's worst fault was his passion for war, and the Dutch War had unleashed all the misfortunes of France. "Your Majesty was driven into it to enhance your glory, but such a motive can never justify a war." A terrible and obviously exaggerated picture is drawn of the plight of France in 1691:

Your peoples are dying of hunger. Agriculture is almost at a standstill; all the industries languish; all commerce is destroyed. France is a vast hospital. The magistrates are degraded and worn out. It is you who have caused all these troubles. The whole kingdom having been ruined, everything is concentrated in you and everyone must feed out of your hand. The people, which loved you so much, is beginning to withdraw its affection, its confidence, and even its respect. Your victories no longer arouse delight. There is only bitterness and despair. Sedition is boiling up. You do not love God; you only fear Him with a slavish fear. It is hell you are afraid of. Your religion consists of superstition and ceremonies. You relate everything to yourself as if you were God on earth.

That the letter was read by the proud monarch is inconceivable.

The death of the dauphin in 1711 turned all eyes to the Duke of Burgundy, who might be expected to succeed his septuagenarian grandfather at any moment; and then, it seemed, was the chance of the ardent reformer at Cambrai. "Our trouble," he wrote to the Duke of Chevreuse, "is that this war has been the personal enterprise of the king, who is ruined and discredited. It should be made the concern of the whole nation, which must save itself." Since he might perhaps be called to power, he felt bound to draft a new policy for the new reign. After prolonged discussions with his old pupil's closest friends, the Duke of Beauvilliers, his ex-governor, and the Duke of Chevreuse, he formulated maxims in which he approached closer to practical issues than ever before. The first tasks were to overcome the active or passive resistance of the court, abolish sinecures, curb the building craze, introduce simpler furniture and cheaper apparel. Such austerity could only become effective if the people joined in the reforming campaign. For this purpose it would be necessary not only to summon the States General, which had not met for a century, but to integrate it into the life of the nation, meeting every three years and sitting as long as circumstances required. Since the members would doubtless be as moderate and loyal as the Estates of Languedoc and Brittany, they could discuss every aspect of policy at home and abroad. In his anxiety to limit the power of the ruler he argued that Gallicanism was no longer necessary since the authority of

Rome had so sharply declined. Give the church a little more free dom, and let the parishes have *curés* of their own choice. The most conspicuous omission in this generous program of reform is the absence of any reference to liberty of conscience, for Fénelon approved the revocation of the Edict of Nantes and had no use for the Jansenists.

A few other points are made in a little essay, *Examen de conscience des devoirs de la royauté,* which urges the sovereign to inform himself in detail of the state of the various classes and the working of central and local institutions. Above all, he must have no favorites and must strive to avoid war, the mother of misery; if forced to fight, he should observe the laws of war. "He is the cleverest and the most fantastical head in the kingdom," grumbled the old king. Had he peered more closely into that scintillating brain he would have recoiled in anger at the audacity of its schemes. That the Duke of Burgundy never came to the throne was the tragedy of Fénelon's life and was a major misfortune for France, for the first seeds of revolution were sown in the closing years of Louis XIV.

A scarcely less formidable critic of the regime, though he attacked on a narrower front, emerged from a different camp. Among the marshals whose triumphs built up the renown of Louis XIV, none occupied a loftier place in the regard of his countrymen and the court than Vauban. Though Condé and Turenne were his superiors on the battlefield, he was the prince of military engineers whose fortresses on the eastern frontiers remained the admiration of Europe long after his death. He was also a man of noble character whose interests embraced the problems of peace no less than war. Staggered by the revocation of the Edict of Nantes, he deplored in a letter to Louvois the blow struck at industry and commerce and the revival of religious strife. He forwarded a copy to Madame de Maintenon, but the appeal fell on deaf ears. The decision, he argued, weakened France by the loss of industrious citizens and strengthened her enemies. Kings were masters of the life and property of their subjects but not of their opinions, and they should not press their prerogative too far.

His next venture was more ambitious and might appear to have more chance of success, for the financial plight of war-worn France was notorious. The Peace of Ryswick in 1697 was merely a truce after a generation of continuous struggle, which emptied the treasury and almost beggared the people. The intendants were instructed to investigate and report on the condition and needs of their districts. It was the wrong method of approach, for they were likely to minimize the evils and in some cases to conceal the causes which brought them gain. Far weightier was the counsel of Vauban, who had studied conditions on the many journeys and marches of his long life. No one since Sully had displayed such deep and unflagging interest in the peasantry, which he regarded as the backbone of the state. When the return of peace afforded him ampler leisure, Vauban summarized his conclusions in *La Dîme royale*. Since France, he estimated, could support twenty-four million but contained only nineteen million, there was no overpopulation; the climate was temperate, the soil good, the peasantry thrifty and industrious. Why then was there such misery? Taxation was heavy but not unbearable if the burden were fairly distributed. The fundamental cause was that many contributed too much while the nobility and the clergy were exempt. The privilege of the former was an inheritance from feudal times, when the landed proprietors were expected to aid the crown from their own resources in time of war. The exemption of the clergy was equally a survival from the ages when the church was a law to itself. These financial entrenchments Richelieu himself had not attempted to storm. The gross injustice was resented by the *Tiers État,* but there were no channels through which it could express discontent. Every year the king's council fixed the sum required from the several districts, and the local collectors required police protection. If the taxpayer could not meet the demand, his animals, agricultural implements, and even his furniture might be seized. The knowledge that a substantial portion of the yield never reached the coffers of the state increased the smart.

Minor changes, argued Vauban, were useless, and a new deal was required. A tax should be levied on all citizens, ranging from 5 to 10 percent according to the needs of the state, in place of the existing *taille,* local *douane,* and *aides.* The idea of a tenth was familiar to the Jews, the Greeks, the Romans, and the early French kings. The church tithe aroused little complaint and involved no corruption. The hated *taille* was not adjusted to the capacity to pay, since the value of properties changed and gross favoritism was rife. To avoid the *taille,* peasants often concealed their resources and went about in rags. Comparing the yield of tithe and *taille* in some fifty parishes, he discovered that the former yielded the larger sum. The *dîme royale* would be assessed on land, houses, mills, fisheries, salaries, pensions, and every other source of income, concealment of assets being punishable by confiscation and doubling the demand. Manual workers should only pay a thirtieth, since they were frequently unemployed and their standard of life was low. Passing to changes in indirect taxation, the author proposed the reduction of the salt tax, which many were too poor to pay, and an extra charge on wine supplied in cabarets, a measure which might help to keep peasants at home and not waste their money on drink. The new system should be introduced gradually so that the whole country could witness its benefits. It was not intended to increase the total yield of taxation but to diminish the burden on those least able to bear it. Vauban expected opposition from the "leeches and harpies." He accepted autocracy but declared war on the swarm of parasites up to the highest levels.

The old soldier wrote not to inflame the public, for his book was not for sale, but to convert the king and his council, expecting that his record of service would ensure attention if not gratitude. A manuscript copy was sent to the king, who, if made aware of its contents, cannot have resented it, for the author was promoted a marshal two years later. When, however, it was printed anonymously in 1707 without seeking the usual permission of the police, which he feared would be refused, a storm blew up. Though the book was presented only to a few influential friends the authorship was no secret, and it was denounced by the tax farmers and other vested interests. A demand was raised that the audacious reformer should be sent to the Bastille and his book destroyed. The shock was too much for the old warrior, who died of a broken heart. When the king heard the news, he exclaimed: "I lose a

man greatly attached to my person and the state." Perhaps he may
have felt a momentary twinge of conscience that he had not held
his shield over a faithful servant who was saluted by Saint-Simon
as the best of Frenchmen. Three years later he was vindicated
when the king imposed a special war levy of a tenth for three successive years.

On the same day, March 14, 1707, which witnessed the condemnation of the *dîme royale,* another formidable indictment of
government action and inaction was suppressed by decree. Speaking with inside knowledge of provincial administration, Bois-
guillebert, a respected official in Normandy, described the sufferings of the people without sparing his superiors. While his *Détail
de la France,* published in 1697, had been mainly statistical, his
Factum de la France, published ten years later when the sky had
become even darker, clamored for the reform of taxation and
the liberation of agriculture, the dominant industry of the country, from the stifling restrictions on purchase and sale. His appeal,
like that of Vauban, fell on deaf ears, and the courageous critic
was disgraced and transferred to the center of France. The *ancien
régime* had scarcely reached its zenith than it began its slow decline. Unfettered absolutism leads to the abuse of power, and the
abuse of power to resistance, at first in thought and later in deed.
Yet the pace was very slow, and nothing could be done till the
middle class, steadily increasing in numbers, wealth, and self-
confidence, took matters into its own hands. During the reign
of Louis XIV far more *roturiers* dreamed, like Molière's *Bourgeois
Gentilhomme,* of buying their way into the privileged classes than
of attempting to alter the social stratification, which reserved the
highest prizes for the chosen few.

III

Louis XIV lived too long for his reputation, and during the
last two decades of his reign he forfeited much of the respect he
had enjoyed in his prime. The Augustan age of French history
had been as brief as it was brilliant. The change from the major
to the minor key was recorded by many witnesses, with Saint-

Simon and Madame, Duchess of Orléans, at their head. He himself was growing old and weary, though he put a brave face on his misfortunes. The distress that had inspired the composition of Vauban's *Dîme royale* rapidly increased as the latest, longest, and fiercest of his many conflicts, the War of the Spanish Succession, dragged on year after year, with the scales turning steadily against France under the hammer blows of Marlborough and Prince Eugène. National bankruptcy was in sight. Critical pamphlets and verses began to appear for the first time since the *mazarinades* in the days of his youth. The fruits of absolutism proved as bitter as those of feudal anarchy. In 1709 nature conspired to swell the mounting tide of misery with the cruelest and most prolonged winter in the history of France. The young Apollo, who had trampled the serpent of faction under his feet and gathered the laurels of victory in a series of campaigns, had withered into a disillusioned old man fighting for his life against a coalition provoked by placing his grandson on the throne of Spain.

He had always been industrious, and when Colbert and Louvois were gone, he worked harder than ever. For eight or nine hours daily he presided over the council of ministers, studied reports from his generals, gave audiences to ambassadors, dictated replies and instructions, and occasionally, as in the correspondence with his grandson, the king of Spain, wrote letters in his own hand. It was an exacting profession. The scandals of the early years were now a distant memory, and Madame de Maintenon had little reason to complain. The secret marriage left her official status unchanged. *La veuve Scarron,* ex-governess of the royal bastards, continued to be styled the Marquise de Maintenon, second *dame d'atours* of the dauphine, but the royal *ménage* told its own tale. From 1685 onward they were inseparable, and her apartments at the various palaces were connected with his own. His free moments were spent with her, and every evening he worked with one or other of his ministers in her room. Though she took no part in the discussions, she knew everything that was going on, and he discussed his many problems with a coolheaded and sympathetic woman who cared as little for money as for intrigue. "She

is a saint," declared the king. "She has all the perfections and plenty
of intelligence, and I have none." One day he remarked: "Madame,
a king is called Your Majesty, the pope Your Holiness, and you
should be Your Solidity."

Dollinger's well-known description of Madame de Maintenon
as the most influential woman in French history is unjust to Joan
of Arc, Catherine de Médicis, and Madame de Pompadour. That
she took a lively interest in ecclesiastical affairs was known to
everyone, but here too the king's will was her law. If he was ever
influenced by any human being it was by his Jesuit confessors.
Knowing the limits of her power, she never dreamed of crossing
the boundary, for unquestioning subordination was the condition
of her hold on that wayward heart. She was fortified by the conviction that her sacrifice—she often felt it to be her martyrdom—
was the will of God; she had rescued the proudest of European
monarchs from a life of sin and enhanced the dignity of the crown.
She was also sustained by her love for the Duke of Maine, the
Duchess of Burgundy, and her little girls in the École de Saint-
Cyr. Romantic love she had never known, for her marriage to
the semiparalyzed Scarron was a legal ceremony and nothing
more, and her second venture was a *mariage de raison*. To understand her character and her trials we must turn from the caricature
of Saint-Simon and the malice of Madame to her letters and to
the affectionate record of her beloved secretary, Mademoiselle
d'Aumale. Saint-Simon's unscrupulous schemer was a woman of
unblemished repute, unfailing tact, culture, and refinement. The
mud hurled at "the old Sultana" and Madame Ordure by Liselotte
does not stick. A fairer verdict was recorded at her death in the
journal of Dangeau, who had studied her at close range for many
years: "a woman of such great merit who had done so much good
and prevented so much harm that one cannot overpraise her." That
this tribute was denounced by Saint-Simon as "a stinking lie" re-
flects discredit on the spiteful little duke, not on the morganatic
wife.

"Do you not see that I am dying of grief," she wrote, "and
am only saved from collapse by the grace of God? Once I was
young and pretty, enjoyed pleasures and was a general favorite.

A little later I spent years in an intellectual circle. Then I came to favor, and I confess it all leaves a terrible void, a disquiet, a weariness, a desire for change." The atmosphere of the Court filled her with disgust, and Mademoiselle d'Aumale often saw her in tears. "I witness every kind of passion, treacheries, meannesses, insensate ambitions, disgusting envy, people with hearts full of rage, struggling to ruin each other, a thousand intrigues, often about trifles. The women of today are insupportable, with their immodest garb, their snuff, their wine, their gluttony, their coarseness, their idleness. I dislike it all so much that I cannot bear it." Yet bear it she did for thirty years. Too reserved to radiate very much warmth, she was respected by those who knew her well and loved by those who knew her best. The notion that she wished or the king wished her to be queen is fantastic. She possessed too much good sense, he too much pride.

Next to Madame de Maintenon the old monarch found his chief happiness in Marie Adelaide, "the Rose of Savoy," grandchild of Monsieur and his first wife Henrietta of England, the child-wife of the Duke of Burgundy, who brought a gleam of sunshine into the gloomy halls of Versailles and, in the words of Madame, Duchess of Orléans, made everyone feel young again, for she was only eleven. "She is a treasure," reported Madame de Maintenon to her mother, the Duchess of Savoy:

> She is the delight of the king, amusing him with her gaiety and pranks, though she never goes too far. One can talk seriously to her without being bored. She dislikes flattery and is grateful for advice. She gets prettier every day. She is growing a little and her figure is perfect. She dances well and no one ever possessed such grace. I never exaggerate. No one dreams of spoiling her. Perhaps it will not always be so. Traps are set for princes as for ordinary folk. I hope God will protect her. She fears and loves Him, and has a great respect for religion. Her education has been excellent and her range of knowledge is surprising.

Her only failing was a passion for the card table, which the king unwisely encouraged by paying her debts. In her combination of youthful levity, natural charm, and warmth of heart she reminds us of Marie Antoinette. During the first phase she appealed more to the king and Madame de Maintenon than to her austere husband, who disliked society and loved to shut himself up with his books; but as motherhood ripened her character she learned to appreciate his noble qualities, and it grew into the first happy marriage in the Bourbon family.

When the shadowy figure of the dauphin, his father's only legitimate child, passed away at Meudon, few tears were shed. The most colorless of the Bourbons had sought relief from his lifelong inferiority complex in the pleasures of the table and the chase; *"sans vice ni vertu"* comments Saint-Simon disdainfully. He had lost his Bavarian wife, and his three sons meant as little to him as he to them. His death at the age of fifty in 1711 was welcomed, not only because it removed the threat of a ruler totally unfitted for his task but because it opened the way for a successor of exceptional promise. In dynastic autocracies the abilities, virtues, and vices of the royal family make history.

Twice in the course of the eighteenth century there seemed to be a chance of the monarchy renewing itself, and twice the cup was snatched away by a cruel fate. When the full measure of the unworthiness of Louis XV came to be realized, the nation looked back nostalgically to the Duke of Burgundy, the pupil of Fénelon. The king was very fond of him, testifies Mademoiselle d'Aumale, and the whole court adored him. He was born a terror, records Saint-Simon, and during his youth he made his entourage tremble by paroxysms of fury, for he could not bear the slightest opposition. Often there were storms so violent that his body seemed ready to burst. He was obstinate to a degree, with a passion for all kinds of pleasures—good cheer, the chase, music. He radiated intelligence. His repartees were astonishing, his answers pointed and profound, the most abstract subjects his delight. From this blend of dross and precious metal his admirable governor the Duke of Beauvilliers, and his preceptor Fénelon, we are told, fashioned a casket of shining gold. "The marvel was that in a very short time their devotion made him another man, changing his faults into corresponding virtues. Out of this abyss we have witnessed the emergence of a prince affable, gentle, human, generous, patient, modest, humble and—for himself—austere. His only thought is to fulfil his duties as a son and a subject as well as those to which he is summoned by destiny." His youthful passion for the card table had been overcome, and Madame de Maintenon, an exacting critic, described him as a saint.

Among the papers found in his desk after his death was a meditation on the call awaiting him, which confirms Saint-Simon's portrait:

> Of all the people who compose a nation the one who deserves most pity and receives least is the sovereign. He has all the disadvantages of grandeur without its delights. Of all his subjects he has the least liberty, the least tranquillity, the fewest moments for himself. Soldiers go into winter quarters, magistrates have vacations, everyone has periods of rest: for the king there are none and never will be. If he changes his residence, his work follows him. A day of inaction involves a crushing task next day, or else everything stagnates. His whole life is spent in a whirlpool of business —a round of ceremonies, anxieties, disagreeable tasks, solicitations without end. His plans go wrong. The people, conscious of their evils, ignore his efforts to help. In appointments he seeks for merit but is deceived. He tries to make someone happy, but he reaps discontent and ingratitude. He has palaces he has not seen and riches he does not enjoy. He fulfils Saint Paul's ideal of a Christian: he has everything and possesses nothing. Strictly speaking, he is the poorest of his subjects, for all the needs of the state are his needs and they always exceed his fortune. A father is never rich when his income does not suffice for the sustenance of his children.

The Duke of Burgundy was fortified by the counsel and affection of friends who composed what Saint-Simon calls *le petit troupeau,* which stood for piety, austerity, and reform. He needed moral support, for the disastrous campaign of 1708, in which he held a high command, had depreciated his stock. The leader of "the little flock" was the Duke of Beauvilliers, one of the few stainless figures, *sans peur et sans reproche,* on the crowded stage at Versailles. At his side stood his brother-in-law, the Duke of Chevreuse, who shared his devotion to the heir to the throne. Both of them looked up to Fénelon, who, though banished from the court, remained in close touch by correspondence. The youngest member of the group was Saint-Simon, who in long private talks urged him to restore the political influence of the *noblesse* when he was called to the helm.

His testing time came sooner than he expected, for his father died of smallpox. During the five days of his illness the duke and his wife held open court and were equally gracious to all comers. In Saint-Simon's glowing phrase it was like the coming of spring. Not only was the whole court there: *tout Paris et tout Meudon* flocked to worship the rising sun. When the news of the dauphin's death reached Versailles late at night, Saint-Simon rushed out of his apartments and found *tout Versailles* assembled or assembling, the ladies emerging from their beds or bedrooms just as they were. The new dauphin—*"tout simple, tout saint, tout plein de ses devoirs"*—embodied the hopes of all that was best in France. He had discussed financial reform with Vauban and was prepared for still more fundamental measures: the machinery of government must be transformed and a popular element introduced. Looking beyond the walls of the palace, he longed to aid the common man and the common soldier, who had never had their chance. It was a false dawn, for within a year the dauphin, his wife, and their eldest son died within ten days. For once Saint-Simon, who could love as well as hate, gave way to passionate grief. The duke, he declares, was born for the happiness of France and all Europe. "We were not worthy of him. I wished to withdraw from the court and the world, and it needed all the wisdom and influence of my wife to prevent it, for I was in despair." To the Duke of Beauvilliers he exclaimed after the last scene at St. Denis, "We have been burying France," and Beauvilliers agreed. Their grief was shared by Madame de Maintenon, who wrote to the Princess of Ursins: "Everything is gone; everything seems empty; there is no more joy. The king does his best to keep up his spirits, but he cannot shake off his sorrow." Never in the history of France has there been such universal regret at the death of a reigning monarch or heir. In the words of Duclos, it would have been an era of justice, order, and morals.

The Duke of Orléans, now marked out as the future regent

for the little boy of two who was to become Louis XV, shared some of the views of the Duke of Burgundy, but he never inspired the devotion and respect that had been so widely entertained for the pupil of Fénelon. The three remaining years of the most memorable reign in the history of France were a gloomy time. The routine of court life, the music, the gambling, continued, but the sparkle had disappeared. The weary old monarch, like Franz Josef at a later date, plodded joylessly through his papers. The fairest flower of the court, the only member of the royal family whom he had taken to his heart, was sorely missed, and Madame de Maintenon, always a restful rather than an exhilarating influence, was nearing eighty. The victory of Villars at Denain saved the French cause on the brink of catastrophe, and procured an honorable settlement in the Treaty of Utrecht, for the king's grandson retained the Spanish throne. Yet the country was exhausted by half a century of warfare, poverty-stricken and depressed, and the ruler felt that he was no longer beloved.

It was time to go, and he died with the dignity that had never deserted him in good and evil times. The sun went down in a bank of dark clouds, for the heir was a delicate lad of five. The second grandson was far away in Madrid and had resigned his claim to the throne. The third grandson, the Duke of Berry, had passed away in 1714. On his deathbed the king sent for his great-grandson and addressed the little boy in words that deeply moved all who were present: "My child, you will one day be a great king. Do not imitate me in my taste for war. Always relate your actions to God, and make your subjects honor Him. It breaks my heart to leave them in such a state. Always follow good advice; love your peoples; I give you Père Le Tellier as your confessor; never forget the gratitude you owe the Duchess of Ventadour." He embraced the child, gave him his blessing, lifted his hands and uttered a little prayer as he watched him leave the room. "Not a day passed," testifies Villars, "without some mark of strength, goodness, and, above all, piety. His instructions for the funeral were given with such clarity and self-control that he seemed to be making arrangements for someone else."

Shortly before his last illness the king drafted instructions for his great-grandson, which he requested Marshal Villeroi to hand to him on reaching the age of seventeen:

My son, if providence allows you to shape your own life, receive this letter from the hands of the faithful subject who has promised me to deliver it. You will find therein the last wishes of your father and your king who, in quitting this world, feels such tenderness for you in your childhood that the troubles he apprehends during your minority cause him more anxiety than the terrors of approaching death. If anything can soften my pain, it is the promise of good subjects who have sworn to me to watch over you and shed their blood for your preservation. Reward them and never forget them or the services of my son the Duke of Maine, whom I find worthy to be placed at your side. This distinction will doubtless be assailed by those whose desire to rule it frustrates. If anything happens to him, or if my dispositions in his favor are set aside, I desire you to restore everything to the position existing at my death, both as regards religion and the Duke of Maine. Have confidence in him. Follow his advice. He is quite able to guide you. If death deprives you of such a good subject, preserve for his children the rank I have bestowed on them, and show them all the friendship you owe to their father, who has sworn to me only to abandon you at death. Let the ties of blood and friendship ever unite you to the King of Spain, and allow no reason or misunderstood political interest to separate you. That is the only way to preserve peace and the European equilibrium. Maintain an inviolable attachment to the common father of the faithful, and never for any reason separate yourself from the bosom of the church. Place all your confidence in God, live rather as a Christian than a king, and never incur His displeasure by moral irregularities. Thank Divine Providence, which so visibly protects this kingdom. Set your subjects the same example as a Christian father to his family. Make them happy if you desire happiness. Relieve them as soon as possible of all the heavy burdens necessitated by a long war that they bore with fidelity and patience. Grant them the long periods of peace, which alone can restore your kingdom. Always prefer peace to the hazards of war, and remember that the most brilliant victory is too dearly bought at the expense of your subjects' blood, which should only be shed for the glory of God. This conduct will earn the blessing of heaven during your reign. Receive my blessing in this last embrace.

The future of France was constantly in his thoughts. Addressing the courtiers and officials from his bed he commended his successor to their care: "He is only five. He will greatly need your zeal and fidelity. I request for him the same sentiments you have often shown for myself. I advise him to avoid wars. I have made too many, and they compelled me to lay heavy burdens on my people. This I deeply regret, and I ask the pardon of God."

A briefer and somewhat similar declaration of faith was embodied in the maxims for his grandson on leaving to assume the crown of Spain in 1700:

> Love your wife, and ask God for one to suit you—not an Austrian. Beware of flatterers. Esteem those who risk your displeasure, for they are your real friends. Only wage war if you are compelled, and then take command yourself. Never have a favorite or a mistress. Be the master. Consult your council but decide yourself. God, who has made you king, will provide all the wisdom you require so long as your intentions are good.

Having by this time dispensed with mistresses, the royal moralist no longer claimed indulgence for the weakness of young rulers, which he had regretfully recognized thirty or more years earlier.

The closing scene was most vividly described by his sister-in-law, the Duchess of Orléans, in a letter written four days before the end.

> Today we have witnessed the saddest and most touching scene imaginable. Our dear king, after preparing himself for death and receiving the last sacraments, sent for the little dauphin and gave him his blessing. Then he summoned the Duchess of Berry, myself, and all the other girls and grandchildren. He bade me farewell with such tenderness that I wonder I did not faint. He said he had always loved me, more than I knew; that he regretted to have hurt me at times; begged me to think of him sometimes, which he believed I should do, since I had always felt affection for him. He gave me his blessing and wished me happiness. I fell at his knees and kissed his hand, and he embraced me. Then he spoke to the others and exhorted them to unity. I thought he was speaking to me, and said I would obey him in that as in every-

thing. He smiled and said: "I was not speaking to you, for I know you are too sensible; I was speaking to the other princesses." The king's self-control is indescribable. He issues his orders as if he were merely going on a journey.

Louis XIV had raised France to the highest pinnacle in the first half of his reign, but he lived long enough to destroy much of his handiwork. "I noticed in my youth," wrote Duclos many years later, "that those who lived longest under his reign were the least favorable to him." The colossal national debt, resulting from many years of war, hung like a millstone round the neck of his descendants, and the system of government could only be operated by a ruler of equal capacity. The population had fallen by one-fifth in half a century, owing to war casualties, the expulsion of the Huguenots, and widespread starvation. Agricultural production had declined in an even more alarming ratio. Considerable areas went out of cultivation, the country swarmed with robbers, and bread riots were frequent. Direct and indirect taxes, tithes, and feudal burdens were a nightmare at a time of bad harvests and dear bread. Old taxes had been increased and new ones—the *capitation* and the *dixième*—imposed. Every possible source of revenue was exploited, including forced loans, lotteries, the issue of paper money, the sale of titles and official posts, and the depreciation of the currency. France, still almost entirely an agricultural country, was sucked nearly dry. Huge annual deficits added to the national debt, and the revenues of the coming years were mortgaged to meet immediate needs. The glitter of a lavish court offered a grim contrast to the specter of hunger that stalked through the land. The sufferings of the people were far more grievous in 1715 than on the eve of the Revolution in 1789. Such was the price his subjects had to pay for the greater glory of the *Roi Soleil.*

DUKE OF SAINT-SIMON

A Tolerably Great King

LOUIS XIV was made for a brilliant court. In the midst of
other men, his figure, his courage, his grace, his beauty, his
grand mien, even the tone of his voice and the majestic and natural
charm of all his person distinguished him till his death. He reigned,
indeed, in little things; the great he could never reach: even in the
former, too, he was often governed. The superior ability of his early
ministers and his early generals soon wearied him. He liked nobody
to be in any way superior to him. Thus, he chose his ministers not
for their knowledge but for their ignorance; not for their capacity
but for their want of it. He liked to form them, as he said; liked

From *Memoirs of the Duc de Saint-Simon,* edited by W. H. Lewis and
translated by Bayle St. John (New York: Macmillan, 1964), pp. 129-146.
Copyright © 1964 by W. H. Lewis. Reprinted by permission of The Macmillan Company and B. T. Batsford Ltd.

to teach them even the most trifling things. It was the same with his generals. He took credit to himself for instructing them; wished it to be thought that from his cabinet he commanded and directed all his armies. Naturally fond of trifles, he unceasingly occupied himself with the most petty details of his troops, his household, his mansions. This vanity, this unmeasured and unreasonable love of admiration, was his ruin. His ministers, his generals, his mistresses, his courtiers soon perceived his weakness. They praised him with emulation and spoiled him. Those whom he liked owed his affection for them to their untiring flatteries. This is what gave his ministers so much authority, and the opportunities they had for adulating him, of attributing everything to him, and of pretending to learn everything from him. Suppleness, meanness, an admiring, dependent, cringing manner—above all, an air of nothingness—were the sole means of pleasing him.

Though his intellect . . . was beneath mediocrity, it was capable of being formed. He loved glory, was fond of order and regularity, was by disposition prudent, moderate, discreet, master of his movements and his tongue. Will it be believed? He was also by disposition good and just! God had sufficiently gifted him to enable him to be a good king; perhaps even *a tolerably great king!* All the evil came to him from elsewhere. His early education was so neglected that nobody dared approach his apartment. He has often been heard to speak of those times with bitterness, and even to relate that one evening he was found in the basin of the Palais Royal garden fountain, into which he had fallen! He was scarcely taught how to read or write and remained so ignorant that the most familiar historical and other facts were utterly unknown to him! He fell, accordingly, and sometimes even in public, into the grossest absurdities.

He was exceedingly jealous of the attention paid him. Not only did he notice the presence of the most distinguished courtiers, but those of inferior degree also. He looked to the right and to the left, not only upon rising but upon going to bed, at his meals, in passing through his apartments, or his gardens of Versailles, where alone the courtiers were allowed to follow him; he saw and noticed everybody; not one escaped him, not even those who hoped to remain unnoticed. He marked well all absentees from the court, found out the reason of their absence, and never lost an opportunity of acting toward them as the occasion might seem to justify. With some of the courtiers (the most distinguished), it was a demerit not to make the court their ordinary abode; with others it was a fault to come but rarely; for those who never or scarcely ever came to it was certain disgrace. When their names were in any way mentioned, "I do not know them," the king would reply haughtily. Those who presented themselves but seldom were thus characterized: "They are people I never see"; these decrees were irrevocable. He could not bear people who liked Paris.

Louis XIV took great pains to be well informed of all that passed everywhere: in the public places, in the private houses, in society, and familiar intercourse. His spies and tell-tales were infinite. He had them of all species; many who were ignorant that their information reached him; others who knew it; others who wrote to him direct, sending their letters through channels he indicated; and all these letters were seen by him alone, and always before everything else; others who sometimes spoke to him secretly in his cabinet, entering by the back stairs. These unknown means ruined an infinite number of people of all classes, who never could discover the cause; often ruined them very unjustly; for the king, once prejudiced, never altered his opinion, or so rarely that nothing was more rare. He had, too, another fault, very dangerous for others and often for himself, since it deprived him of good subjects. He had an excellent memory; in this way, that if he saw a man who, twenty years before, perhaps, had in some manner offended him, he did not forget the man, though he might forget the offense. This was enough, however, to exclude the person from all favor. The representations of a minister, of a general, of his confessor even, could not move the king. He would not yield.

The most cruel means by which the king was informed of what was passing—for many years before anybody knew it—was that of opening letters. The promptitude and dexterity with which they were opened passes understanding. He saw extracts from all the letters in which there were passages that the chiefs of the post office, and then the minister who governed it, thought ought to go before him; entire letters, too, were sent to him, when their contents seemed to justify the sending. Thus, the chiefs of the post, nay, the principal clerks, were in a position to suppose what they pleased and against whom they pleased. A word of contempt against the king or the government, a joke, a detached phrase was enough. It is incredible how many people, justly or unjustly, were more or less ruined, always without resource, without trial, and without knowing why. The secret was impenetrable; for nothing ever cost the king less than profound silence and dissimulation.

This last talent he pushed almost to falsehood, but never to deceit, pluming himself upon keeping his word—therefore he scarcely ever gave it. The secrets of others he kept as religiously as his own. He was even flattered by certain confessions and certain confidences; and there was no mistress, minister, or favorite who could have wormed them out, even though the secret regarded themselves.

Never did man give with better grace than Louis XIV, or augmented so much, in this way, the price of his benefits. Never did man sell to better profit his words, even his smiles, nay, his looks. Never did disobliging words escape him; and if he had to blame, to reprimand, or correct, which was very rare, it was nearly always with goodness. Never was man so naturally polite, or of a politeness so measured, so graduated, so adapted to person, time, and place. Toward women his politeness was without parallel. Never did he pass the humblest petticoat without raising his hat; even to chambermaids, that he knew to be such, as often happened at Marly. For ladies he took his hat off completely, but to a greater or less extent; for titled people, half off, holding it in his hand or against his ear some instants, more or less marked. For the nobility he contented himself by putting his hand to his hat. He took it off for the princes of the blood, as for the ladies. If he accosted ladies, he did not cover himself until he had quitted them. All this was out of doors, for in the house he was never covered. His reverences, more or less marked, but always light, were incomparable for their grace and manner; even his mode of half raising himself at supper for each lady who arrived at table. Though at last this fatigued him, yet he never ceased it; the ladies who were to sit down, however, took care not to enter after supper had commenced.

If he was made to wait for anything while dressing, it was always with patience. He was exact to the hours that he gave for all his day, with a precision clear and brief in his orders. If in the bad weather of winter, when he could not go out, he went to Madame de Maintenon's a quarter of an hour earlier than he had arranged (which seldom happened), and the captain of the guards was not on duty, he did not fail afterward to say that it was his own fault for anticipating the hour, not that of the captain of the guards for being absent. Thus, with this regularity, which he never deviated from, he was served with the utmost exactitude.

He treated his valets well, above all those of the household. It was among them that he felt most at ease and that he unbosomed himself the most familiarly, especially to the chiefs. Their friendship and their aversion have often had great results. They were unceasingly in a position to render good and bad offices. The ministers, even the most powerful, openly studied their caprices; and the princes of the blood—nay, the bastards—not to mention people of lower grade, did the same.

The king loved air and exercise very much, as long as he could make use of them. He had excelled in dancing, and at tennis and mall. On horseback he was admirable, even at a late age. He liked to see everything done with grace and address. To acquit yourself well or ill before him was a merit or a fault. He said that with things not necessary it was best not to meddle, unless they were done well. He was very fond of shooting, and there was not a better or more graceful shot than he. He had always in his cabinet seven or eight pointer bitches and was fond of feeding them, to make himself known to them. He was very fond, too, of stag hunting, but in a *calèche,* since he broke his arm while hunting at Fontainebleau, immediately after the death of the queen. He rode alone in a species of "box," drawn by four little horses—with five or six relays—and drove himself with an address and accuracy unknown to the best coachmen. His postilions were children from ten to fifteen years of age, and he directed them.

He liked splendor, magnificence, and profusion in everything: you pleased him if you shone through the brilliancy of your houses, your clothes, your table, your equipages.

As for the king himself, nobody ever approached his magnificence. His buildings, who could number them? At the same time, who was there who did not deplore the pride, the caprice, the bad taste seen in them? St. Germain, a lovely spot, with a marvellous view, rich forest, terraces, gardens, and water he abandoned for Versailles, the dullest and most ungrateful of all places, without prospect, without wood, without water, without soil; for the ground is all shifting sand or swamp, the air accordingly bad.

But he liked to subjugate nature by art and money. He built at Versailles, on, on, without any general design, the beautiful and the ugly, the vast and the mean, all jumbled together. His own apartments and those of the queen are inconvenient to the last degree, dull, close, stinking. The gardens astonish by their magnificence but cause regret by their bad taste. You are introduced to the freshness of the shade only by a vast torrid zone, at the end of which there is nothing for you but to mount or descend; and with the hill, which is very short, terminate the gardens. The violence everywhere done to nature repels and wearies us despite ourselves. The abundance of water, forced up and gathered together from all parts, is rendered green, thick, muddy; it disseminates humidity, unhealthy and evident; and an odor, still more so.

At last, the king, tired of the cost and bustle, persuaded himself that he should like something little and solitary. He found behind Lucienne a deep narrow valley, completely shut in, inaccessible from its swamps, and with a wretched village called Marly upon the slope of one of its hills. The king was overjoyed at his discovery. The hermitage was made. At first, it was only for sleeping in three nights, from Wednesday to Saturday, two or three times a year, with a dozen at the outside of courtiers, to fill the most indispensable posts.

By degrees, the hermitage was augmented, the hills were pared and cut down, to give at least the semblance of a prospect; in fine, what with buildings, gardens, waters, aqueducts, the curious and well-known machine, statues, precious furniture, the park, the ornamental enclosed forest, Marly has become what it is today, though it has been stripped since the death of the king. Great trees were unceasingly brought from Compiègne or farther, three-fourths of which died and were immediately after replaced; vast spaces covered with thick wood, or obscure alleys, were suddenly changed into immense pieces of water, on which people were rowed in gondolas; then they were changed again into forests (I speak of what I have seen in six weeks); basins were changed a hundred times; cascades the same; carp ponds adorned with the most exquisite painting, scarcely finished, were changed and differently arranged by the same hands; and this an infinite number of times; then there was that prodigious machine just alluded to, with its immense aqueducts, the conduit, its monstrous resources solely devoted to Marly, and no longer to Versailles.

Let me now speak of the amours of the king, which were even more fatal to the state than his building mania. Louis XIV in his youth more made for love than any of his subjects, tired of gathering passing sweets, fixed himself at last upon La Vallière. The progress and the result of his love are well known.

Madame de Montespan was she whose rare beauty touched him next, even during the reign of Madame de La Vallière. She soon perceived it and vainly pressed her husband to carry her away into Guienne. With foolish confidence, he refused to listen to her. She spoke to him more in earnest. In vain. At last the king was listened to, and carried her off from her husband, with that frightful hubbub, which resounded with horror among all nations and which gave to the world the new spectacle of two mistresses at once! The king took them to the frontiers, to the camps, to the armies, both of them in the queen's coach. The people ran from all parts to look at the three queens and asked each other in their simplicity if they had seen them. In the end, Madame de Montespan triumphed, and disposed of the master and his court with an éclat unconcealed.

Madame de Montespan was cross, capricious, ill-tempered, and of a haughtiness in everything, which reached to the clouds and from the effects of which nobody, not even the king, was exempt.

The courtiers avoided passing under her windows, above all when the king was with her. They used to say it was equivalent to being put to the sword, and this phrase became proverbial at the court. It is true that she spared nobody, often without other design than to divert the king; and because she had infinite wit and sharp pleasantry, nothing was more dangerous than the ridicule she, better than anybody, could cast on all. With that, she loved her family and her relatives and did not fail to serve people for whom she conceived friendship. The queen endured with difficulty her haughtiness—very different from the respect and measure with which she had been treated by the Duchesse de La Vallière, whom she always loved. But of Madame de Montespan she would say, "That strumpet will cause my death." . . .

During her reign she did not fail to have causes for jealousy. There was Mademoiselle de Fontanges, who pleased the king sufficiently to become his mistress. But she had no intellect, and without that it was impossible to maintain supremacy over the king. Her early death quickly put an end to this amour. Then there was Madame de Soubise, who, by the infamous connivance of her husband, prostituted herself to the king and thus secured all sorts of advantages for that husband, for herself, and for her children. The love of the king for her continued until her death, although for many years before that he had ceased to see her in private. Then there was the beautiful Ludre, Canoness of Lurraine, and maid of honor to Madame, who was openly loved for a moment. But this amour was a flash of lightning, and Madame de Montespan remained triumphant.

Let us now pass to another kind of amour, which astonished all the world as much as the other had scandalized it, and which the king carried with him to the tomb. Who does not already recognize the celebrated Françoise d'Aubigné, Marquise de Maintenon, whose permanent reign did not last less than thirty-two years?

Born in the American islands, where her father, perhaps a gentleman, had gone to seek his bread, and where he was stifled by obscurity, she returned alone and at haphazard into France. She landed at La Rochelle and was received in pity by Madame de

Neuillant, mother of the Maréchale Duchesse de Navailles, and was reduced by that avaricious old woman to keep the keys of her granary, and to see the hay measured out to her horses. . . . She came afterwards to Paris—young, clever, witty, and beautiful, without friends and without money—and by lucky chance made acquaintance with the famous Scarron. Marriage with this joyous and learned cripple appeared to her the greatest and most unlooked-for good fortune.

The marriage being brought about, the new spouse pleased the company that went to Scarron's house. It was the fashion to go there: people of wit, people of the court and of the city, the best and most distinguished went. Scarron was not in a state to leave his house, but the charm of his genius, of his knowledge, of his imagination, of that incomparable and ever fresh gaiety that he showed in the midst of his afflictions, that rare fecundity, and that humor, tempered by so much good taste that is still admired in his writings, drew everybody there.

Madame Scarron made at home all sorts of acquaintances, which, however, at the death of her husband, did not keep her from being reduced to the charity of the parish of St. Eustace. She took a chamber for herself and for a servant, where she lived in a very pinched manner.

Step by step, she was introduced to the Hôtel d'Albret, and thence to the Hôtel de Richelieu, and elsewhere; so she passed from one house to the other. In these houses Madame Scarron was far from being on the footing of the rest of the company. She was more like a servant than a guest.

To the intimacy between the Maréchal d'Albret and Madame de Montespan, Madame de Maintenon owed the good fortune she met with fourteen or fifteen years later. Madame de Montespan continually visited the Hôtel d'Albret and was much impressed with Madame Scarron. She conceived a friendship for the obliging widow, and when she had her first children by the king—Monsieur du Maine and Madame la Duchesse, whom the king wished to conceal—she proposed that they should be confided to Madame Scarron. A house in the Marais was accordingly given to her, to lodge in with them, and the means to bring them up, but in the utmost secrecy. Afterward, these children were taken to Madame de Montespan, then shown to the king, and then by degrees drawn from secrecy and avowed. Their governess, being established with them at the court, more and more pleased Madame de Montespan, who several times made the king give presents to her. He, on the other hand, could not endure her; what he gave to her, always little, was by excess of complaisance and with a regret that he did not hide.

The estate of Maintenon being for sale, Madame de Montespan did not let the king rest until she had drawn from him enough to buy it for Madame Scarron, who thenceforth assumed its name. She obtained enough also for the repair of the château, and then attacked the king for means to arrange the garden, which the former owners had allowed to go to ruin.

It was at the toilette of Madame de Montespan that these demands were made. The captain of the guards alone followed the king there. Monsieur le Maréchal de Lorges, the truest man that ever lived, held that post then, and he has often related to me the scene he witnessed. The king at first turned a deaf ear to the request of Madame de Montespan and then refused. Annoyed that she still insisted, he said he had already done more than enough for this creature; that he could not understand the fancy of Madame de Montespan for her and her obstinacy in keeping her after he had begged her so many times to dismiss her; that he admitted Madame Scarron was insupportable to him, and, provided he never saw her more and never heard speak of her, he would open his purse again, though, to say truth, he had already given too much to a creature of this kind! Never did Monsieur le Maréchal de Lorges forget these words; and he has always repeated them to me and others precisely as they are given here, so struck was he with them, and much more after all that he saw since, so astonishing and so contradictory. Madame de Montespan stopped short, very much troubled by having too far pressed the king.

Monsieur du Maine was extremely lame; this was caused, it was said, by a fall he had had from his nurse's arms. Nothing done for him succeeded; the resolution was then taken to send him to various practitioners in Flanders, and elsewhere in the realm, then to the waters, among others to Barèges. The letters that the governess wrote to Madame de Montespan, giving an account of these journeys, were shown to the king. He thought them well written, relished them, and the last ones made his aversion for the writer diminish.

The ill humor of Madame de Montespan finished the work. She had a good deal of that quality, and had become accustomed to give it full swing. The king was the object of it more frequently than anybody; he was still amorous; but her ill humor pained him. Madame de Maintenon reproached Madame de Montespan for this, and thus advanced herself in the king's favor. The king, by degrees, grew accustomed to speak sometimes to Madame de Maintenon, to unbosom to her what he wished her to say to Madame de Montespan, at last, to relate to her the chagrins this latter caused him and to consult her thereupon.

Admitted thus into the intimate confidence of the lover and the mistress, and this by the king's own doing, the adroit waiting woman knew how to cultivate it, and profited so well by her industry that by degrees she supplanted Madame de Montespan, who perceived, too late, that her friend had become necessary to the king. Arrived at this point, Madame de Maintenon made, in her turn, complaints to the king of all she had to suffer, from a mistress who spared even him so little; and by dint of these mutual complaints about Madame de Montespan, Madame de Maintenon at last took her place and knew well how to keep it.

It was while the king was in the midst of his partiality for Madame de Maintenon that the queen died. It was at the same time, too, that the ill humor of Madame de Montespan became more and more insupportable. This imperious beauty, accustomed to domineer and to be adored, could not struggle against the despair that the prospect of her fall caused her. What carried her beyond all bounds was that she could no longer disguise from herself that she had an abject rival whom she had supported, who owed everything to her, whom she had so much liked that she had several times refused to dismiss her when pressed to do so by the king; a rival, too, so beneath her in beauty, and older by several years; to feel that it was this lady's maid, not to say this servant, that the king most frequently went to see; that he sought only her; that he could not dissimulate his uneasiness if he did not find her; that he quitted all for her; in fine, that at all moments she (Madame de Montespan) needed the intervention of Madame de Maintenon, in order to attract the king to reconcile her with him, or to obtain the favors she asked for. It was then, in times so propitious to the enchantress, that the king became free by the death of the queen.

He passed the first few days at Saint-Cloud, at Monsieur's, whence he went to Fontainebleau, where he spent all the autumn. It was there that his liking, stimulated by absence, made him find that absence insupportable. Upon his return it is pretended—for we must distinguish the certain from that which is not so—it is pretended, I say, that the king spoke more freely to Madame de Maintenon, and that she, venturing to put forth her strength, retrenched herself behind devotion and prudery; that the king did not cease, that she preached to him and made him afraid of the devil, and that she balanced his love against his conscience with so much art that she succeeded in becoming what our eyes have seen her, but what posterity will never believe she was.

But what is very certain and very true is that some time after the return of the king from Fontainebleau, and in the midst of the winter that followed the death of the queen (posterity will with difficulty believe it, although perfectly true and proved), Père de La Chaise, confessor of the king, said Mass at the dead of night in one of the king's cabinets at Versailles. Bontems, governor of Versailles, chief valet on duty, and the most confidential of the four, was present at this Mass, at which the monarch and Maintenon were married in presence of Harlay, archbishop of Paris, as diocesan, of Louvois (both of whom drew from the king a promise that he would never declare this marriage), and of Montchevreuil.

The satiety of the honeymoon, usually so fatal, and especially the honeymoon of such marriages, only consolidated the favor of Madame de Maintenon. Soon after she astonished everybody by the apartments given to her at Versailles, at the top of the grand staircase facing those of the king and on the same floor. From that moment the king always passed some hours with her every day of his life; wherever she might be, she was always lodged near him, and on the same floor if possible.

Madame de Maintenon was a woman of much wit, which the good company, in which she had at first been merely suffered but in which she soon shone, had much polished and oranamented with knowledge of the world, and which gallantry had rendered of the most agreeable kind. Incomparable grace, an easy manner, and yet measured and respectful, which, in consequence of her long obscurity, had become natural to her, marvellously aided her talents—with language gentle, exact, well expressed, and naturally eloquent and brief. Her best time, for she was three or four years older than the king, had been the dainty phrase period—the super-fine gallantry days—in a word, the time of the *"ruelles,"* * as it was called; and it had so influenced her that she always retained evidences of it.

Her inconstancy was of the most dangerous kind. With the exception of some of her old friends, to whom she had good reasons for remaining faithful, she favored people one moment only to cast them off the next. You were admitted to an audience with her, for instance; you pleased her in some manner; and forthwith she unbosomed herself to you as though you had known her from childhood. At the second audience you found her dry, laconic, cold. You racked your brains to discover the cause of this change. Mere loss of time!—Flightiness was the sole reason of it.

Devoutness was her strong point; by that she held her place. The profound ignorance in which the king had been kept all his life rendered him from the first an easy prey to the Jesuits, for he was devout with the grossest ignorance.

The magnificent establishment of Saint-Cyr followed closely upon the revocation of the Edict of Nantes. Madame de Montespan had founded at Paris an establishment for the instruction of young girls in all sorts of fine and ornamental work. Emulation gave Madame de Maintenon higher and vaster views which, while

---

* *Ruelle* is, properly speaking, the space left between the bed and the wall, where intimate visitors sometimes sat; but it came by degrees to sig-nify any little *sanctum* where ladies received their gossips.

gratifying the poor nobility, would cause her to be regarded as protectress in whom all the nobility would feel interested.

It must not be imagined that in order to maintain her position Madame de Maintenon had need of no address. Her reign, on the contrary, was one of continual intrigue.

Ordinarily, as soon as she rose, she went to Saint-Cyr, dined in her apartment there alone, or with some favorite, directed the affairs of the house, and returned to Versailles just as the king was ready to enter her rooms.

Toward nine o'clock in the evening two waiting women came to undress her. Immediately afterwards, her *maître d'hôtel,* or a *valet de chambre* brought her her supper—soup, or something light. As soon as she had finished her meal, her women put her to bed, and all this in the presence of the king and his minister, who did not cease working or speak lower. This done, ten o'clock had arrived; the curtains of Madame de Maintenon were drawn, and the king went to supper, after saying good night to her.

When with the king in her own room, they each occupied an armchair, with a table between them, at either side of the fireplace, hers toward the bed, the king's with the back to the wall, where was the door of the antechamber; two stools were before the table, one for the minister who came to work, the other for his papers.

During the king's working hours Madame de Maintenon read or worked at tapestry. She heard all that passed between the king and his minister, for they spoke out loud. Rarely did she say anything, or, if so, it was of no moment. The king often asked her opinion; then she replied with great discretion.

For the king was constantly on his guard, not only against Madame de Maintenon but against his ministers also. Many a time it happened that when sufficient care had not been taken, and he perceived that a minister or a general wished to favor a relative or protégé of Madame de Maintenon, he firmly opposed the appointment on that account alone, and the remarks he uttered thereupon made Madame de Maintenon very timid and very measured when she wished openly to ask a favor.

When the king traveled, his coach was always full of women:

his mistresses, afterwards his bastards, his daughters-in-law, sometimes Madame, and other ladies when there was room. In the coach, during his journeys, there were always all sorts of things to eat, [such] as meat, pastry, fruit. A quarter of a league was not passed over before the king asked if somebody would not eat. He never ate anything between meals himself, not even fruit; but he amused himself by seeing others do so, aye, and to bursting. You were obliged to be hungry, merry, and to eat with appetite; otherwise he was displeased and even showed it. And yet after this, if you supped with him at table the same day, you were compelled to eat with as good a countenance as though you had tasted nothing since the previous night. He was as inconsiderate in other and more delicate matters; and ladies, in his long drives and stations, had often occasion to curse him. The Duchess of Chevreuse once rode all the way from Versailles to Fontainebleau in such extremity that several times she was well-nigh losing consciousness.

The king, who was fond of air, liked all the windows to be lowered; he would have been much displeased had any lady drawn a curtain for protection against sun, wind, or cold. No inconvenience or incommodity was allowed to be even perceived.

Madame de Maintenon, who feared the air and many other inconveniences, could gain no privilege over the others. All she obtained, under pretence of modesty and other reasons, was permission to journey apart; but whatever condition she might be in, she was obliged to follow the king and be ready to receive him in her rooms by the time he was ready to enter them. She made many journeys to Marly in a state such as would have saved a servant from movement. She made one to Fontainebleau when it seemed not unlikely that she would die on the road! In whatever condition she might be, the king went to her at his ordinary hour and did what he had projected, though several times she was in bed, profusely sweating away a fever.

Nothing remains but to describe the outside life of this monarch, during my residence at the court.

At eight o'clock the chief *valet de chambre* on duty, who alone had slept in the royal chamber and who had dressed himself, awoke the king. The chief physician, the chief surgeon, and the nurse (as long as she lived), entered at the same time. The latter kissed the king; the others rubbed and often changed his shirt, because he was in the habit of sweating a great deal. At the quarter, the grand chamberlain was called (or, in his absence, the first gentleman of the chamber), and those who had, what was called the *grandes entrées*. The chamberlain (or chief gentleman) drew back the curtains which had been closed again, and presented the holy water from the vase, at the head of the bed. These gentlemen stayed but a moment, and that was the time to speak to the king, if any one had anything to ask of him, in which case the rest stood aside. When, contrary to custom, nobody had aught to say, they were there but for a few moments. He who had opened the curtains and presented the holy water presented also a prayer book. Then all passed into the cabinet of the council. A very short religious service being over the king called; they reentered. The same officer gave him his dressing gown; immediately after, other privileged courtiers entered, and then everybody, in time to find the king putting on his shoes and stockings, for he did almost everything himself and with address and grace. Every other day we saw him shave himself; and he had a little short wig in which he always appeared, even in bed, and on medicine days. He often spoke of the chase and sometimes said a word to somebody. No toilette table was near him; he had simply a mirror held before him.

As soon as he was dressed, he prayed to God, at the side of his bed, where all the clergy present knelt, the cardinals without cushions, all the laity remaining standing; and the captain of the guards came to the balustrade during the prayer, after which the king passed into his dressing room.

He found there, or was followed by all who had the *entrée,* a very numerous company, for it included everybody in any office. He gave orders to each for the day; thus within a half a quarter of an hour it was known what he meant to do; and then all this crowd left directly. The bastards, a few favorites, and the valets alone were left. It was then a good opportunity for talking with the king, for example, about plans of gardens and buildings; and conversation lasted more or less according to the person engaged in it.

All the court meantime waited for the king in the gallery, the captain of the guard being alone in the chamber seated at the door of the dressing room. During this pause the king gave audiences when he wished to accord any, spoke with whoever he might wish to speak secretly to, and gave secret interviews to foreign ministers in presence of Torcy.

The king went to Mass, where his musicians always sang an anthem. He did not go below except on grand fetes or at ceremonies. While he was going to and returning from Mass, everybody spoke to him who wished, after apprising the captain of the guard, if they were not distinguished; and he came and went by the door of the dressing room into the gallery. During the Mass the ministers assembled in the king's chamber, where distinguished people could go and speak or chat with them. The king amused himself a little upon returning from Mass and asked almost immediately for the council. Then the morning was finished.

On Sunday, and often on Monday, there was a council of state; on Tuesday, a finance council; on Wednesday, council of state; on Saturday, finance council. Rarely were two held in one day or any on Thursday or Friday. Once or twice a month there was a council of dispatches on Monday morning; but the order that the secretaries of state took every morning between the king's rising and his Mass much abridged this kind of business. All the ministers were seated according to rank, except at the council of dispatches, where all stood except the sons of France, the chancellor, and the Duke of Beauvilliers.

Thursday morning was almost always blank. It was the day of audiences that the king wished to give—often unknown to any—back-stair audiences. It was also the grand day taken advantage of by the bastards, the valets, and so forth, because the king had nothing to do. On Friday, after the Mass, the king was with his confessor, and the length of their audiences was limited by nothing and might last until dinner. At Fontainebleau on the mornings when there was no council, the king usually passed from Mass to

Madame de Maintenon's, and so at Trianon and Marly. It was the time for their tête-à-tête without interruption. Often on the days when there was no council the dinner hour was advanced, more or less for the chase or the promenade. The ordinary hour was one o'clock; if the council still lasted, then the dinner waited and nothing was said to the king.

The dinner was always *au petit couvert,* that is, the king ate by himself in his chamber upon a square table in front of the middle window. It was more or less abundant, for he ordered in the morning whether it was to be "a little," or "very little" service. But even at this last, there were always many dishes, and three courses without counting the fruit. The dinner being ready, the principal courtiers entered; then all who were known; and the first gentlemen of the chamber on duty informed the king.

I have seen, but very rarely, Monseigneur and his sons standing at their dinners, the king not offering them seats. I have continually seen there the princes of the blood and the cardinals. I have often seen there also Monsieur, either on arriving from Saint-Cloud to see the king, or arriving from the council of dispatches (the only one he entered), give the king his napkin and remain standing. A little while afterward, the king, seeing that he did not go away, asked him if he would not sit down; he bowed, and the king ordered a seat to be brought for him. A stool was put behind him. Some moments after, the king said, "Nay then, sit down, my brother." Monsieur bowed and seated himself until the end of the dinner, when he presented the napkin.

At other times when he came from Saint-Cloud, the king, on arriving at the table, asked for a plate for Monsieur, or asked him if he would dine. If he refused, he went away a moment after, and there was no mention of a seat; if he accepted, the king asked for a plate for him. The table was square, he placed himself at one end, his back to the dressing room. Then the grand chamberlain (or the first gentleman of the chamber) gave him drink and plates, taking them from him as he finished with them, exactly as he served the king; but Monsieur received all this attention with strongly marked politeness. When he dined thus with the king, he much enlivened the conversation. The king ordinarily spoke

little at table unless some familiar favorite was near. It was the
same at his rising. Ladies scarcely ever were seen at these little
dinners.

Upon leaving the table the king immediately entered his dressing room. That was the time for distinguished people to speak to
him. He stopped at the door a moment to listen, then entered;
very rarely did any one follow him, never without asking him for
permission to do so; and for this few had the courage. If followed,
he placed himself in the embrasure of the window nearest to the
door of the dressing room, which immediately closed of itself and
which you were obliged to open yourself on quitting the king.
This also was the time for the bastards and the valets.

The king amused himself by feeding his dogs and remained
with them more or less time, then asked for his wardrobe, changed
before the very few distinguished people it pleased the first gentleman of the chamber to admit there, and immediately went out by
the backstairs into the court of marble to get into his coach. From
the bottom of that staircase to the coach, any one spoke to him
who wished.

The king was fond of air and when deprived of it his health
suffered; he had headaches and vapors caused by the undue use
he had formerly made of perfumes, so that for many years he
could not endure any, except the odor of orange flowers; therefore, if you had to approach anywhere near him you did well not
to carry them.

Since he was but little sensitive to heat or cold, or even to rain,
the weather was seldom sufficiently bad to prevent his going
abroad. He went out for several objects: stag hunting, once or
more each week; shooting in his parks (and no man handled a
gun with more grace or skill), once or twice each week; and
walking in his gardens for exercise, and to see his workmen. Sometimes he made picnics with ladies, in the forest at Marly or at
Fontainebleau; and in this last place, promenades with all the
court around the canal, which was a magnificent spectacle. Nobody followed him in his other promenades but those who held
principal offices, except at Versailles or in the gardens of Trianon.
Marly had a privilege unknown to the other places. On going out

from the château, the king said aloud, "Your hats, gentlemen," and immediately courtiers, officers of the guard, everybody, in fact, covered their heads, because he would have been much displeased had they not done so; and this lasted all the promenade, that is, four or five hours in summer—or in other seasons, when he dined early at Versailles to go and walk at Marly, and not sleep there.

The stag-hunting parties were on an extensive scale. The king did not like too many people at these parties. He did not care for you to go if you were not fond of the chase. He thought that ridiculous, and never bore ill-will to those who stopped away altogether.

It was the same with the playing table, which he liked to see always well frequented—with high stakes—in the saloon at Marly, for lansquenet and other games. He amused himself at Fontainebleau during bad weather by seeing good players at tennis, in which he had formerly excelled; and at Marly by seeing mall played, in which he had also been skillful. Sometimes when there was no council, he would make presents of stuff, or of silverware, or jewels, to the ladies, by means of a lottery, for the tickets of which they paid nothing. Madame de Maintenon drew lots with the others, and almost always gave at once what she gained. The king took no ticket.

Upon returning home from walks or drives, anybody, as I have said, might speak to the king from the moment he left his coach till he reached the foot of his staircase. He changed his dress again, and rested in his dressing room an hour or more, then went to Madame de Maintenon's, and on the way any one who wished might speak to him.

At ten o'clock his supper was served. The captain of the guard announced this to him. A quarter of an hour after the king came to supper, and from the antechamber of Madame de Maintenon to the table again, any one spoke to him who wished. This supper was always on a grand scale, the royal household (that is, the sons and daughters of France) at table, and a large number of courtiers and ladies present, sitting or standing. And on the evening before the journey to Marly [there were] all those ladies who wished to take part in it. That was called presenting yourself for Marly. Men asked in the morning, simply saying to the king, "Sire, Marly." In later years the king grew tired of this, and a valet wrote up in the gallery the names of those who asked. The ladies continued to present themselves.

After supper the king stood some moments, his back to the balustrade of the foot of his bed, encircled by all his court; then, with bows to the ladies, passed into his cabinet, where on arriving, he gave his orders. He passed a little less than an hour there, seated in an armchair, with his legitimate children and bastards, his grandchildren, legitimate and otherwise, and their husbands or wives. Monsieur in another armchair; the princesses upon stools, Monseigneur and all the other princes standing.

The king, wishing to retire, went and fed his dogs; then said good night, passed into his chamber to the *ruelle* of his bed, where he said his prayers, as in the morning, then undressed. He said good night with an inclination of the head, and while everybody was leaving the room stood at the corner of the mantelpiece, where he gave the order to the colonel of the guards alone. Then commenced what was called the *petit coucher,* at which only the specially privileged remained. That was short. They did not leave until he got into bed. It was a moment to speak to him.

On medicine days, which occurred about once a month, the king remained in bed, then heard Mass. The royal household came to see him for a moment, and Madame de Maintenon seated herself in the armchair at the head of his bed. The king dined in bed about three o'clock, everybody being allowed to enter the room, then rose, and the privileged alone remained. He passed afterward into his dressing room, where he held a council, and afterward went, as usual, to Madame de Maintenon's and supped at ten o'clock, according to custom.

During all his life, the king failed only once in his attendance at Mass. It was with the army, during a forced march; he missed no fast day, unless really indisposed. Some days before Lent, he publicly declared that he should be very much displeased if any one ate meat or gave it to others, under any pretext. He ordered the *grand prévôt* to look to this and report all cases of disobedience.

But no one dared to disobey his commands, for they would soon have found out the cost. They extended even to Paris, where the lieutenant of police kept watch and reported. For twelve or fifteen years he had himself not observed Lent, however. At church he was very respectful. During his Mass everybody was obliged to kneel at the *Sanctus* and to remain so until after the communion of the priest; and if he heard the least noise, and saw anybody talking during the Mass, he was much displeased. He took the Communion five times a year, in the collar of the Order, band, and cloak. On Holy Thursday he served the poor at dinner; at the Mass he said his chaplet (he knew no more), always kneeling, except at the Gospel.

He was always clad in dresses more or less brown, lightly embroidered, but never at the edges, sometimes with nothing but a gold button, sometimes black velvet. He wore always a vest of cloth, or of red, blue, or green satin, much embroidered. He wore no ring and no jewels, except in the buckles of his shoes, garters, and hat, the latter always trimmed with Spanish point, with a white feather. He had always the *cordon bleu* outside, except on fetes, when he wore it inside, with eight or ten millions of precious stones attached.

Rarely a fortnight passed that the king did not go to Saint Germain, even after the death of King James the Second. The Court of Saint Germain came also to Versailles, but oftener to Marly, and frequently to sup there; and no fete or ceremony took place to which they were not invited, and at which they were not received with all honors. Nothing could compare with the politeness of the king for this court, or with the air of gallantry and of majesty with which he received it at any time.

The king was but little regretted. His valets and a few other people felt his loss, scarcely anybody else. Monsieur le Duc d'Orléans could scarcely be expected to feel much grief for him. And those who may have been expected to did not consider it necessary to do their duty.

Paris, tired of a dependence that had enslaved everything, breathed again in the hope of liberty, and with joy at seeing at an end the authority of so many people who abused it. The provinces, in despair at their ruin and their annihilation, breathed again and leaped for joy; and the *parlement* and the robe destroyed by edicts and by revolutions flattered themselves: the first that they should figure, the other that they should find themselves free. The people, ruined, overwhelmed, desperate, gave thanks to God, with a scandalous éclat, for a deliverance their most ardent desires had not anticipated.

No foreign court exulted: all plumed themselves upon praising and honoring his memory. As for our ministry and the intendants of the provinces, the financiers and what may be called the *canaille,* they felt all the extent of their loss. We shall see if the realm was right or wrong in the sentiments it held, and whether it found soon after that it had gained or lost.

VOLTAIRE

A Neo-Augustan Age

WHAT GREAT CHANGES Louis XIV brought about in
the state! And such changes were useful since they are
still in force. [Louis XIV's] ministers vied with each other in
their eagerness to assist him. The details, indeed the whole execution of such schemes, was doubtless due to them, but his was
the general organization. There can be no shadow of doubt that
the magistrates would never have reformed the laws, the finances
of the country would not have been put on a sound basis, or
discipline introduced into the army, or a regular police force instituted throughout the kingdom; there would have been no fleets,

From Voltaire, *Age of Louis XIV,* edited by Ernest Rhys and translated
by Martyn P. Pollack (Everyman's Library, n.d.), pp. 333–338.

no encouragement accorded to the arts; all these things would never have been peacefully and steadily accomplished in such a short period and under so many different ministers had there not been a ruler to conceive of such great schemes, and with a will strong enough to carry them out.

His own glory was indissolubly connected with the welfare of France, and never did he look upon his kingdom as a noble regards his land, from which he extracts as much as he can that he may live in luxury. Every king who loves glory loves the public weal; he had no longer a Colbert or a Louvois when, about 1698, he commanded each comptroller to present a detailed description of his province for the instruction of the Duke of Burgundy. By this means it was possible to have an exact record of the whole kingdom and a correct census of the population. The work was of the greatest utility, although not every comptroller had the ability and industry of Monsieur de Lamoignon of Baville. Had the comptroller of every province carried out the king's intent so well as the magistrate of Languedoc with regard to the numbering of the population, this collection of records would have been one of the finest achievements of the age. Some of them are well done, but a general scheme was lacking since the same orders were not issued to each comptroller. It is to be wished that each one had given in separate columns a statement of the number of inhabitants of each estate, such as nobles, citizens, laborers, artisans, workmen, cattle of all kinds, fertile, mediocre, and poor land, all clergy, both orthodox and secular, their revenues, and those of the towns and communes.

In most of the records submitted all these details are confused; the matter is not well thought out and inexact; one must search, often with great difficulty, for the needed information such as a minister should have ready to hand and be able to take in at a glance so as to ascertain with ease the forces, needs, and resources at his disposal. The scheme was excellent and, had it been methodically carried out, would have been of the greatest utility.

The foregoing is a general account of what Louis XIV did or attempted to do in order to make his country more flourishing. It seems to me that one can hardly view all his works and efforts

without some sense of gratitude, or without being stirred by the
love for the public weal which inspired them. Let the reader picture to himself the condition today, and he will agree that Louis
XIV did more good for his country than twenty of his predecessors
together; and what he accomplished fell far short of what he might
have done. The war that ended with the Peace of Ryswick began
the ruin of that flourishing trade established by his minister Colbert, and the war of the succession completed it.

Had he devoted the immense sums which were spent on the
aqueducts and works at Maintenon for conveying water to Versailles—works that were interrupted and rendered useless—to beau-
tifying Paris and completing the Louvre, had he expended on Paris
a fifth part of the money spent in transforming nature at Versailles,
Paris would be in its entire length and breadth as beautiful as the
quarter embracing the Tuileries and the Pont-Royal; it would
have become the most magnificent city in the world.

It is a great thing to have reformed the laws, but justice has
not been powerful enough to suppress knavery entirely. It was
thought to make the administration of justice uniform; it is so in
criminal cases, in commercial cases, and in judicial procedure; it
might also be so in the laws that govern the fortunes of private
citizens.

It is in the highest degree undesirable that the same tribunal
should have to give decisions on more than a hundred different
customs. Territorial rights, doubtful, burdensome or merely troublesome to the community, still survive as relics of a feudal government that no longer exists; they are the rubbish from the ruins of
a gothic edifice.

We do not claim that the different classes of the nation should
all be subject to the same law. It is obvious that the customs of
the nobility, clergy, magistrates, and husbandmen must all be different, but it is surely desirable that each class should be subject
to the same law throughout the kingdom; that what is just or
right in Champagne should not be deemed unjust or wrong in
Normandy. Uniformity in every branch of administration is a
virtue; but the difficulties that beset its achievement are enough to
frighten the boldest statesman. It is to be regretted that Louis XIV

did not dispense more readily with the dangerous expedient of employing tax farmers, an expedient to which he was driven by the continual advance drawings he made on his revenues. . . .

Had he not thought that his mere wish would suffice to compel a million men to change their religion, France would not have lost so many citizens. Nevertheless, this country, in spite of the shocks and losses she has sustained, is still one of the most flourishing in the world, since all the good that Louis XIV did for her still bears fruit, and the mischief that was difficult not to do in stormy times has been remedied. Posterity, which passes judgment on kings, and whose judgment they should continually have before them, will acknowledge, weighing the greatness and defects of that monarch, that though too highly praised during his lifetime, he will deserve to be so forever, and that he was worthy of the statue raised to him at Montpellier, bearing a Latin inscription whose meaning is "To Louis the Great after his death." A statesman, Don Ustariz, who is the author of works on the finance and trade of Spain, called Louis XIV "a marvel of a man."

All these changes that we have mentioned in the government and all classes of the nation inevitably produced a great change in customs and manners. The spirit of faction, strife, and rebellion, which had possessed the people since the time of Francis II, was transformed into a rivalry to serve their king. With the great land-owning nobles no longer living on their estates, and the governors of the provinces no longer having important posts at their command, each man desired to earn his sovereign's favor alone: and the state became a perfect whole with all its powers centralized.

It was by such means that the court was freed from the intrigues and conspiracies which had troubled the state for so many years. There was but a single plot under the rule of Louis XIV, which was instigated in 1674 by La Truaumont, a Norman nobleman, ruined by debauchery and debts, and aided and abetted by a man of the house of Rohan, master of the hounds of France, of great courage but little discretion.

The arrogance and severity of the Marquis de Louvois had irritated him to such a point that on leaving him one day he entered

Monsieur Caumartin's house, quite beside himself, and throwing himself on a couch, exclaimed: "Either Louvois dies . . . or I do." Caumartin thought that this outburst was only a passing fit of anger, but the next day, when the same young man having asked him if he thought the people of Normandy were satisfied with the government, he perceived signs of dangerous plans. "The times of the Fronde have passed away," he told him; "believe me, you will ruin yourself, and no one will regret you." The chevalier did not believe him, and threw himself headlong into the conspiracy of La Truaumont. The only other person to enter into the plot was a chevalier of Préaux, a nephew of La Truaumont, who, beguiled by his uncle, won over his mistress, the Marquise de Villiers. Their object and hope was not and could not have been to raise a new party in the kingdom; they merely aimed at selling and delivering Quillebeuf into the hands of the Dutch and letting the enemy into Normandy. It was rather a base and poorly contrived piece of treachery than a conspiracy. The torture of all the guilty parties was the only result of this senseless and useless crime, which today is practically forgotten.

The only risings in the provinces were feeble disorders on the part of the populace, which were easily suppressed. Even the Huguenots remained quiet until their houses of worship were pulled down. In a word, the king succeeded in transforming a hitherto turbulent people into a peace-loving nation, who were dangerous only to their foes, after having been their own enemies for more than a hundred years. They acquired softer manners without impairing their courage.

The houses that all the great nobles built or bought in Paris, and their wives who lived there in fitting style, formed schools of gentility, which gradually drew the youth of the city away from the tavern life, which was for so long the fashion and which only encouraged reckless debauchery. Manners depend upon such little things that the custom of riding on horseback in Paris tended to produce frequent brawls, which ceased when the practice was discontinued.

We have finally come to enjoy luxury only in taste and convenience. The crowd of pages and liveried servants has disappeared, to allow greater freedom in the interior of the home. Empty pomp and outward show have been left to nations who know only how to display their magnificence in public and are ignorant of the art of living. The extreme case that [one] obtains in the intercourse of society, affable manners, simple living and the culture of the mind have combined to make Paris a city that, as regards the harmonious life of the people, is probably vastly superior to Rome and Athens during the period of their greatest splendor.

These ever-present advantages, always at the service of every science, every art, taste, or need; so many things of real utility combined with so many others merely pleasant and coupled with the freedom peculiar to Parisians, all these attractions induce a large number of foreigners to travel to take up their residence in this, as it were, birthplace of society. The few natives who leave their country are those who, on account of their talents, are called elsewhere, and are an honor to their native land; or they are the scum of the nation who endeavor to profit by the consideration which the name of France inspires; or they may be emigrants who place their religion even before their country, and depart elsewhere to meet with misfortune or success, following the example of their forefathers who were expelled from France by that irreparable insult to the memory of the great Henry IV—the revocation of his perpetual law of the Edict of Nantes; or finally they are officers dissatisfied with the ministry, culprits who have escaped the vigorous laws of a justice that is at times ill-administered, a thing that happens in every country in the world.

People complain at no longer seeing that pride of bearing at court. There are certainly no longer petty autocrats, as at the time of the Fronde, under Louis XIII, and in earlier ages; but true greatness has come to light in that host of nobles so long compelled in former times to demean themselves by serving overpowerful subjects. Today one sees gentlemen—citizens who would formerly have considered themselves honored to be servants of these noblemen—now become their equals and very often their superiors in the military service.

The more that services rendered are accounted above titles of nobility, the more flourishing is the condition of the state.

The age of Louis XIV has been compared with that of Augustus. It is not that their power and individual events are comparable; Rome and Augustus were ten times more considered in the world than Louis XIV and Paris, but it must be remembered that Athens was the equal of the Roman Empire in all things whose value is not dependent upon might and power.

We must also bear in mind that there is nothing in the world today to compare with ancient Rome and Augustus, yet Europe taken as a whole is vastly superior to the whole of the Roman Empire. In the time of Augustus there was but a single nation, while at the present day there are several nations—all civilized, warlike, and enlightened—that cultivate arts unknown to the Greeks and Romans; and of these nations, there is none that has shone more brilliantly in every sphere for nearly a century than the nation molded to a great extent by Louis XIV.

ERNEST LAVISSE

The Self-Defeating Reign
of Louis XIV

WE HAVE ARRIVED at certain conclusions about this long reign after each of the principal chapters of its history. Our over-all conclusion must be based on the fact that the monarchy survived the king for only seventy-four years, a period of approximately the same length as his reign. Louis XIV had exhausted the French monarchy.

The endless wars, the immense sums spent on luxuries, the errors of an exaggerated Colbertism that Colbert himself would

From Ernest Lavisse, *Histoire de la France depuis les origines jusqu'à la Revolution: Louis XIV, la fin du règne*. Vol. VIII, Part I (Paris: Hachette, 1911), pp. 476–480. Translation © 1972 Hill and Wang, a division of Farrar, Straus & Giroux, Inc.

have repudiated, a system of taxation that tended to discourage production, the revocation of the Edict of Nantes and its drain upon the resources of the country—all these factors converged to reduce an industrious country to a condition of poverty that has been amply and painfully documented. The financial mismanagement of the state may be compared with that of the private individual who, born rich, spends every year beyond his means, keeps his head above water by ruinous expedients, loses his credit with tradespeople, makes gestures of selling his silver and offering to let his steward pawn his jewelry, stoops to fraud, and winds up in bankruptcy.

Louis XIV considered his religious policies the most important concern of his government, but he had no success with them. He wished his reign to be an "edifying pontificate," but the ecumenical pontiff, the pope, would tolerate no rivalry from this provincial pontiff. After some sweeping gestures and haughty invective Louis XIV submitted like a shamefaced penitent who begs that his admission of error be kept secret. Louis XIV had no greater luck in restoring his subjects to the unity of the faith. He had declared that he was prepared to make any sacrifice to defend the faith within his realm. His sacrifices, although great, remained futile: the last years of his reign witnessed a revival of Protestantism and Jansenism. The Protestants and the Jansenists remained the enemies of the government that had persecuted them, for hatred and bitterness stemming from religious conflict tend to last as long as the religion itself. The victims of religious persecution would rally to the approaching struggle against absolute monarchy. Political and religious issues were already hopelessly entangled. Gallicanism, more or less betrayed by the king, took refuge in the *parlements;* it would break its sullen silence immediately after the king's death.

Louis XIV scored his clearest success in the imposition of political obedience. The cost of this success was high. Every year there were fresh revolts, some of which were quite serious. The detailed history of these insurrections reveals many premonitory symptoms of the revolution. Still the rumblings of this far-off thunder were brief and intermittent; only a few foresaw the actual storm, and perhaps even these few did not trust their own presentiments. Besides, it was usually only the poorest of "private persons" who rose in revolt, and these were quickly dispatched by the firing squad, the gallows, or sentence to the hulks. What counted was the obedience of the corps, that is, the *parlements,* the nobility, and the clergy.

Did Louis XIV ever ask himself if there were some other way for people to serve the state beyond obedience? Others quite close to him did. Fénelon decided that they should "recall the true form of the kingship and moderate despotism, the cause of all our troubles." They should "persuade the nation as a whole that it alone could protect the monarchy from the consequences of its ruinous course." If Louis XIV did in fact "recall the ancient form of the kingship," it was merely with disdain, and he most assuredly did not believe the course of the monarchy to be "ruinous." He described Fénelon as "a fine mind given to fantasy." For him all the prognostications of the reformers were fantasy; he acknowledged no reality beyond himself. He assumed complete mastery; he became an autocrat whispering his commands in the ear of the man who must execute them. His ministers imitated him, each in his own sphere of authority; in this way the bureaucracy took form. Through the activity of the intendants it made inroads everywhere, even into the smallest communities and the most insignificant workshops, heaping rule upon rule and regulation upon regulation, until the mass of statutes governing merchants and artisans were equal in volume to the whole corpus of Roman law. It was impossible to draw one free breath anywhere within the kingdom.

Louis XIV was not the "enlightened" despot that Colbert wanted him to be. He ignored anything that did not bother him personally as king and everything that had been so bothersome to Colbert: the disparities of the provinces in customs, weights and measures, tax assessment and collection. In all these areas anarchy lurked beneath the smooth surface of monarchical order. In the same way he continued the privileges of the church and the politically subjugated nobility, and preserved the *parlements* even though he had withdrawn "their authority and, as it were, their distinction." What was soon to be called the *ancien régime*—an amalgam of outworn custom, shabby décor, and rights without duties, ruins of the past huddling beneath an omnipotence that shut its eyes to the future—cannot be ascribed entirely to Louis XIV, but it was he who aggravated its imperfections and thus consigned it to its eventual destruction.

He extended the frontiers of the realm. The annexation of Roussillon, Artois, and Alsace cannot be ascribed to him; that had been the work of Louis XIII and the two cardinals. But he did conquer and hold Franche-Comté, part of Flanders, part of Hainaut, Cambrésis, and Strasbourg. With a ring of splendid fortresses he made his kingdom an "entrenched camp of twenty million men." These annexations were important events in the history of the French national territory, but important as they were, the strength of France in 1661 and the relative weakness of the rest of Europe permitted one to hope for more.

Here we must reiterate that the annexation of the Spanish Netherlands would have been a great boon to France, for it would have placed Paris at the geographical center of the realm and corrected its dangerous proximity to the frontier. What is more, it would have balanced the geniuses and temperaments of north and south in the national character, recruited prosperous and hardworking subjects, extended the coastline to the mouth of the Scheldt, and added the port of Antwerp to the ports of Dunkirk, Bordeaux, and Marseille. This conquest might have been accomplished without undue violence to natural boundaries or serious offense to the regional loyalties of the inhabitants. What would be a crime in our day would not have been so then. Only the play of chance operating through marriage and inheritance had left these Belgian provinces subject to Madrid. It is true, of course, that these provinces, linked since Burgundian times, had the sense of a common destiny, and were as little fond of their neighbors in France as they were of their neighbors in Holland. The idea of a Belgian homeland, however, was still far in the future. The towns of Artois and Flanders had quickly become French and even patriotic. Alsace too, after its separation from an as yet unintegrated Germany, had readily turned toward France.

The France of Colbert and Seignelay, the France of Dunkirk, Brest, Rochefort, Bordeaux, and Marseille, which had colonized

Canada, Louisiana, and the West Indies, was capable of becoming as "powerful on the sea as it was on land," in the words of Colbert, who wished to assure France of full "might of arms" through the combination of land and naval forces. As late as 1689 the king's navy had been equal to the combined naval forces of England and Holland.

No doubt, the annexation of the Spanish Netherlands and the development of France into a great maritime power would have encountered stiff resistance, and we have been careful to concede that it has always been difficult for France to pursue her amphibious vocation. Nonetheless, we are free to imagine that, given the exceptional opportunities that were offered to him, Louis XIV might have accomplished far more, had he not based his somewhat contradictory policies on the fixed idea of gaining glory for himself through the humiliation of others. His behavior may be characterized as a mixture of prudence, guile, and eruptions of vainglory that in a single moment undid the work of long and patient calculation. At some point he had outraged, insulted, or duped everyone, and coalitions against him continued to widen until they had embraced all of Europe. His interminable wars were conducted by a man who had all the qualifications of a good staff officer but lacked the mind of a general and the courage of a soldier.

The love of France for its king approached adoration. In his words and gestures France admired the reflection of its own grandeur and glory. When it began to suffer cruelly in consequence of his errors, anger welled up within, and it seemed as if the glory of Louis XIV was quite extinguished, although it was soon to blaze forth anew. At the beginning of the following reign there would be attempts to do things differently. These were doomed to failure, for Louis XIV had given old France its definitive political form— despotism. None of his successors knew how to conduct this form of government, and the strange situation arose in which one could "find despotism everywhere, but the despot nowhere." Domestic and foreign policy suffered from weakness and incoherence, and France declined. At this point Voltaire redirected attention to the glory of Louis XIV, whose faults had been forgotten.

Since that time the Great King's reputation has survived the assaults of harsh critics and impartial historians. Although reason may discern the destructive undercurrents of his reign, its brilliant surface continues to seduce our imagination. It is all very pleasant to evoke the memory of this colorful man, who was by no means an evil one and was possessed of numerous qualities, even virtues, as well as grace, beauty, and a talent for saying things nicely. While France shone brightly, he represented its brilliance; when it was exhausted, he refused to acknowledge its exhaustion. From the splendid opening until the gloomy scenes of the final act, the king sustained his role amid a setting of fantastic splendor. Palaces rose from nowhere; fountains sprang forth from dry earth; trees came from Fontainebleau and Compiègne. His retinue sang the part of the chorus in a tragedy so remote from us that it seems to take on the charm and grandeur of classical antiquity.

PIERRE GOUBERT

A Man in the Universe

L UCIEN FEBVRE, one of the guiding lights of French historical studies, once wrote that the historian had no business
"to pronounce judgment . . . to set himself up as acting judge of
the valley of Jehosaphat." He said many times that the historian's
besetting sin was the sin of anachronism, although he stated also
that history was "a child of her time" and that none of her practitioners could detach themselves from the preoccupations, currents
of thought, and general "climate" of their own times. One might

From Pierre Goubert, *Louis XIV and Twenty Million Frenchmen,* trans.
Anne Carter (New York: Pantheon Books, Inc., 1970), pp. 289–315. Copy-
right © 1969 by Anne Carter. Reprinted by permission of Pantheon Books,
Inc., a division of Random House, Inc., and Penguin Books Ltd.

also maintain that a degree of passion is necessary to the historian, that it is those works which are most vibrant with personality which remain the most vivid and fertile, even if only because they provoke contradiction and are bound to produce the more important work of analysis and painstaking research inseparable from any serious study.

So let us leave to the sovereign judges, of Jehosaphat or anywhere else, the honor or ridicule of passing judgment on Mazarin's godson. In any case, whoever judges Louis *le dieudonné,* judges chiefly himself. But for the would-be impartial historian, there is one question which cannot be avoided and which does seem to belong genuinely to the historian's province. That is the question of what were the precise extent and limits of King Louis's own personal acts in the course of fifty-five long years which were no more than so many seconds in the whole history of the world.

THE KING'S ACTS: HIS PERSONAL SPHERE

As early as 1661, as he declared in his *Mémoires,* Louis meant to have sole command in every sphere and claimed full responsibility, before the world and all posterity, for everything that should happen in his reign. In spite of constant hard work, he soon found he had to entrust the actual running of certain departments, such as finance or commerce, to a few colleagues, although he still reserved the right to make major decisions himself. There were, however, some aspects of his *métier de roi* to which he clung absolutely and persistently, although his persistence was not invariably absolute. Consequently, it is permissible to single out a kind of personal sphere which the king reserved to himself throughout his reign, although this sphere might vary, while the rest still remained, as it were, under his eye.

As a young man, Louis had promised himself that his own time and posterity should ring with his exploits. If this had been no more than a simple wish, and not an inner certainty, it might be said to have been largely granted.

As a hot-headed young gallant, he flouted kings by his extravagant gestures and amazed them by the brilliance of his court, his entertainments, his tournaments, and his mistresses. As a new Augustus he could claim, for a time, to have been his own Maecenas. Up to the year 1672, all Europe seems to have fallen under the spell of his various exploits and his youthful fame spread even as far as the "barbarians" of Asia. For seven or eight years after that, the armies of Le Tellier and Turenne seemed almost invincible while Colbert's youthful navy and its great admirals won glory off the coast of Sicily. Then, when Europe had pulled itself together, Louis still showed amazing powers of resistance and adaptability. Even when he seemed to be aging, slipping into pious isolation amid his courtiers, he retained the power to astonish with the splendors of his palace at Versailles, his opposition to the pope and the will to make himself into a "new Constantine," and later by allying himself with Rome to "purify" the Catholic religion. When practically on his death bed, he could still impress the English ambassador who came to protest at the building of a new French port next door to the ruins of Dunkirk.

Dead, he became a kind of symbolic puppet for everyone to take over and dress up in his chosen finery. Voltaire used him, in the name of "his" age, as ammunition against Louis XV. On the other side, he long stood as the type of blood-thirsty, warlike, and intolerant despot. Even the nineteenth-century Bourbons preferred to celebrate their descent from "good king Henri" with his white cockade, or from the "martyr" of January 21. The great school of historians which flourished from 1850 until 1915 did not spare him, but studied his entourage and his reign most carefully. In the twentieth century, the royalist academicians Bertrand, with superb naïveté, and Gaxotte, with more talent and disingenuousness, have made him a symbol of order and greatness, of patriotism and even of virtue. At the same time, the teaching of Lavisse which, although hostile, also shows great subtlety and unrivaled scholarship, still dominates the field in the scholarly academic tradition. Finally, there are the young historians, strongly influenced by philosophers, sociologists, and certain economists, who pass over the king's personality and entourage—to be left to the purveyors of historical gossip and romance—in favor of concentrating on those problems of institutions, attitudes of mind, religious observances, social strata, and the great movements of fundamental economic forces which, in their view, transcend mere individuals and events. While all this is going on, the general public is subjected to diatribes on "classicism," which is an illusion, on Versailles and its "significance," the man in the iron mask, the affair of the poisons, on the king's mistresses, successive or contemporaneous, and on the "policy of greatness."

For precisely three centuries, Louis XIV has continued to dominate, fascinate, and haunt men's minds. "The universe and all time" have certainly remembered him, although not always in the way he would have wished. From this point of view, Louis's personal deeds have been a great success. Unfortunately, his memory has attracted a cloud of hatred and contempt as enduring as that which rises from the incense of his worshipers or the pious imitations of a later age.

In his personal desire to enlarge his kingdom, the king was successful. The lands in the north, Strasbourg, Franche-Comté, and the "iron belt" are clear evidence of success. In this way Paris was better protected from invasion. But all these gains had been made by 1681 and later events served only to confirm, rescue, or reduce them. It has even been maintained that considering his strong position in 1661, surrounded by so many kings who were young, unsure of their thrones, or simply incompetent, Louis might have hoped for greater things. He might have aimed at the annexation of the Spanish Netherlands, although Holland and England would always have managed to prevent him. Lorraine was vulnerable and Louis was less powerful there in 1715 than in 1661, while with a little shrewdness or cunning, there were Savoy and Nice to be had, to say nothing of the colonies which he tended to disregard, leaving them to traders, adventurers, priests, and a few of his colleagues. He was satisfied with losing one West Indian island and the gateway to Canada while a handful of brave men were striving to win him an empire in America and another in India.

As absolute head of his diplomatic service and his armies, from beginning to end, he was well served while he relied on men who had been singled out by Mazarin or Richelieu, but he often made a fool of himself by selecting unworthy successors. He was no great warrior. His father and his grandfather had reveled in the reek of the camp and the heady excitement of battle. His preference was always for impressive maneuvers, parades, and good safe sieges rather than the smoke of battle, and as age grew on him he retreated to desk strategy. Patient, secretive, and subtle in constructing alliances, weaving intrigues, and undoing coalitions, he marred all these gifts by ill-timed displays of arrogance, brutality, and unprovoked aggression. In the last analysis, this born aggressor showed his greatness less in triumph than in adversity, but there was never any doubt about his effect on his contemporaries whose feelings toward him were invariably violent and uncompromising. He was admired, feared, hated, and secretly envied.

If, as a good libertine and a poor theologian, he began by taking little interest in the matter of religion, this became, from his fortieth year onward, one of his favorite "personal spheres." But here he met with total lack of success. In his conflict with the great authoritarian and pro-Jansenist pope, Innocent XI, he was forced to give way and, from a passionate Gallican became ultramontane to the point of embarrassing later popes. Against the Jansenists as a matter of policy rather than of doctrine, he only succeeded, despite repeated acts of violence, in strengthening the sect and uniting it with Gallicans in the *parlements* and the Sorbonne and with the *richériste* priests suppressed by the edict of 1695. Whatever may be claimed, the extirpation of the "Calvinist heresy" resulted in the weakening of the kingdom, the strengthening of her neighbors, and a formidable amount of hatred, national and European, whether real or assumed. In the end, not many *religionnaires* were converted. They recanted, resisted, revolted, or appealed to the enemy, and calmly rebuilt their churches in the Midi, while in Paris, the great Huguenot businessmen were generally tolerated because they were indispensable. The Catholic counter-reformation undoubtedly made great strides during the reign owing to the missions, the seminaries which were finally established, and the admirable Jansenist parish priests, but the basic foundations had in fact been laid long before 1661.

For some fifteen or twenty years, it was Louis's ambition to gather around his person the cream of artists and writers. In this field Colbert, who had learned his trade from Mazarin, was able to help him considerably while he had the power and the money. After 1673, money grew short and from 1689 downright scarce, while in the ill-fated year of 1694 even such a magnificent undertaking as the Gobelins very nearly failed. On the other hand, Louis very early began concentrating his efforts on his works at Versailles and later at Marly, and neglecting the rest. After 1680, patronage as a whole slipped away from the monarchy. Ideas became freer and more diversified and the main themes of the eighteenth century began to appear while the critical and scientific spirit progressed rapidly, shaking the old dogmatic ideas, and by that time Louis had largely lost interest in intellectual matters unless it was a case of checking some dangerous "innovation." But for fifteen years, there was a happy meeting of talents which shed, as it were, a luster on the finest period of the reign. The young king had given proof of taste and even of daring. There was in him a very great *"honnête homme,"* in the sense of the period, capable of appreciating, singling out, and making others appreciate (even Molière), and sometimes showing great tolerance. As time went on and he was burdened with other cares, less ably supported and in any case he was growing set in his ways, turning his back on changes in manners and ideas, he became obstinate or frankly gave up. The so-called *"grand siècle,"* with the "Great King" as its patron was a brilliant firework display which lasted no more than fifteen years.

Louis was a child of the Fronde and, although its detailed execution was left to the small fry among his servants, the humbling of all the great "Corps and Estates" of the realm remained his constant concern. The officers' companies were debased, humiliated, and taxed out of existence; the *parlements,* states, communes, and consulates annihilated; the arrogant nobility reduced to begging for his favors where they had once been conspirators and instigators of provincial revolts. Most of the clergy were turned into courtiers, and all the ancient nobility tamed and barred from his councils, while the new were treated with contempt for all the cheapness of their titles. Last of all the Béarnais, Catalans, Cévenols, Bordelais, Poitevins, and, above all, the Bretons, with any others who persisted in untimely uprisings were massacred outright. Such repressive measures were bound, by their very violence, to lead to passionate reactions. The new regency and the new century were certainly to give striking occasion for them.

As the head of a dynasty which he could trace back to Charlemagne and which was, it went without saying, the first in the world, Louis maintained the interests and dignity of his whole family with great arrogance. It was, in the last resort, for his grandson's sake that he embarked on and pursued the War of the Spanish Succession. Once Philip V's future was assured, he turned his attention to his own survival through his remaining legitimate and illegitimate descendants by means of the will of 1714 which he altered in 1715, only to have it broken as soon as he was dead, a will of which we may well ask ourselves whether it was the work of a stubborn, a benighted, or a desperate man.

Everlasting glory, territorial aggrandizement, and dominion abroad; at home mastery of all political and administrative life, of religion, society, and thought, and the protection of the dynasty and the succession: these were the vast spheres which, for all or part of the time, Louis dared to reserve for his sole jurisdiction. The results of his actions varied from dazzling success, through partial or temporary success, to semi-failure and absolute disaster.

For all his bravery and diligence, his frequent opportunism and his sense of greatness, he was, after all, no more than a man with a varied and honorable mixture of virtues and weaknesses. His ministers, also, varied in quality; his executives often lacked means of persuasion, and he was surrounded on all sides by forces which opposed his will and his glory. It remains to take a look at the actions of the men who served him and at the forces with which he had to contend.

The King's Responsibilities:
The Spheres of His Agents

More often than not, and permanently in some cases, administrative details and the complete running of certain sectors of the administration were left to agents appointed by the king and responsible to him. Louis rarely resorted to the cowardly expedient of laying the blame for failure on his subordinates. Not until the end of his life, and notably in the case of the bishops, did he indulge in such pettiness. Everything that was done during his reign was done in his name and Louis's indirect responsibility in matters he had delegated was the same as his direct responsibility in his own personal spheres. Moreover, the two sectors could not help but be closely connected.

A policy of greatness and prestige demanded an efficient and effective administration as well as adequate resources, both military and financial. We have followed the various endeavors undertaken in this field down the years. Now it is time to add up the reckoning.

In order to disseminate the king's commands over great distances and combat the complex host of local authorities, a network of thirty intendants had been established over the country. These were the king's men, dispatched by the king's councils and assisted by correspondents, agents, and *subdélégués* who by 1715 were numerous and well organized. By this time the system was well established and more or less accepted (even in Brittany). It met with reasonable respect and sometimes obedience. Sometimes, not always, since we only have to read the intendants' correspondence to be disabused swiftly of any illusions fostered by old-fashioned textbooks or history notes. The difficulties of communication; the traditions of provincial independence, inalienable rights, and privileges; and the sheer force of inertia all died hard. Lavisse used to say this was a period of absolutism tempered by disobedience. In the depths of the country and the remote provinces, the formula might almost be reversed. Nevertheless, there is no denying that a step forward had been made and that the germ of the splendid administrative systems of Louis XV and of Napoleon was already present in the progress made between 1661 and 1715. Some of the great administrative bodies which subsequently set the tone and example for others, such as the registry office, the postal service, the highway department, were even then in existence, although it must be admitted that the first of these was introduced as a purely fiscal measure, the second farmed out, and the third in an embryonic state.

In one adjacent but vital field, ministers and jurists labored valiantly to reach a unified code of French law, giving the king's laws priority over local custom and simplifying the enormous tangled mass of statute law. Colbert's codes and two or three great collections of law and practice, such as those of Ricard, Domat, and Savary, will serve as examples. But how did all these excellent works fit in with the spirit of the time and with the daily march of justice? Every tiny province still persisted in judging cases according to its own local custom, fixed and written down in the sixteenth century with a mass of later glosses added. The king's law was only one law among many. It had to be ratified by the sovereign courts which, since they could not reject it, had become most skillful in the arts of delay and prevarication. Moreover, royal decrees, even the revocation of the Edict of Nantes, seldom applied to the whole kingdom. Ordinances regulating the maximum rate of interest (the *denier*), for example, varied from one province to the next and were easily circumvented. As for the monetary ordinances, every man turned them to his own advantage: the merchants had their own rates and *équivalences* and the time was not far off when ordinary farm contracts would be coolly inscribed "actions of the prince notwithstanding" in stipulating means of payment. As for the notorious regulations put out by Colbert and his successors, we have already seen, in passing, the extent to which they could be ignored and flouted daily in one city, Beauvais, which was less than eighty kilometers from Paris. Too much interest, routine, privilege, and sheer habit stood in the way for royal legislation to be properly applied. The great efforts toward centralization and unification which were made were only partially successful but they did pave the way for the great legislators and unifiers of the eighteenth century and still more for those of the Revolution and the Empire.

Of the means to the achievement of power and glory, one, diplomacy, was in the hands of individuals rather than institutions. Long before the "great reign" a great tradition had existed which is called to mind in the mere mention of such names as Servien, de Lionne, d'Avaux, not to mention the two formidable cardinal-diplomats. They, their colleagues, their successors, and their children continued the tradition. In their different ways, Louis XIV's diplomats were among the best in Europe but they were up against brilliant adversaries in the Dutch, the British, and the Romans. Two novelties, perhaps, were a degree of "institutionalizing" of a "career in diplomacy" and, more important, the emergence of a much higher level of negotiation of men like Mesnager of Rouen, the great merchants of the realm, whose activities had previously been cloaked in a certain obscurity.

The navy, rescued from virtual oblivion by Colbert who gave it arsenals, shipwrights, gunners, talented designers, its finest captains, and fresh personnel obtained by means of seaboard conscription, distinguished itself particularly from 1672 to 1690. After that, it declined for lack of resources and any real interest on the part of a king who was a landsman at heart, and private enterprise took the lead once more. Even then, Louis and the excellent staff of his navy office did not fail to encourage and make use of the fleets belonging to the shipowners and merchants of the great ports, the capitalists who backed them, and the bold captains who brought them both glory and profit.

The greatest of all the king's great servants were those who helped him to build up an army, which in size and striking force was for the most part equal to all the other armies of Europe put together. They were first Le Tellier and Turenne and later, Louvois and Vauban. Many others of less fame, such as Chamlay, Martinet, Fourilles, and Clerville, would also deserve a place in this unusually lengthy roll of honor if the historian's job were the awarding of laurels, especially military ones. The fighting strength was increased at least fourfold, discipline was improved, among generals as well as officers and men, and a civil administration superimposed, not without a struggle, on the quarrelsome, short-sighted, and in many cases incompetent and dishonest military one. New ranks and new corps were introduced; among them the artillery and the engineers, as well as such new weapons as the flintlock and the fixed bayonet, and a new military architect,

Vauban, all helped to make the army more efficient. Most important of all, the army at last possessed a real *intendance* with its own arsenals, magazines, and regular staging posts. Uniforms became more or less general, providing employment for thousands of workers. The first barracks were an attempt to put an end to the notorious custom of billeting troops in civilian households. The Hôtel des Invalides was built, on a grand scale. The instrument which these invaluble servants placed at their master's disposal was almost without parallel in their time, a genuine royal army, growing ever larger and more diversified, modern and disciplined.

Naturally, the people of the realm were not always bursting with pride in it. The army was very expensive. It still went in for billeting and foraging, even within the borders of the kingdom, and still, like the navy with its "press gang" in the ports, claimed far too many young men who would have preferred to stay at home in their own villages. Too much conscription and, to an even greater extent, the militia were the cause of much of the king's unpopularity in his old age.

To please his trusted servant Colbert, the king, while a young man, did try for a time to study his finances and to keep simple accounts of his private income and expenditure, but he always believed in his heart of hearts that such occupations were beneath his royal dignity. [It can be] shown in some detail how Colbert's work was endangered by the first coalition (1673) and ruined by the two which followed. Quite obviously, it was not the king's building program, his court, his "favors," or his petty cash which wrecked the kingdom's finances once they had been put in order by a good finance minister. The one and only reason was the length of the wars and the ever-broadening fronts on which they were fought.

Louis's finance ministers, remarkable both for honesty and ingenuity, did what they could to provide for the constantly renewed wars. They acquiesced in or invented measures which, with more courage and determination, might have been real and radical reforms: the capitation tax, the *dixième,* the *Caisse des Emprunts,* and even the introduction of paper money. But all in all, they could not do more than scrape the utmost from a financial, social, and administrative system so petrified that it rejected even the slightest attempt at reform. The richest went on paying ludicrously little or nothing at all. The state failed to maintain its credit or to set up a national bank, while England was managing to do so in spite of all her difficulties. The *ancien régime* under Louis XIV was an accumulation of old forms, old habits, and old ideas, the more deeply respected the older they were, which proved incapable of reshaping or even of reforming its financial system. To do so would have meant denying its very nature, tearing down the antiquated edifice which had been shored up a score of times although it still presented a glittering façade to the world, and daring to face up to the march of time and the nature of things. The old house stood for another seventy-five years. No one in 1715 could have foreseen how comparatively imminent was its collapse.

For all this, successes, good intentions, failures, inadequacies, and refusals, Louis XIV remains, through his ministers, ultimately responsible.

Responsible, that is, if it can be truly said that any man, even a king and a great king, has the power to act effectively against the great political, demographic, economic, and intellectual forces which may, after all, finally command the over-all development of a kingdom which is not alone in the world. Among these forces were some which, whether the king knew it or not, were acting directly against him. Others, working more slowly and obscurely and almost invariably unknown to the king, had nonetheless a powerful long-term effect which some historians have regarded as crucial.

THE OPPOSING FORCES

An ambition to astonish the world with magnificence and great armies is all very well so long as the world is prepared to be astonished.

At the beginning of his reign, when Louis surveyed the rest of Europe, he saw nothing but weakness and decline. Some of his observations, as regards Spain and Italy, were perfectly correct. In others, he was mistaken. He stupidly underestimated the United Provinces, as though a small, bourgeois, and Calvinist population were an inevitable sign of weakness. Yet another observation was swiftly belied by the changes which occurred in two highly dissimilar entities—England and the Empire.

Louis XIV found himself balked at every turn by the diplomacy and dogged courage, as well as by the seapower and the immense wealth of the United Provinces. It is no longer fashionable to believe that the "Golden Age" of the Dutch was over in 1661. For a long time after that, their Bank, their Stock Exchange, their India Company, their fleets, and their florins remained as powerful as ever. The invasion of 1672 weakened them only temporarily and even in 1715, whatever may be said to the contrary, the Dutch sent as many or even more ships than before to the Baltic, to Japan (where they were the only nation to trade), to Batavia, to Asia, and all over the high seas. Their wealth, currency, and bankers remained powerful and respected and often decisive. Their policy was not yet tied directly to England's. It was simply that they no longer enjoyed undivided supremacy: another nation's economy had reached the same level and was about to overtake them.

Louis XIV always did his best to ignore economic factors, but they would not be denied and they took their revenge. In addition, Louis's aggression in 1672 had a miraculous effect upon the patriotic feelings of the Dutch and brought about the revolution which carried William of Orange to the leadership of the Republic. The last quarter of the seventeenth century belongs, in fact, as much to William as to Louis. Stubborn, clever, with the whole wealth of the Republic behind him, William was a determined enemy, in spite of his bad luck in the field, and he was the soul and the financier of all the coalitions. No sooner was he dead than his place was taken by a Dutchman of no less greatness who had already seconded him on the continent, Heinsius.

With masterly ineptitude, the king of France, having made William master of the United Provinces, went on to help make him king of England. For a long time, Louis XIV believed he had England at his mercy because he thought himself sure of both Charles II, who was in his pay, and the papist James II, and also because he was convinced that the island kingdom must have been greatly weakened by a revolution and by Cromwell. This was to reckon without the English constitutional traditions, without the deeply anti-Catholic religious feelings of most Englishmen, and without the fleet, the London merchants, and the pound sterling. Louis XIV's English policy from 1685 to 1712 was one long series of mistakes and almost continual provocations. During that time, the power of Parliament, of trade, of seapower, and of the Bank of England was growing and reaching out across the seas to lay the firm foundations of a strong empire, which would ultimately devour the French empire and was, indeed, already nibbling at it. The final quarter of the seventeenth century was marked by the rise of Britain, spectacularly endorsed by the treaties of 1713, much more than by the dominance of France.

Even the Empire, for which Louis had nothing but contempt, though impotent and enfeebled by the treaties of Westphalia, was ruled by a monarch who, despite his initial youth, nervousness, and timidity, succeeded gradually in making an unexpected recovery and emerging as the leader of a crusade against the Turks. He had good advisers and with the support of the pope, the majority of the German princes, and kings like Sobieski, more Catholic than politic, he succeeded in halting the infidel advance for the first time in three hundred years and then in driving them back to their Balkan fastnesses. By liberating Vienna, Hungary, and Transylvania, he enlarged his domains much more than Louis had extended his and relieved Europe of the Ottoman pressure once and for all. As a result he became, in his own lands, the great emperor who had succeeded where all others had failed. Artists and writers sang his praises and for all good Germans this end of the century was the time, not of Louis the Devastator but of Leopold the Victorious.

Louis XIV, for his part, put off such German sympathizers as he possessed in 1661, offending them by his ravages and his measures against the Protestants and no longer able to attract them with his impoverished treasury which was powerless in competition with the florins and the sterling which could now purchase new allegiances across the Rhine. It may be that the absence of any French contingent from the great Catholic victory of Kahlenberg in 1683 was considered shameful. It was undoubtedly a mistake, which was more serious. Violent propaganda began to issue from certain quarters in the Empire, lambasting the errors of the king of France and the sanguinary excesses of his troops. In this way, Louis XIV made his own contribution to the birth of German national feeling. Not even Leopold's death in 1705 released him, for he had earned the undying hatred of his successors. By an additional irony, Prince Eugène, who had at first asked nothing better than to be allowed to serve France, outlived Leopold as Heinsius and Marlborough had outlived William.

What of the suggestion that, as a kind of compensation, French language, art, and letters were making a peaceful conquest of the Europe of the coalition? It is true that every ruler and every petty princeling was, or soon would be, longing to have his own Versailles and his own Maintenon and set about reproducing them with varying success, but even so, we incorrigibly patriotic Frenchmen should not be in too great a hurry to proclaim a triumph of the French spirit. To do so would be, firstly, to ignore the real character of baroque art, with its strong Austrian and Spanish elements. And then, what of Locke and Leibniz, to mention only two, whose influence was by no means negligible? And were the prodigious advances in the scientific field a purely French affair? And finally, if it did become fashionable in certain foreign circles to adopt French airs and graces, how many eminent Frenchmen from Descartes onward also went abroad, to Holland and still more to England, to find a breath of freedom?

Louis found other forces of opposition within the borders of his kingdom. We have seen how he dealt with the most obvious and persistent and there is no need for a repetition. We have also seen that they, or others like them, appeared again at the end of his reign, while some waited until the despot was dead before bursting into the full light of day. And we have seen, lastly, those which would not be put down: the small, determined flock of Christians who did not follow Rome; the proud, intelligent, and tenacious little group of Jansenists; and the Gallicans with whom they ultimately joined.

But is there, in fact, no more to be said? There is one thing: to try to convey some idea of the ancient, traditional, and heavily calculated weight of inertia possessed by that collection of "nations," *pays, seigneuries,* fiefs, and parishes which together made up the kingdom of France. Each of these entities was accustomed to living independently, with its own customs, privileges, and even language, snug in its own fields and within sound of its own bells. The king consecrated at Rheims was a priest-king to be revered and almost worshiped, but from afar. When someone sent by him turned up in the village accompanied by an escort of armed or black-clad men, or merely bearing an order in writing, he was met, on principle, with suspicion or even open hostility. What "new-fangled idea" had he brought with him? A blow struck at local custom? Or a levy of money, horses, or men? There is no end to the amount which might be written about this sequestered existence with its local patriotism, its deep-rooted horror of all novelty, its fears and terrors which made up the very texture of life in France under the *ancien régime.* Making the king's voice heard in the depths of the countryside was easier said than done when the *curé.* who was the only means of spreading it, garbled, scamped, or merely forgot a task which was clearly no part of his duties; when courts of law were far off, costly, unreliable, and even less respected, the forces of law and order never there, the intendant a mystery, and his assistants powerless. We have only to look at poor Colbert, trying to establish his manufactures, his tentative regulations, and his companies. No one wanted them because all had their own traditions, habits, and interests and clung fiercely to their own independence. We have only to look at every administrator, religious or secular, striving to apply contradictory instructions regarding the "so-called reformed church" to his own particular province. We have only to look at the books of the forestry department and the papers concerned with the *gabelle,* to see the incredible number and variety of infringements which appeared whenever the well-armed dared to set foot in a region to put them down. We have only to stress, in addition, the rash of desertion prevalent in the regular army and still more in the militia (where it may have been as high as 50 percent) at a time when parishes and even whole provinces were ready to condone, hide, and feed the deserters.

If, dazzled by the splendors of Versailles, we let ourselves forget the constant presence of these seething undercurrents, we will have understood nothing of the France of Louis XIV and of the impossible task which the king and his ministers had set themselves, or of the massive inertia which made it so difficult. Moreover, we have said nothing of the inertia of the clergy and of the nobility and their refusal to make any contribution to progress in the kingdom beyond a few prayers and rapier thrusts and some small, grudging alms, when they might have placed all their power, wealth, and talent at the service of these grand designs. But was it even asked of them? They remained the first and second orders, and the only service which they owed was by prayer and the sword. This was yet another instance of the inertia, the rejection of all change and progress toward efficiency, in a regime whose end no one could as yet foresee.

THE FORGOTTEN FORCES

The inherent inertia of that great, tradition-ridden body which was the monarchy of the *ancien régime,* the growing antagonism of the major European states, the forces, vague or precise, foreseen or unforeseen, of which Louis XIV was more or less consciously aware, were all ultimately and undeniably in strong opposition to his designs. But were there no other forces at work, more mysterious and perhaps more powerful but for which no allowance was made in state affairs and which may not even have occurred to the minds of those who ruled it? These, surely, were the forces which ultimately controlled the very life of the kingdom, reducing the activities of one small king of one small country to nothing more than the meaningless gesticulations of insects in relation to the universe.

For some years now, younger historians of a certain school have tended to ignore the bustle of individuals and events in favor of what they call revealing, measuring, defining, and illustrating the great, dominant rhythms which move world history as a whole. These rhythms emerge as largely economic. The method may have a certain rashness and temerity but it bears fruit. Suppose we give way to it for a moment.

Setting aside the gesticulations of the human insects, the economic, social, and political life of France and half the world may well have been dictated by the pace of extracting, transporting, and circulating the "fabulous metal." The discovery of the "Indies," and the mines of Mexico and Peru, which poured ever-increasing amounts of precious metals into Europe, goes a long way to explain the prosperity, brilliance, ostentation, and sheer wealth of the seventeenth century just as, later on, Brazilian gold was behind the mounting prosperity of the eighteenth century and California gold gave rise to the *belle époque* of Badinguet. But from 1600 onward, the quantities of silver reaching Spain from America grew less and less until by 1650 the imports were only a fifth of what they had been in 1600. A probable revival of the mines of central Europe was insufficient to make up the deficit. First gold and then silver grew scarce, giving rise to hoarding. Copper from Sweden or Japan (via Holland) tended to take their place but it was a poor substitute. The whole age of Louis XIV was an age that Marc Bloch has called "monetary famine." The king had difficulty in paying the English for Dunkirk. Ministers and private citizens complained of "shortages of cash" and "hoarding" and everyone paid their debts in *rentes*, which meant pledges on the future. We have laid some stress on the way in which this situation might explain some aspects of Colbert's work and their lack of success as well as some continuous problems of government and also a certain style of opposition. But money was not the only thing.

Historians and economists have long been aware that the seventeenth century as a whole and the period from 1650–90 in particular, or even 1650–1730, was marked by a noticeable drop in the cost of basic foodstuffs as well as of a great many other things—a drop quite separate from annual "accidents." Landed incomes, offices, and possibly moneylending: all seem to have been affected by the same general reduction. François Simiand and later Ernest Labrousse, collating and studying these observations in the 1930s, came to the conclusion that in between the great phases of economic expansion which occurred between the sixteenth and eighteenth centuries, the seventeenth, and particularly the time of Louis XIV, was a period bearing all the signs of, at best, stagnation and at worst economic recession and depression. They were followed by other historians who carried the idea further, sometimes to the point of crude exaggeration. Huguette and Pierre Chaunu, following the same general lines and supported by a remarkable statistical analysis of relations between Spain and America, drew a sweeping cross through the whole of the seventeenth century from a maritime angle from 1600 onward, although still recognizing that elsewhere, in the north and on the continent, the natural rhythm of growth persisted longer, an observation confirmed by others. The same authors, again supported by impressive documentary evidence, go on to describe a new linking up of circumstances favorable to maritime development about 1700, a move toward a new expansion which spread slowly inland from the great ports. Similar observations have been made for Provence, Dauphiné, and the region of Beauvais.

René Baehrel, on the other hand, argues fiercely against this cross which seems to stand by the name of the "sad seventeenth century," although admittedly he argues only on behalf of the rural south of Provence, where he sees economic growth continuing, while at the same time agreeing that the rate of this growth slowed down considerably between 1655 and 1690. But rural southern Provence is not representative either of France or of Western Europe. It is a corner of the Mediterranean, and the man who studies it is a born controversialist.

Setting aside these scholarly arguments, what was the real overall bearing of the great movements of the economic conjuncture, movements rarely perceived at the time unless in some vague way by one or two exceptional minds? Do they, to echo Chaunu, reveal the "deep breathing of history"?

There remains a strong impression that the period of Louis's reign was one of economic difficulties, suffering both from sudden, violent crises and from phases of stagnation and of deep depression.

It is not easy to govern under such conditions, especially when, like the king and most of his councilors, one is unaware of them. But what they tried to do and sometimes, despite such obstacles, achieved, remains nonetheless worthy of interest and even of admiration.

It is possible, therefore, that France under Louis XIV may have been unconsciously subject to powerful economic forces which are still much disputed and not fully understood. Social, demographic, mental, and other factors, wholly or partly incomprehensible to the rulers, may have played their part also. How and within what limits would they have affected the nation's course?

In a century which possessed no mass media of communication, Louis and his champions of scholasticism fought a pale rearguard action against the irresistible advance of science and of the spirit of criticism. But Descartes, Harvey, Newton, and Bayle were not to be gainsaid, and neither was the swing which was to follow the apogee of the Roman Catholic faith with a compensating downward trend. If the seventeenth century was "the age of saints" (and the church certainly needed such champions), its last decades, as we have seen, looked forward to the age of enlightenment, when Voltaire was king. Bossuet died defeated, like Louis XIV, by his confessors and his dragoons. There is no going against nature.

About the great mass of French society and its slow, ponderous development, we know almost nothing—only a few glimmers here and there. How did it happen? Louis XIV seems to have thought the existing social structures all very well so long as he was in control, and he was ruthless in his determination to remain so. But apart from such superficial movement, the society of the *ancien régime* seems to have petrified more than it evolved. The nobility, in its anxiety to remain pure and predominant, may have made some efforts to confirm its position but continued to live in the same spendthrift fashion, drawing wealthy bourgeois into its ranks, hunting their fortunes and their daughters. At the end of the reign, social life seemed dominated by the great businessmen, bankers, merchants, tax-farmers, shipowners, and tradesmen of Paris, Lyons, and the other great ports with their great fortunes, often made almost overnight, their credit, and their patronage, but had things been so very different at the end of the preceding reign, in the time of Mazarin, with the triumph of Fouquet and the Italian or German banks?

And yet, in the manufacturing towns, the small, independent tradesmen seemed to be disappearing, social distinctions becoming more clear-cut, and relations between bosses and workers hardening. A tendency to concentration? The growth of a proletariat? Perhaps, but all we know at present concerns Beauvais and Amiens. In the heart of the country, around Paris and still much further north, but also in Languedoc, some elements of a similar process seem to have been found: the small, independent peasant-farmers grew fewer and less influential, there was a vast number of impoverished day laborers and a sudden increase of powerful middlemen, a kind of rural bourgeoisie in close touch with the great landowners, whether noble or otherwise, clerical or secular. In the same regions, it has been possible to distinguish the early signs (1660–70) of some kind of seigneurial (or feudal) reaction, characterized by a renewed interest in landed property, more scrupulous collection of tithes and dues, revival of old rights, and fresh encroachments on to common lands. But here, too, René Baehrel has stated, and perhaps proved conclusively, that nothing had changed in southern Provence and there remain any number of provinces in the southwest, the center and the west still unexplored. All that can be said for certain is that the acts of the king and his administration, wherever we find them, tended to preserve and maintain the rights of the most powerful section of this mixed and largely landed aristocracy which always came off best in the courts whenever its vassals and dependents dared to plead against it.

Apart from one small, passing effort of Colbert's, the state of Louis XIV seems to have taken little thought for any kind of demographic policy. The general feeling was that fertility in France was more than adequate to cope with the ravages of plague and "mortality," and people were convinced that the population of the kingdom, the densest in Europe, was in no danger of diminution. For the most part, they did not think at all, or thought about other things, and nature took its course. Apart from Vauban and a few others now forgotten, no one took much interest in "the people" except in terms of taxation. The chief demographic victory of the regime, the control of the plague, is largely to the credit of the local authorities. But this did not stop the unknown masses from suffering all through the reign from the individual and collective miseries of shortages and epidemics. Except among the very small ruling class, the demographic characteristics of the kingdom changed very little, or if they did, these changes have not yet emerged. The numbers in each age group varied wildly, but the population as a whole (within fixed limits) may have grown from time to time in Brittany and one or two other places. More often than not, it certainly decreased or possibly remained static. Within this population, the cycles of poverty and ease, the many christenings and hasty interments went on, very much as they had done in Biblical times. There was no apparent sign of change and hardly anyone expected it.

The court, the kingdom, and the collection of princes which, for Louis, constituted the chief of the old continent: these were the accustomed limits of his royal horizon. Far, far beyond them, Muscovy, Asia, the Americas, and the whole world continued to exist for all that and to develop. A new Caesar arose in Russia but his peculiarities were of interest only to the court and to the city. Only a few missionaries and traders concerned themselves with China, at the other end of the world, or had any inkling of her incomparable civilization. Only the Dutch had access to one small hostile Japanese island, and they reaped huge profits from it. War was soon to break out in India, but Louis took little notice of such pagan empires. Africa provided Negro slaves and some other merchandise, but two or three poorly protected trading posts were his only interest there. The English, while making thrifty investments in the Spanish Main, were moving farther north and beginning to win a decisive battle which did not interest the Great King, who cared little for Canada or Louisiana. Brought up by Mazarin in a world of court intrigues, dynastic squabbles, and problems of successions and of frontiers, Louis rarely looked beyond his own lands and almost never to the world at large. Twenty nuns at Port-Royal-des-Champs, a few buildings at Marly, and two or three strongholds seemed to him worthier objects of glory.

It is true that Louis XIV, like most men who grew up between 1640 and 1660, was incapable of rising beyond the limits of his education, let alone of taking in, at one glance, the whole of the planet on which he lived, to say nothing of infinite space. A king to the depths of his being, and a dedicated king, he had a concept of greatness which was that of his generation: military greatness, dynastic greatness, territorial greatness, and political greatness which expressed itself in unity of faith, the illusion of obedience, and magnificent surroundings. He left behind him an image of the monarchy, admirable in its way, but already cracking if not outworn at the time of his death. Like most men, and many kings, he had grown stiff and sclerotic with old age.

By inclination a man of taste, and a politician by nature, education, and desire, he always despised those material accidents called economy and finance. Such commonplace things were merely appendages to his great plane. It never occurred to him that they could one day topple the throne of the next king but one. For him, all social upheavals and ideals were lumped together as "uprisings" and "cabals" to be forcibly suppressed.

Isolated at Versailles at an early stage by his own pride, the machinations of a woman, and a few priests and courtiers, he neither knew nor cared that his age was becoming the age of reason, of science, and of liberty. From first to last, he refused to recognize the power of Holland, the nature of England, or the birth of an embryo German nation. He gave Colbert little support in his courageous maritime and colonial policies and failed to pursue them seriously. He was always more excited by one fortress in Flanders or the Palatinate than by all of India, Canada, and Louisiana put together.

And yet he and his colleagues left behind them a France that was territorially larger, militarily better defended, with a more effective administration, and to a large extent pacified. And although he neglected it and often fought against it, there was a time when he built up and maintained what was to be, for a long time to come, the real greatness and glory of France. The age of enlightenment was dominated, at least in part, by the language and the culture of France.

Like many another king of France, he went to his grave amid general dislike and the particular execration of Parisians. His dead body had already become a symbol. Louis was turning into the stuffed mummy singled out for future deification by the nostalgic and for supreme contempt by his passionate enemies.

All we have tried to do is to understand Louis XIV against the background of his own time without attempting to idolize him.

Bibliography

Ashley, M. H. *The Splendid Century: Some Aspects of French Life in the Reign of Louis XIV* (London, 1953).

Carston, F. L., ed. *The Ascendency of France, 1648–1688,* New Cambridge Modern History, vol. V (London, 1961).

Church, W. F. *The Greatness of Louis XIV, Myth or Reality* (Boston, 1959).

Cronin, Vincent. *Louis XIV* (Boston, 1965).

Eccles, W. J. *Canada Under Louis XIV, 1663–1701* (Toronto, 1964).

Erlanger, P. *Louis XIV,* trans. Stephen Cox (New York, 1970).

Gaxotte, Pierre. *The Age of Louis XIV,* trans. Michael Shaw (New York, 1970).

Goubert, Pierre. *Louis XIV and Twenty Million Frenchmen,* trans. Anne Carter (New York, 1970).

Hatton, Ragnhild. *Europe in the Age of Louis XIV* (New York, 1970).

—— and J. S. Bromley, eds. *William III and Louis XIV* (Liverpool, 1968).

Knackel, Philip A. *England and the Fronde* (Ithaca, 1967).

Nussbaum, F. L. *The Triumph of Science and Reason, 1660–1685* (New York, 1953).

Ogg, David. *Louis XIV* (London, 1933).

Rothkrug, Lionel. *Opposition to Louis XIV* (Princeton, 1965).

Rule, John, ed. *Louis XIV and the Craft of Kingship* (Columbus, Ohio, 1970).

Sonnino, Paul, ed. and trans. *Louis XIV: Mémoires for the Instruction of the Dauphin* (New York, 1970).

Wolf, John B. *The Emergence of the Great Powers, 1685–1715* (New York, 1951).

—— *Louis XIV* (New York, 1968).

—— *Toward a European Balance of Power, 1640–1715* (Chicago, 1970).

Contributors

Louis André (1867–1948), professor at the University of Lille, wrote significantly on the organization of the army under Le Tellier and Louvois (*Michel Le Tellier et l'organisation de l'armée monarchique* [1906] and *Michel Le Tellier et Louvois* [1942]). He also edited several volumes of the *Sources de l'histoire de France,* 1909–35, either alone or in cooperation with Professor Bourgeois. He wrote general histories and many articles, as well as the volumes cited here.

Louis Bertrand (1866–1941) was, strictly speaking, not a historian but rather a journalist, man of letters, and popular biographer. He is included in this collection because his writings on Louis XIV illustrate the rightist position in French politics during the period between the two wars of the first half of the twentieth century.

PIERRE GAXOTTE is a popular rather than an academic historian. He has had a noted career as editorial journalist as well as man of letters and historian.

G. P. GOOCH (1873–1969) was one of the most distinguished of the English historians of the first half of this century. He wrote significantly on German history in the nineteenth century, on historians of the nineteenth century, on nineteenth-century diplomacy, and on four eighteenth-century rulers: Frederick the Great, Maria Theresa, Catherine the Great, and Louis XV.

PIERRE GOUBERT is one of the most distinguished contemporary French historians interested in the seventeenth century. He is professor at the University of Nanterre and is widely known for his work on Beauvais (*Beauvais et le Beauvaisis de 1600 à 1730*), as well as for many articles and the volume from which a chapter is published in this collection.

DUKE DE LA FORCE (1878–1962) also was not a professional academic historian but rather a man of letters and writer of popular history. His most serious work, however, will long be used, for he finished the last four volumes of Hanataux's projected six-volume life of Cardinal Richelieu. His other works include books on Lauzun, La Grande Mademoiselle, Conti, Chateaubriand, his distinguished ancestor the Maréchal de La Force, and others.

ERNEST LAVISSE (1842–1922) was the dean of French historians at the turn of the twentieth century. He is best known for his monumental work on Louis XIV in the equally monumental multi-volume history of France that he edited: *Histoire de la France depuis les origines jusqu'à la Revolution* and *Histoire de la France depuis la Revolution jusqu'à la paix de 1919*—eighteen volumes in all. These books have long been the standard secondary work on the history of France.

A. DE SAINT-LÉGER (born 1866) and PHILIPPE SAGNAC (born 1868) were both students of Lavisse and contributed to the third volume of Lavisse's history of Louis XIV, cited above. They were also well-known scholars in their own right. Saint-Léger was professor of history at Lille, and Sagnac was professor of history at the Sorbonne. Both men have published extensively, including Sagnac's two-volume *La Formation de la société française moderne.*

The DUKE OF SAINT-SIMON's (1675–1755) *Mémoires* are an unavoidable source for the history of his era. Even though they are inaccurate, highly biased, and quite untrustworthy, they present a literary picture of the time that has had great influence upon all subsequent histories of Louis XIV. No discussion of the Sun King would be complete if it ignored Saint-Simon.

VOLTAIRE (1694–1778) was the foremost French literary figure of the eighteenth century. He was historian, playwright, man of letters, polemicist, and social critic. His history of the reign of Louis XIV was one of the first attempts to evaluate the success of the reign.

JOHN B. WOLF—A.B. and A.M., University of Colorado; Ph.D., University of Minnesota—taught at the University of Missouri and the University of Minnesota, and since 1966 has been Professor of History at the University of Illinois, Chicago Circle. He has received grants from the Social Science Research Council and the Guggenheim Foundation and has been a Fulbright Research Professor at the Sorbonne. Dr. Wolf is a past president of the Society of French Historical Studies. His books include *The Diplomatic History of the Bagdad Railroad; Early Modern Europe; The Emergence of the Great Powers, 1685–1715; France, 1814–1919; Louis XIV;* and *Toward a European Balance of Power, 1640–1715.*

AÏDA DIPACE DONALD holds degrees from Barnard and Columbia and a Ph.D. from the University of Rochester. A former member of the History Department at Columbia, Mrs. Donald has been a Fulbright Fellow at Oxford and the recipient of an A.A.U.W. fellowship. She has published *John F. Kennedy and the New Frontier* and *Diary of Charles Francis Adams.*